KU-613-626

March to
VICTORY
THE FINAL MONTHS OF WWII

From D-Day, June 6, 1944 to
the Fall of Japan, August 14, 1945

March to
VICTORY

THE FINAL MONTHS OF WWII

From D-Day, June 6, 1944 to
the Fall of Japan, August 14, 1945

Edited by Tony Hall

a Salamander book

Published by Salamander Books Limited
LONDON

V

A Salamander Book

Above and Right:
War Memorial Museum of Virginia

Published by Salamander Books Ltd
129–137 York Way
London N7 9LG

© Salamander Books Ltd 1994

ISBN 0 86101 776 5

10 9 8 7 6 5 4 3 2 1

All rights reserved. No part of this book may be reproduced, stored in a retrieval system or transmitted in any form or by any means, electronic, mechanical, photocopying, recording or otherwise, without prior permission of Salamander Books Ltd.

All correspondence concerning the content of this volume should be addressed to Salamander Books Ltd.

CREDITS
Editor: Tony Hall

Designer: Paul Johnson

Captions: Chris Chant, Tony Hall

Index: David Linton

Commissioned colour photographs: Michael Dyer Associates, London; Don Eiler, Richmond, Virginia; Terry Dilliway. © Salamander Books Ltd.

Filmsetting: SX Composing, Rayleigh, Essex

Colour and mono reproduction: P&W Graphics PTE, Singapore

Printed in Italy

PICTURE CREDITS
BUND: Bundesarchiv, Koblenz, Germany; IWM: Imperial War Museum, London; NA: US National Archives; NOV: Novosti Photo Library, London; RAF: RAF Museum, Hendon; SAL: Salamander Books.
t, Top; b, Bottom; l, Left; r, Right
Prelims: 1: Pistols of Lt. Gen. Omar N. Bradley, *US Army Military History Institute, Carlisle, Pa;* 2: Staff car pennant of a German field marshal, *West Point Museum, NY;* Standard of the 70th Tank Battalion, *Patton Museum of Cavalry and Armor.*
6, IWM; 8, SAL; 9, IWM; 10, SAL; 11, NA; 12(b) NA; 13, National Archives of Canada, Ottawa; 15, IWM; 16, BUND; 18, IWM; 20, RAF; 21(b), NA; 22, NOV; 24, 25 SAL; 27, 30-31(b), 32(t), 33(t), 34 NOV; 35(t), SAL; 36, NOV; 38, NA; 42, NA; 44, Mainichi Newspaper, Tokyo; 47, 48, 49, 51, NA; 52, 54, 56, 60(b) IWM; 61(t), SAL, (b), IWM; 63(t), IWM; 64, 66, 67, 69, NA; 70, IWM; 72, RAF; 74(t,b), 75(t) IWM, (b) Jeffrey Ethell; 79, SAL; 81(t,b) Alfred Price; 82, SAL; 84, 85 Jeffrey Ethell; 86, NOV; 87, IWM; 88(1) Battle of Britain Prints International, (r) Alfred Price; 89, 90, 91 IWM; 92, 95 SAL; 96(b), 97(t) IWM; 98(b) BUND; 99, IWM; 100(t), NOV, (b), IWM; 101(b), NA; 102, 104, 105, 106, 108 IWM; 111, Peter Newark's Military Pictures; 112, 113, 114, 116, 118, 119, 120 IWM; 121 NA; 122(t), 123 IWM; 125, 126, 127, 128, 130 NA; 131, SAL; 132-133, NA; 134(b) SAL; 135, NA; 138-139, SAL; 140, 141, 142 IWM; 143, NA; 144, IWM; 145(b) IWM; 146, 147, 148, 149, 151, 154, 155, 156, 157, 159, 160 NOV; 162, IWM; 164, NA; 165(b), 166 IWM; 168(b), 169(b) NA; 171, Mainichi Newspaper, Tokyo; 172, IWM; 173(t), NA; 174, NA; 175(b), 176, 177, 179, 180 IWM; 182, NA; 184, SAL; 187, NA; 189, IWM; 190, NA; 192(b) NOV; 193(t), IWM, (b) NOV; 194, NOV; 195(t), IWM, (b), Battle of Britain Prints International; 198, 200(t), 201, 202-203, 204, 205, 206(b), 207, 208(t), 209, 210(b) NOV; 211(t), IWM, (b), NOV; 212, 214(l) NOV; 214-215 Battle of Britain Prints International; 215(b), NOV; 216, 218, 219, 221 NA; 222, 223(b) SAL; 224(t), 226 NA; 227(t) SAL; 228(b), NA; 230-231, Smithsonian Institute; 232, SAL; 233, NA; 234, NOV; 236, 237 Science Photo Library; 238, SAL; 239(b), NA; 240, 241 IWM; 242, 243 NOV; 244(t,b), 245 IWM; 246, 247, 248, 249, NOV; 250, IWM; 251, NOV; 252-253, 254-255 NA

Contents

THE WAR'S NOT OVER 'til our last man is free

● STAY ON THE JOB!
● BUY BONDS
● PLAY FAIR

V One
Europe Invaded

John Pimlott

"The time has come to deal the enemy
a terrific blow in western Europe ...
With stout heart and with enthusiasm for
the contest, let us go
forward to victory."
Gen. Sir Bernard Montgomery, June 1944

At 00:16 on Tuesday June 6, 1944 three Horsa gliders, carrying men of Company D, 2nd Battalion, Oxfordshire and Buckinghamshire Light Infantry, swooped down out of the night sky over Normandy. The lead glider, containing a section of men under Lt. Den Brotheridge, landed with its nose less than 60 feet (18m) from its objective – the Bénouville Bridge over the Caen Canal. The German sentry, Pvt. Helmut Romer, dived for cover as British soldiers, their faces blackened, rushed forward. A short burst of machine gun fire killed Brotheridge, but the bridge (later renamed Pegasus Bridge) was in British hands within three minutes. A few miles to the east, men from other gliders seized another bridge over the Orne River.

These soldiers were the spearhead of an immense Allied air and naval armada that was about to assault the shores of Normandy. Its task was to establish a beachhead, out of which Anglo–American armies would sweep forward to liberate those countries of western Europe – France, Belgium, Luxembourg, The Netherlands and Denmark – preparatory to an advance on Berlin. The invasion was codenamed Operation *Overlord*, with landings taking place on D-Day.

It was an enormous undertaking, only made possible once the Americans, with their seemingly limitless resources, had entered the war in late 1941. US President Franklin D. Roosevelt pressed for a cross-Channel invasion as soon as possible – as did the Soviet leader Josef Stalin, desperate to relieve German pressure on the Eastern Front – but British Prime Minister Winston Churchill urged caution. At the Casablanca Conference

Left: The view from German entrenchments down onto *Omaha* Beach. Untouched by the Allied naval bombardment that was meant to obliterate them, it was from these dugouts that men of the German 352nd Division pinned down the American assault for most of D-Day.

Above: The German beach defenses in northern France included vast numbers of mine-fitted obstacles below the high-water mark, and these were specifically designed for the destruction of landing craft.

in January 1943, the invasion was finally set for May 1, 1944.

Two months later Maj. Gen. Frederick Morgan was appointed Chief of Staff to the Supreme Allied Commander (COSSAC) and ordered to work out an invasion plan. His first priority was to gather information about the German coastal defenses, which stretched from northern Norway to the Franco–Spanish frontier. Royal Air Force reconnaissance Spitfires provided detailed photographs that were supplemented by information from Resistance agents on the ground. Small teams of specially trained commandos – known as Combined Operations Pilotage Parties (COPPs) – were also tasked to look at specific beaches.

Other factors had to be taken into account. The invasion force would be large – in the event, 150,000 men to seize the beachhead, with over two million to carry out the campaign – and they would have to be kept supplied. This meant that the landing beaches could not be too far from supply ports in England, so that ships could return to reload; while it was also desirable to capture a continental port quickly to ease the pressure. The landing area had also to be within range of Allied fighter aircraft stationed in England.

Norway and the Bay of Biscay were too far from England and beyond fighter range. The coasts of Denmark and The Netherlands were too risky – the former because the Germans could easily contain any landings, the latter because the coast was flooded. The Pas de Calais, 22 miles (35km) from southeast England, seemed ideal, but was heavily defended; the Brittany Peninsula was too rocky. That left an area from Le Havre to the Cotentin Peninsula: the coast of Normandy. It was not too far from England, German defenses were known to be relatively weak and the port of Cherbourg was within striking distance. In June 1943, Morgan proposed a landing by three divisions (about 60,000 men), with airborne (parachute and glider) flank support along this stretch of coast.

The next step was to put together the command team: Supreme Headquarters Allied Expeditionary Force (SHAEF). In December 1943 US Gen. Dwight D. Eisenhower, currently commanding Allied troops in the Mediterranean, was appointed Supreme Allied Commander, with Britain's Air Chief Marshal Sir Arthur Tedder as his deputy. Air Chief Marshal Sir Trafford Leigh-Mallory was given command of Allied air forces, and Adm. Sir Bertram Ramsay of sea forces, for the invasion. Gen. Sir Bernard Montgomery was to be in charge of land operations until the breakout from the beachhead, with lieutenant generals Omar N. Bradley and Miles Dempsey commanding the actual assault troops – the US First and Anglo-Canadian Second Armies respectively. It was a formidable team, experienced not just in amphibious landings (in Northwest Africa, Sicily and Italy) but also in the delicate art of inter-Allied planning and cooperation.

Eisenhower and Montgomery increased the assault force to five divisions, and retained the airborne support. This imposed a delay while extra landing craft were despatched from the United States, but it was not the only problem. An integral part of the plan was to soften up German defenses all along the coast, a task that had to be carried out by heavy bombers. At first, the commanders of the bomber fleets in Britain – the US Eighth Army Air Force and RAF Bomber Command – objected to any diversion from operations against Germany, and it was only when Eisenhower threatened to resign that he got his way. From April 1, 1944, the bombers began to hit targets that would disrupt enemy movement, making sure that more bombs were dropped outside Normandy than within it so as not to alert the enemy. As a further deception, a "spoof" army group was created around Dover, chiefly by diverting radio traffic from real armies further west, to make the enemy think that the Pas de Calais was the true objective. This was so successful that, even after June 6, German commanders remained convinced that the Normandy attack was a feint.

By spring 1944, over a million Allied troops were packed into southern England, and an invasion fleet of nearly 5,000 ships was concentrated in ports throughout the British Isles. In addition, special prefabricated harbors, known as *Mulberry*, were constructed – to be placed off the invasion beaches until Cherbourg had been captured – and training exercises stepped up. On May 15, SHAEF commanders outlined the plan to King George VI. The landing area was to extend 60 miles (96km) from the Dives River in the east to the base of the Cotentin Peninsula in the west. Prior to the beach assaults, Allied airborne divisions were to secure the flanks. Just before dawn, a massive naval bombardment would hit German defenses, followed by air attacks on specific locations once it grew light. Under cover of these attacks, US forces would go ashore across beaches codenamed *Utah* and *Omaha* in the west, followed an hour later (as the tide moved along the coast) by Anglo–

Left: Senior commanders for the invasion of France included (standing left to right) Lt. Gen. H.D.G. Crerar, Lt. Gen. William H. Simpson and Lt. Gen. Sir Miles Dempsey, and (seated left to right) Gen. Sir Bernard Montgomery, Gen. Dwight D. Eisenhower and Lt. Gen. Omar N. Bradley.

Above: The destruction of this Parisian oil depot and marshaling yard is strong evidence of the importance attached by the Allies to the destruction of Germany's ability to reinforce and fuel its defense of northern France.

Canadian units across beaches codenamed *Gold*, *Juno* and *Sword*. The plan was to land just after low tide, when German beach obstacles were exposed, and to use the rising tide to ensure a rapid build-up. Eisenhower set the date for attack (D-Day) as June 5, but rain and overcast skies imposed a 24-hour delay.

The poor weather helped to ensure surprise, for German forces in Normandy – men of Gen. Friedrich Dollmann's Seventh Army, part of Field Marshal Erwin Rommel's Army Group B – were convinced that an invasion under such conditions was impossible. On June 6, Rommel was absent in Germany and many of his senior commanders were attending a war game at Rennes. Although Rommel had improved defenses along the Normandy coast, covering the beaches with obstacles and planting elaborate minefields, the Pas de Calais always took priority. Moreover, Adolf Hitler, as supreme commander, had withdrawn better units from Normandy to fight the Soviets, leaving second-rate formations behind. Finally, there was a shortage of panzer (armored) divisions with which to mount a counterattack. On June 6, the only panzer division close to the Normandy beaches was Lt. Gen. Edgar Feuchtinger's 21st at Caen, but it had received no orders about what to do in the event of an attack. Rommel wanted an immediate counterattack to catch the enemy on the beaches, but his superior officer, Field Marshal Gerd von Rundstedt (Commander-in-Chief West), favored holding the tanks back in case of an Allied feint.

Once Eisenhower had made his decision, the Allied plan swung into action. A total of 137 warships, including 7 battleships, 23 cruisers and 77 destroyers, sailed toward the Normandy coast behind more than 200 minesweepers, tasked to clear lanes through minefields in the Channel. The assault troops were packed into landing ships and landing craft, while a total of 11,500 aircraft were ready to support them. French Resistance cells, alerted by BBC radio broadcasts on June 5, carried out over 1,000 sabotage attacks, and dummy parachutists were dropped all over northern France. Finally, motor launches and RAF bombers operated off the Pas de Calais, giving the impression of a large invasion force.

Despite the accuracy of the attack on the Bénouville Bridge, the airborne landings on the flanks of the assault area were chaotic. In the British sector, where men of Maj. Gen. Richard Gale's 6th Airborne Division were tasked to seize objectives in an area between the Orne and Dives Rivers, the paratroopers were scattered by high winds. Lt. Col. Terence Otway, commanding the 9th Parachute Battalion, for example, had to take a coastal battery at Merville, overlooking *Sword* beach, with only 150 men, half of whom were killed in the attack. By dawn, the British flank was secure, but at a cost of 800 airborne troops dead or wounded.

On the western flank, transports carrying Maj. Gen. Matthew B. Ridgway's 82nd Airborne Division and Maj. Gen. Maxwell D. Taylor's 101st Airborne Division were disrupted by antiaircraft fire and dropped their men over a wide area, some of them landing in the sea and drowning. Their objectives were causeways linking *Utah* beach to less flooded terrain inland, as well as crossings over the Merderet River to the west. These, however, had not been fully secured by dawn. Although the village of Ste. Mère-Eglise was taken, severing the road between Carentan and Cherbourg, elsewhere it was a case of groups of isolated troops taking on German defenders. This had the advantage of confusing the enemy but, again, the cost was heavy: 2,400 members of the US airborne forces killed or wounded.

Men of the US 4th Infantry Division, part of Lt. Gen. J. Lawton Collins' VII Corps, set off in landing craft for *Utah* beach, on the east coast of the Cotentin Peninsula between the villages of la Madeleine and les Dunes de Varreville, at 04:55. The naval bombardment opened 45 minutes later; at dawn (05:58) Allied bombers hit targets in the vicinity of the beach. The first wave of 600 infantrymen landed on time at 06:30, but in the wrong place, drifting with the tide to come ashore about a mile (1.6km) too far south. However, this turned out to be a bonus, as the landing area was virtually undefended. Following waves were directed to the new beach – another 900 men plus 32 Duplex Drive (DD) amphibious tanks. By 11:05 lead elements of the 4th Division had made contact with the 101st Airborne, securing the first of the vital causeways. It was a model invasion; by nightfall,

Below: One of the Allies' most important weapons for D-Day was the deep-wading version of its Sherman medium tank, which was specially adapted so that it could wade ashore from comparatively deep water.

Above: Shoulder patch of the US 1st Infantry Division, 'Big Red One.' The division arrived in England in 1942 and took part in campaigns in North Africa, Sicily and Northwest Europe. *Salamander Books*

Below: Men of the 3rd Battalion of the US 1st Infantry Division's 16th Regimental Combat Team rest against the cliffs below Colleville sur Mer, one of the targets for the units landed on *Omaha* Beach.

over 21,000 men had landed at *Utah*, at a cost of only 106 killed and wounded.

The same could not be said of the landings on *Omaha*, carried out by the US 1st Infantry Division, part of Lt. Gen. Leonard T. Gerow's V Corps. They were to come ashore across open beaches between the villages of Colleville-sur-Mer and Vierville-sur-Mer, behind which lay marshy ground leading to grassy bluffs. At both ends of the beach the bluffs turned into cliffs, forcing troops to move inland along four distinct valleys. The area was defended by the German 352nd Infantry Division, recently moved into Normandy without the Allies knowing. German gun positions were built into the bluffs and the beaches were covered with obstacles.

Naval and air bombardments took place between 05:50 and 06:27 but most of the targets were missed because of poor visibility. Thereafter, the problems multiplied. A force of 64 DD tanks, scheduled to spearhead the assault, were launched too far out in heavy seas and most of them sank, leaving ordinary tanks to come ashore from landing craft into the teeth of the German guns. The infantry landed in scattered groups because of high seas, while special demolition teams, ordered to destroy the beach obstacles, were decimated. Surviving infantry took what shelter they could on a beach that rapidly became jammed. Bradley, offshore in the cruiser USS *Augusta*, contemplated calling off the assault, but as the morning wore on small groups of determined soldiers slowly fought their way inland, inspired by surviving officers. One of them, Col. George A. Taylor of the 16th Regimental Combat Team, was heard to shout: "Two kinds of people are staying on this beach, the dead and those who are about to die – now let's get the hell out of here." The crisis passed. By nightfall, 25,000 men had been put ashore, but at a high cost – nearly 3,000 dead or wounded.

A disadvantage of "Bloody *Omaha*" was that the beachhead was shallow. This was particularly worrying for a group of 226 men of the US 2nd Ranger Battalion, whose task on June 6 was to scale cliffs at Pointe du Hoc, midway between the two US beaches. They landed at about 07:00, aiming to destroy a German gun battery on the clifftop; when they arrived amid heavy enemy fire, they discovered that the battery had been resited further inland. They had to wait until June 8 to be relieved; by then only 90 men were still on their feet.

The most westerly of the Anglo–Canadian beaches – *Gold* – lay about 15 miles (24km) to the east of *Omaha*, comprising a straight stretch of sand between the villages of le Hamel and la Rivière. The assault, carried out by men of the British 50th (Northumbrian) Infantry Division, backed by the 8th Armoured Brigade, part of Lt. Gen. C. Bucknall's XXX Corps, went remarkably

smoothly. At 04:45 two Royal Navy midget submarines surfaced at the extremities of the Anglo–Canadian landing area to act as guides and small teams of frogmen swam ashore to start clearing obstacles. The naval bombardment began at 05:30 and continued until 07:20, five minutes before the first wave of infantry came ashore, landing a full hour after the Americans because of the tide. This extra bombardment time helped to prepare the way, but the British had other advantages. Their opponents on *Gold* were the German 716th Infantry Division, a second-rate unit, and their forces were well organized for the assault. Special armored vehicles, known as "Funnies," accompanied the infantry: not just DD tanks but also Flails to clear minefields, and Armoured Vehicles Royal Engineers (AVREs), armed with large caliber mortars, to breach defenses. Within 30 minutes of the first-wave landing, la Rivière had been captured and, although le Hamel proved to be more difficult, by nightfall over 25,000 men were ashore and contact had been made with the Canadians on *Juno* beach to the east. To the west, No. 47 Commando Royal Marines had failed to link up with *Omaha*, and the town of Bayeux was not to be taken until early on June 7, but a strong foothold had been gained.

Juno beach, next to *Gold*, extended from la Rivière in the west to St. Aubin in the east. It was assaulted by the 3rd Canadian Infantry Division, supported by the 2nd Canadian Armoured Brigade, part of Lt. Gen. John Crocker's British I Corps. Initially, problems were experienced – the naval and air bombardments were less effective than on *Gold* and the assault was delayed for 20

Above: Men of the North Nova Scotia Highlanders and Highland Light Infantry of Canada, two of the 9th Brigade's three battalions, come ashore near Bernières sur Mer on the Canadian 3rd Division's *Juno* Beach.

Above: A collapsible bicycle (seen here restored) of the type issued to many British and Canadian units during the landings.
D-Day Museum, Portsmouth

minutes because of rocks offshore – but the Canadians were determined fighters. Despite German 88mm guns in concrete emplacements, machinegun positions and a high seawall, the infantry, supported by "Funnies," took the villages of Courseulles and Bernières before advancing in the direction of the city of Caen. On the extreme left, men of No. 48 Commando Royal Marines, part of the 4th Special Service Brigade attached to I Corps, landed at St. Aubin in an attempt to link up with No. 41 Commando Royal Marines of the same brigade, landing on *Sword* beach, but by nightfall no firm contact had been made.

The fifth and most easterly beach, codenamed *Sword*, stretched from Lion on the right flank to just beyond the port of Ouistreham on the left. The main assault was carried out by the British 3rd Infantry Division, also part of I Corps, with Commando landings on either flank – 41 Commando at Lion and elements of Lord Lovat's 1st Special Service Brigade (which included Free-French Commandos) at Ouistreham. The landings began at 07:25 after naval and air bombardments, and although some of the DD tanks, launched too far offshore, floundered in the heavy surf, enough survived to support the infantry. Five beach exits were open within an hour; by 10:00 lead units were in Hermanville, a mile (1.6km) inland. Lovat's commandos, led by a piper, linked up with glider troops at the Bénouville Bridge at 13:15.

Three hours later, the only organized German counterattack of June 6 materialized, as some 40 tanks of the 21st Panzer Division, with infantry support, probed toward the coast from Caen. They were too late, reflecting German confusion. Hitler had not been informed of the Allied landings until midday and had refused to release his panzer reserve in case Normandy was a feint. By then, the Allies were able to deal with any local attack. Problems still existed – there were worrying gaps between some of the beaches, while Caen, a vital road center, had not been taken – but with 150,000 men ashore by the end of June 6, a firm foothold had been established. In addition, the costs had been lighter than anticipated: a total of 2,500 dead.

Success had to be exploited. The Allies' first priority was to link the various beaches – a process completed by June 12 – while bringing in the forces needed to effect a breakout from the beachhead area. Two *Mulberry* harbors were built, one off *Omaha* and the other off *Gold*, but there were limits to their capacity. It was imperative that a French port should be captured quickly. Elements of the US VII Corps attacked west from *Utah*, linking up with the airborne around Ste. Mère-Eglise on June 7, but found the going hard. Attempts to reach the west coast of the Cotentin Peninsula prior to an advance north towards Cherbourg were blocked by flooded river valleys and determined enemy opposition.

Meanwhile, men of the US 1st Infantry Division had probed forward from *Omaha* along the valley of the Aure River. Montgomery, as Land Force Commander, tried to widen this apparent gap in German defenses by committing the British 7th Armoured Division. The attack did not succeed. Early on June 13, men of the 4th County of London Yeomanry (Sharpshooters) and 1st Battalion, Rifle Brigade moved out of Villers-Bocage, a village to the south of Bayeux. They were engaged by just five German tanks, commanded by SS Lieutenant Michael Wittmann; 27 British tanks were destroyed for no German loss. Montgomery pulled the spearheads back.

Aware that, further east, British airborne troops were fighting hard to maintain positions beyond the Orne River, Montgomery faced acute problems. When he briefed King George VI on his overall plan in May he spoke of a need to "jab at the Germans from both flanks"

Below: The creation of two *Mulberry* artificial harbors was essential for the supply of the Allied forces before French ports such as Le Havre and Cherbourg could be captured and brought into operation.

Above: Men of the 12th SS Panzer Division 'Hitlerjugend' ride roward the front on an SdKfz 251 half-track carrier. This division posed the greatest single German threat to the Allies on D-Day.

to find a weakness that could be exploited, but within a week of the D-Day landings he was finding lines of possible advance blocked. One of the main problems was the terrain – a network of small fields, surrounded by sunken lanes, known as *bocage* – that was imposing delays on both the Americans and the British. Each field was a defender's dream, taking little more than a well placed machinegun to inflict heavy casualties on attacking infantry. Supporting tanks were vulnerable to anti-tank ambushes. Moreover, the Germans began to recover their balance and, although Hitler still insisted on keeping reserves in the Pas de Calais, fresh units from further afield began to arrive in Normandy. The 2nd SS Panzer Division 'Das Reich,' for example, took two weeks to move from Toulouse through Resistance ambushes (one of which triggered the destruction by the SS of the village of Oradour-sur-Glane).

An apparent breakthrough occurred in the American sector when infantry and airborne finally crossed the Merderet River and, on June 18, reached the west coast of the Cotentin Peninsula. As they turned north toward Cherbourg, new urgency was added to their task by a five-day Channel storm that destroyed one of the *Mulberry* harbors and seriously damaged the second. Cherbourg was now vitally important. By June 21, most of the US VII Corps had reached the outskirts of the port; when the 16,000-strong German garrison refused to surrender, over 1,000 Allied aircraft hit their positions. The infantry moved forward to take Cherbourg in hand-to-hand fighting. On June 29, the Germans surrendered, but they left the port facilities wrecked. It would take a month to clear the way for merchant ships, leaving the Allies dependent for supplies on what could be landed across the invasion beaches.

Montgomery decided to increase his attacks around Caen, in the Anglo–Canadian sector. In his memoirs, published after the war, he insisted that he had always planned to keep the Germans tied down in the east while the Americans in the west built up their forces before advancing south to break the deadlock, but at the time things were not that clear-cut. This was reflected in Operation *Epsom*, initiated on June 26. Over 60,000 men and 600 tanks of Lt. Gen. Sir Richard O'Connor's British VIII Corps were to move into the valley of the Odon River, outflanking Caen from the west and south. The intention was to force the enemy out of Caen, leaving the Allies in control of a road and rail network that would allow them to break out of the *bocage* into more open terrain, regardless of events in the US sector.

It did not work. A preliminary artillery bombardment failed to subdue enemy defenses manned by crack formations such as the 12th SS Panzer Division 'Hitlerjugend,' and as British infantry advanced, the weather

deteriorated. When O'Connor unleashed his tanks they encountered strong opposition in a sea of mud, and although lead elements of the 11th Armoured Division did cross the Odon on June 28, they could go no further. Two days later they were recalled, the Allies having received secret information (via the *Ultra* decrypts of German *Enigma* signals) that the II SS Panzer Corps was being moved in to mount a counterattack. *Epsom* cost over 4,000 casualties for no real gain.

By now Montgomery was under mounting pressure from London to break the deadlock. Heavy fighting had left Allied infantry units short of trained men and Churchill was concerned about recent attacks on London by German V1 pilotless flying bombs, the launch sites of which could be seized if a breakout occurred. In addition, Allied air forces, still operating from bases in southern England, were demanding the capture of more open terrain so that airfields could be built in Normandy. Montgomery's response was to order a direct assault on Caen: Operation *Charnwood*. On July 7, nearly 500

Above: Waffen-SS uniforms worn during the Normandy fighting. The camouflage smock is of the 1st pattern and features reversible fall (autumn) colors. Note the sniper's rope faced veil on the helmet. The uniform on the right was worn by an SS-sturmmann (lance corporal) of the 17th Panzer Grenadier Division 'Götz von Berlichingen.'
Memorial Museum, Bayeux

Above: The beautiful city of Caen was not taken as planned on D-Day, and the subsequent fighting resulted in enormous damage as indicated by this photograph taken after the British and Canadians had finally won the city.

Allied bombers reduced the city to rubble; 24 hours later Canadian troops moved forward against German defenders who took full advantage of the ruins to block their progress. The attack was called off on July 10, by which time the Canadians had penetrated as far as the Orne River, leaving the eastern suburbs of the city still in enemy hands. It looked as if the Allies were stalled.

But the balance was beginning to tilt in favor of Montgomery's forces. On the western flank the Americans were steadily increasing their strength, while there was no doubt that the Germans were concentrating around Caen. If the pressure could be maintained in the east, Bradley might soon be able to break out in the west against relatively weak enemy opposition. It was decided that two new operations would be mounted. To the east of Caen, the British would attack German positions on the Bourguébus Ridge, covering the approaches to Falaise (Operation *Goodwood*), to ensure that no enemy reinforcements moved west to face an American drive from St. Lô towards Avranches (Operation *Cobra*).

Goodwood began on July 18. Three British armored divisions – the Guards, 7th and 11th – were ordered to cross the Orne River into the bridgehead carved out by the airborne on D-Day, preparatory to an advance over open farmland to the Bourguébus Ridge, about four miles (6km) from the start-line. Meanwhile, other elements of Dempsey's Second Army would take the eastern suburbs of Caen. But a host of problems arose. Despite Allied intelligence assessments to the contrary, German defenses in the area were strong, using stone-built villages, railway embankments and low ridges as cover. Panzer reserves were hidden in woods to the south of the Bourguébus Ridge. A massive air, naval and artillery bombardment early on July 18 inflicted damage on these defenses, but did not destroy them. As British armor moved forward it came under attack from the villages, many of which contained 88mm guns and Tiger tanks. What little infantry the British had with them was soon tied down, leaving the tanks to continue unsupported. They could not call in air attacks because of a breakdown in ground-to-air communications; as they advanced they quickly went beyond the range of artillery, still on the west bank of the Orne. The attack ground to a halt beneath the Bourguébus Ridge and, as the weather broke on July 20, the operation was called off. By then, the British had lost over 400 tanks.

Tactically, *Goodwood* was a disaster, but strategically it did succeed. As the Germans were fighting in the east, Bradley's forces further west were preparing for *Cobra*. The going had not been easy – attacks in early July to seize a line running from Coutances through St. Lô to Caumont had bogged down in appalling terrain – and the weather was deteriorating. On July 24, *Cobra* was postponed for 24 hours, although the message did not reach some of the US bombers tasked to hit enemy defenses. When they arrived they dropped their bombs short, killing 25 US soldiers. A similar tragedy occurred on the 25th, this time killing 111 (including Lt. Gen. Lesley J. McNair, commander of US Army Land Forces), but the ground offensive did begin. It failed to make headway until July 26, when US armored divisions smashed through toward Coutances, ignoring enemy minefields and taking the town two days later. By then, the armor was under the command of Lt. Gen. George S. Patton, whose style of leadership was well suited to mobile warfare. By July 30, the Americans had taken Avranches and were poised to move west into the Brittany peninsula. On the following day Patton's US Third Army was activated, with Bradley taking command of the 12th Army Group (the US First and Third Armies together).

Maj. Gen. Troy H. Middleton's US VIII Corps, part of Patton's army, poured through the Avranches gap to capture the Breton ports. It proved to be a difficult task. Although St. Malo fell on August 16, followed by Brest a month later, Lorient and St. Nazaire were to remain in German hands until the end of the war in May 1945. Bradley, concerned that operations in Brittany were irrelevant – the bulk of the enemy was, after all, in Normandy – altered the thrust of the American advance. On August 3, he ordered Patton to leave a covering force in Brittany and divert the rest of his army to a wide

Below: A 'Sexton' self-propelled howitzer bearing the distinctive winged helmet insignia of the 1st Polish Armoured Division. The 'Sexton' was a variant of the American M7 'Priest', and though also based on a M3 Grant tank chassis mounted a 25 pounder gun instead of the M7's 105mm.
Memorial Museum, Bayeux

Above: The clandestine Forces Francaises de l'Intérieur played a major part in the liberation of Paris, and here men of this organization take the surrender of German soldiers on August 26, 1944.

encircling move to the east, aiming for the Seine River, south of Paris. This would outflank German forces facing the Anglo–Canadians around Caen and leave them with no option but to withdraw. Montgomery accepted this, directing Dempsey to attack toward Vire to ensure that the enemy did not redeploy to counter the American advance.

Despite a German counterattack at Mortain, east of Avranches, on August 6/7 – a desperate gamble that diverted panzers from defensive tasks elsewhere and was blunted by US troops holding high ground – the American plan worked well. Patton's men took Le Mans on August 8, then swept forward to liberate Nantes and Angers before approaching the Seine through Chartres and Orléans. But it had already occurred to Allied commanders that an opportunity existed for a more decisive operation, designed to trap the enemy rather than force his withdrawal. As Le Mans fell, Patton was authorized to divert some of his units north toward Argentan to link up with Anglo–Canadians attacking south from Caen and Falaise. This would create an enormous pocket of enemy forces that could then be destroyed.

Men of Maj. Gen. Wade Haislip's US XV Corps reached Argentan on August 12, but were under orders to go no further for fear of clashing with Canadian (and Polish) troops moving south. As it turned out, there was little danger of this happening. Attempts to attack Falaise by Lt. Gen. Henry Crerar's newly activated Canadian First Army had stalled on August 9 – the town was not liberated until the 16th, after particularly heavy fighting – and this left a 15-mile (24km) gap between the Allied pincers. About 40,000 German troops escaped to the east before the Falaise Pocket was finally closed on August 20.

Even so, substantial German forces were destroyed. As the Allied armies edged closer together to create the pocket, artillery and rocket-firing fighter-bombers pounded the area. They did enormous damage to enemy units caught in narrow lanes to the south of Falaise, killing an estimated 10,000 Germans and capturing more than 50,000. Many of the prisoners were deeply shocked by what they had experienced – "alive, but inside dead, numbed by . . . the horrible scenes" of destruction. The Germany army defending Normandy had ceased to exist.

This left the way clear for the Allies to cross the Seine River. Patton led the assault, creating a bridgehead at Mantes-Gassicourt, 30 miles (48km) to the northwest of Paris, on August 20. By then communist-led members of the French Forces of the Interior (FFI) had seized various public buildings in Paris, convinced that liberation was close at hand. In fact, Eisenhower was not keen to become bogged down in urban fighting, intending instead to bypass the city and leave the German garrison to "wither on the vine." Gen. Charles de Gaulle, leader of the Free French, recognized the danger of a communist takeover and, without consulting the Americans, ordered Maj. Gen. Jacques Philippe Leclerc to lead his French 2nd Armored Division into Paris. Presented with such a *fait accompli*, Eisenhower had no choice but to authorize US units to follow.

As French troops fought through the suburbs, the population of Paris rose in revolt against their occupiers, building barricades and triggering a response from the Germans that threatened the destruction of key historic sites. It was not until late on August 24 that tanks of the 2nd Armored Division reached the Hotel de Ville in the center of the city, and it was to take a further 24 hours of chaotic fighting to complete the liberation. On August 26, despite German snipers, de Gaulle led a victory parade down the Champs Elysées, ensuring that he, rather than the communists, held the reins of political power in France.

By then, the Germans were facing a new threat. On August 15, Anglo–American and Free French forces invaded southern France in an operation codenamed *Dragoon*. Originally scheduled to coincide with the cross-Channel landings, *Dragoon* had been delayed by Allied debates about its strategic value – Churchill saw it as an unnecessary diversion from the Italian campaign – and by a shortage of landing craft. In the event, it was a success, because by August Hitler had denuded southern France of troops, sending them north to Normandy.

Air bombardment of enemy defenses between Cannes and St. Tropez began on August 6, while an invasion fleet of 880 ships was prepared in Naples. Just after 04:00 on the 15th Allied airborne troops secured the left flank of the beachhead, followed four hours later by three US infantry divisions (the 3rd, 36th and 45th) which landed from the sea against minimal opposition. Free French units swept forward to liberate Toulon and Marseilles, forcing the Germans to retreat northward up the Rhône River. As they did so, other formations in western France, realizing they were about to be trapped, also withdrew, closely pursued by Allied infantry. By the end of August, the Allies were approaching the Belfort Gap (a pass between the Vosges and Jura mountains to the east of Dijon) and were about to link up with Patton's US Third Army advancing from the Seine.

On September 1, Eisenhower took over personal command of all Allied forces in Northwest Europe. He inherited a strategic situation ripe with opportunity. Most of France had been liberated, substantial German forces had been destroyed and Allied armies were poised to sweep forward into the Low Countries and towards the German border. It was a remarkable achievement.

Above: The German Flag which flew over the city of Paris throughout the city's occupation.
Museum of the Liberation, Paris

Below: Smoke rises above the rooftops of Paris during the fighting for the city. Unlike much of the other urban fighting of World War II, the battle for Paris was small in scale and entailed little damage or losses.

Two
The Soviet
Summer Offensive, 1944

David Glantz

As Operation *Overlord* began in the west, on the Eastern Front the summer of 1944 would see over one million men of the Red Army launched on an offensive that would take them to the eastern border of Germany.

By spring 1944, the ultimate concern of the German–Russian War was no longer in doubt. It was clear to most that without a German miracle the Soviets would achieve victory. The only questions were how long would it take and at what cost.

The back of the German Army had been broken during the preceding sixteen months. During the Winter Campaign of 1942–43 the Germans had lost their most powerful army (the Sixth) at Stalingrad, together with Romanian Second and Third Armies. Thereafter, along the Don River, the German Second Army was severely mauled and the Italian Eighth and Hungarian Second Armies were utterly destroyed. Bereft of most of its allied forces, in spring the Wehrmacht mustered its strength for one final lunge at Soviet defenses. The Battle of Kursk and the subsequent Soviet strategic offensive smashed German forces and drove them back to the line of the Dnieper River. In November and December 1943, Soviet forces penetrated the vaunted German "Eastern Wall" along the Dnieper and plunged deep into the Ukraine. With scarcely a halt, by April, four Soviet *fronts* (army groups) spearheaded by six tank armies cleared the Crimea and most of the Ukraine of German forces, simultaneously encircling and severely damaging German First Panzer and new Sixth Armies. By April, only the most optimistic German could anticipate their survival. Those few who did, took solace in the hope that Soviet forces would bleed themselves white or the Allied coalition would collapse. In their view, Germany could survive only as a result of Soviet ineptitude or diplomatic duplicity in their opponent's camp. The

Left: Morally and physically broken by the bitterness of the war on the Eastern Front, a German soldier collapses on the trail of a piece of artillery shattered by Soviet fire in the Battle of Kursk during July 1943.

23

Above: The Germans were poorly prepared for winter campaigning in the USSR, and in 1941-42 this season was notably bitter. Yet the Soviets chose this time for a major offensive, and the Germans had to fight on.

Soviet High Command (the *Stavka*) prepared to meet these challenges as it planned for its summer campaign of 1944.

On June 1, 1944 the Wehrmacht in the east numbered 2,460,000 troops supplemented by 550,000 allied forces. These troops were supported by 2,608 tanks and assault guns and 7,080 artillery pieces. On March 2, 1944, the closest available figure, Soviet Army ration strength on the Eastern Front was 6,394,500 troops with another 727,000 in hospitals. Soviet armored strength on June 1, 1944 was 7,753 tanks and self-propelled (SP) guns, and over 100,000 guns and mortars. Theoretically, successful defense was possible, but only if the Germans could anticipate Soviet plans and redeploy to counter Soviet offensive concentrations. Experience had shown that this was becoming increasingly difficult due to Soviet successes with deception. And continued Soviet successes with deception promised to turn twofold strategic force superiority into tenfold operational dominance. If this were to be the case, no German force could successfully defend.

The Soviet winter offensive of 1943–44 continued well into the spring. Successive and, finally, simultaneous Soviet front offensive operations across southern Russia ultimately drove German forces from the Ukraine to the Polish and Romanian borders. By late April, offensive momentum had ebbed, and the Soviets began planning where to resume the offensive after refitting.

There were several enticing offensive options. First, Soviet forces could continue their offensive southward into the Balkans and reap considerable political as well as military rewards. This option, however, would extend their armies, leave large areas of the Soviet Union under German control, and pose a threat to their over-extended northern flank. Second, they could launch a major offensive from the northern Ukraine across central and eastern Poland to the Baltic Sea, entrapping both German Army Groups Center and North. This option, however, would involve maneuver beyond Soviet capabilities and would also leave German forces on the flanks. A third option, to attack into the Baltic States and Finland, would engage strong German defenses on difficult terrain and lead virtually nowhere.

Finally, the Soviets could advance through Belorussia to the Baltic Sea, crushing German Army Group Center in the so-called Belorussian balcony (which jutted westward north of the Pripiat marshes) and isolating German Army Group North. This would clear German troops from Soviet soil and permit future operations on the direct route to Berlin. The Soviets selected this option because victory there would place Soviet forces on the frontiers of the Third Reich and facilitate subsequent victories in other Eastern Front sectors.

In April 1944, the *Stavka*, General Staff, and Soviet *front* commanders jointly planned the upcoming operations. They chose Belorussia as the priority target and then planned a time-phased series of operations spanning the entire front, each of which would capitalize on the preceding victory. When planning was complete, the summer offensive consisted of the following five distinct operations:

Karelian Isthmus–south Karelia – June 10, 1944
Belorussia – June 23, 1944
Lvov–Sandomierz – July 13, 1944
Lublin–Brest – July 18, 1944
Iassy–Kishinev – August 20, 1944

The *Stavka* reconfigured its operating *fronts* to match offensive requirements. It subdivided Western Front, facing northern and central Belorussia, into 2nd and 3rd Belorussian Fronts, and the Belorussian Front, operating against southern Belorussia and central Poland, became the 1st Belorussian Front. This reorganization focused the strength of three and one half *fronts* against German forces in Belorussia, half of 1st Belorussian and all of 1st Ukrainian Front against central and southern Poland, and 2nd and 3rd Ukrainian Fronts against German forces in Romania.

Soviet offensive success depended on secret movement and concentration of large forces between *fronts*, specifically movement of a tank army from southern Ukraine to Belorussia, two armies from the Crimea to

Below: Ever increasing Soviet armored strength forced the Germans to many expedients such as the creation of potent tank-destroyers such as this Nashorn with an 88mm gun on a hybrid PzKpfw III/IV tank chassis.

Belorussia, one army from the southern Ukraine to Belorussia, two armies from Moldavia (on the Romanian border) to northern Ukraine, and one army from the Baltic to northern Belorussia. The Soviets were able to do so undetected by virtue of a successful large-scale deception plan. With *Stavka* campaign planning, complete detailed *front* planning proceeded as each operation unfolded.

The opening act of the impending summer drama played out north of Leningrad, where combat had stabilized since late 1941. As if by tacit agreement, in the first months of war, Finnish troops had advanced to the northern outskirts of Leningrad and into Karelia; and, then, to the Germans' consternation, they had halted along the former 1939 borders. For almost three years, the Finns, had stood by as the Germans sought in vain to seize the city. As pleased as the Soviets were over Finnish inactivity, the very presence of the Finns had tied down Soviet forces. Moreover, the Soviets were intent on retaking the territory they had seized in the Russo–Finnish War of 1939–40 but lost in 1941.

The Karelian operations were designed to drive Finland from the war, divert attention from Soviet offensive preparations further south, and embarrass the Germans, politically, by driving one of their allies from the war.

The *Stavka* ordered the Leningrad and Karelian Fronts to secure the Karelo–Finnish region and the Karelian isthmus northwest and north of Leningrad. Gen. L. A. Govorov's Leningrad Front, supported by the warships of the Baltic Fleet, was to attack on June 10, to secure Vyborg by the tenth day of the operation, and, on

Below: An array of World War II medals from the Republic of Finland, including from the left: Cross of Liberty, Third Class with oak leaf; Cross of Liberty, Third Class; Order of the White Rose, First Class; commemorative medal of the Winter War 1939–40 (the Russo-Finnish War); commemorative medal of the Continuation War 1941–45 (for political reasons not instituted until 1957).
Salamander Books

June 21, Gen. K. A. Meretskov's Karelian Front would strike north of Lake Ladoga.

Finnish defenses on the Karelian isthmus were elaborate, and the Soviets painfully recalled their difficulties in 1939 when numerically inferior Finnish forces had frustrated Soviet attackers for almost four months. Consequently, planning was careful, and, prior to the operation, the Soviets built up a considerable superiority in manpower and equipment over their Finnish foes.

The offensive began on June 10, and developed according to plan. On June 20, Soviet forces secured Vyborg, and on the following day, Meretskov's Karelian Front commenced operations north of Lake Ladoga, ultimately forcing the Finns to sue for peace. The Vyborg and Karelian operations were clearly peripheral in nature and had only limited effect on the more important operations which, on June 23, began to unfold further south.

Stavka planning for the Belorussian operation was complete by May 30, and the next day offensive directives went to each *front*. As had been the custom since late 1942, *Stavka* representatives, Marshal A. M. Vasilevsky for 1st Baltic and 3rd Belorussian Fronts and Marshal G. K. Zhukov for 1st and 2nd Belorussian Fronts, then coordinated detailed planning for the operation.

The concept of operations for Operation *Bagration* required simultaneous penetration of German Army Group Center defenses in six sectors and encirclement and destruction of enemy forces in Vitebsk, Orsha,

Above: Forced back by the weight of the Soviet offensive driving through the main defenses of their Mannerheim Line, the Finns fired the towns they were compelled to abandon in June 1944. This is Viipuri in flames.

Mogilev, and Bobruisk. Subsequently, the remainder of Army Group Center would be encircled and destroyed around Minsk by three converging *fronts*, and Soviet forces would then advance to the western borders of the Soviet Union. Once Minsk had fallen, 2nd and 3rd Baltic Fronts would expand the offensive with attacks towards Riga against Army Group North, 1st Belorussian Front's left wing would advance into central Poland, and 1st Ukrainian Front would begin a major operation toward Lvov and the Vistula River in eastern Poland.

Above: The summer uniform and service cap of the Red Army. Introduced in 1943, it is of cotton twill and designed as a conscious revival of the old Tsarist uniform. The distinctive gymnasturka blouse bears the shoulder board insignia of an infantry private (krasnoarmeyets). The leather belt has an alloy buckle. The weapon is a 7.62mm Tokarev SVT40 semi-automatic rifle with pattern bayonet. *Imperial War Museum, London*

Above: Marshal Georgi Zhukov was the most successful Soviet commander of World War II. Here he plans operations near the Polish city of Modlin during summer 1944, when the Soviets seized most of eastern Poland.

Below: Men of the Soviet 2nd Baltic Front ford a water barrier on their approach to Riga on the coast of the Baltic Sea. The city fell on October 15, 1944 after a doomed German defense had been crushed.

Success in the first phase of the operation depended largely on the secret movement into the region of 6th Guards Army to reinforce the 1st Baltic Front, 28th Army to reinforce the 1st Belorussian Front, 5th Guards Tank Army to exploit in 3rd Belorussian Front's sector, and numerous other units. All of these movements were covered by an elaborate deception plan, which was designed to convince the Germans that the offensive would take place further south.

The destruction of Army Group Center was no small task. On June 1, elements of the four Soviet *fronts* (1st Baltic, 1st, 2nd, and 3rd Belorussian) confronted the four armies of Army Group Center (Third Panzer, Fourth, Ninth, and Second). Approximately one million Soviet troops confronted over 700,000 Germans (426,168 in combat units), a ratio not to Soviet planners' liking. To establish force superiority necessary for success involved a massive secret strategic redeployment into Belorussia of three combined-arms armies, one tank and one air army, and several mobile corps. Once regrouping was complete, Soviet strength had risen to over 1.2 million troops.

The operation, which began with strong and successful reconnaissance action on June 22, developed more rapidly than had been planned. Army mobile tank groups exploited the rifle forces' success on the first or second day of the assault. In the Vitebsk area, tank-heavy forward detachments and follow-on rifle forces quickly encircled the bulk of Third Panzer Army. Further south, 2nd Guards Tank Corps outflanked German Fourth Army forces at Orsha and advanced deep towards Minsk. The cavalry-mechanized group began its exploitation toward Lepel' and the Berezina River northeast of Minsk, and Gen. Pavel A. Rotmistrov's 5th Guards Tank Army, with almost 600 tanks and SP guns, advanced directly toward the Berezina River and Minsk.

The German command responded belatedly by dispatching 5th and 12th Panzer Divisions into Belorussia

to restore the situation. Despite gallant actions by these two divisions along the Berezina and west of Bobruisk, the two divisions were forced by the weight of the attack to join the swelling stream of German fugitives escaping west from the Soviet juggernaut.

In the Bobruisk region, Soviet 9th and 1st Guards Tank Corps, spearheading 1st Belorussian Front's advance, reached Bobruisk and encircled major portions of German Ninth Army, while a second cavalry-mechanized group thrust northwestward to cut German communications running into Minsk from the south and southwest. By July 3, Soviet forces linked up west on Minsk, secured the city without costly urban combat, and encircled the bulk of German Fourth Army. While almost 300,000 Germans were being reduced, Soviet mobile forces pushed on westward towards Vilnius, Bialystok, and Brest in an operation which, by late August, had pushed the remnants of Army Group Center to the borders of East Prussia. In the north, the Baltic Fronts advanced painstakingly towards Riga on the Baltic Sea against stiffening German resistance.

The vicious fighting in Belorussia cost the Germans over 400,000 men, more than were lost at Stalingrad, at a cost to the Soviets of over half a million casualties. At this stage of the war, however, such losses were far more catastrophic for the Germans.

The 1st Ukrainian Front's operations in southern Poland against Germany Army Group North Ukraine were designed to capitalize on successes already achieved in Belorussia. The Stavka ordered Marshal I.S. Konev's Front to destroy enemy groups in the Lvov and Rava-Russkaia regions by two simultaneous blows. Konev's attacks were to be spearheaded in the north by Gen. M. E. Katukov's 1st Guards Tank Army, which had been secretly redeployed from the south, and a cavalry-mechanized group, and in the south by Gen. P. S. Rybalko's and D. D. Leliushenko's 3rd and 4th Guards Tank Armies and a second cavalry-mechanized group.

Above: A Soviet medal for bravery instituted in 1938. In 1942 these classless awards began to be replaced by campaign and defense medals and awards specifically for senior officers, such as the Order of Victory (1943). *Salamander Books*

Above: Marshal Ivan Konev watches the progress of the fighting from a forward observation post as men of his 1st Ukrainian Front battle for Krosno in southeastern Poland during the autumn of 1944.

Below: The standard service rifle of the Red Army, the Nagant Model 91/30. The rifle fired a 7.62 × 54mm rimmed cartridge carried in a five round magazine.
Imperial War Museum, London

Meanwhile, to the south two armies would conduct a feint in the foothills of the Carpathian Mountains.

The most challenging task Konev faced was to carry out the required massive regrouping of forces, which involved movement of 1,300 tanks/SP guns, 1,910 guns and mortars, and 7,200 vehicles organized into 37 rifle divisions, 32 tank and mechanized brigades, and 87 artillery regiments. By virtue of this regrouping, at the time of his attack Konev had established marked numerical superiority over his foes.

The Soviet offensive in the northern sector began on July 13, when 3rd Guards' and 13th Army's reconnaissance units found German forward positions unmanned. Immediately, forward battalions and main forces joined the attack and, by day's end, had penetrated 5–9 miles (8–15km) into the German defenses east of Rava-Russkaia. Further south, opposite Lvov, German resistance was heavier, and Soviet forward battalions were halted. Soviet 60th Army succeeded in penetrating German defenses in 3rd Guards Tank Army's sector of commitment, but 38th Army failed to pierce German defenses in the sector where 4th Tank Army was to advance. Consequently, Konev committed both tank armies and several tank corps, about 1,000 tanks and SP guns, through the narrow 3.5 mile (6km) corridor (the Koltov corridor) in 60th Army's sector. Once committed and after fending off heavy German counterattacks, the two tank armies succeeded in enveloping German defenses around Lvov and forced the Germans to abandon the city.

Even more damaging to the Germans was 1st Guards Tank Army's operations with the Cavalry-Mechanized Group in the north. Prior to his army's advance, Katukov ordered his army's forward detachment, 1st Guards Tank Brigade, to attack westward and deceive the Germans regarding the direction of his attack. Once German operational reserves (16th and 17th Panzer Divisions) had responded to the threat, thinking it to be the bulk of 1st Guards Tank Army, Katukov led his army southwest, breaking cleanly through German defenses and driving deep into their operational rear.

The subsequent development of the operation demonstrated the impact of 1st Guards Tank Army's success. Under pressure from the north, German resistance also broke east of Lvov. The 3rd Guards and 4th Tank Armies penetrated into the depths, bypassed Lvov and, together with 1st Guards Tank Army, began a race toward the Vistula River. By July 30, lead elements of Soviet tank and rifle armies secured key bridgeheads across the Vistula, which, despite heavy German counterattacks, they would not relinquish. The tank armies had advanced up to 186 miles (300km) in as many as 15 days of continuous operations. Although the bulk of the Germans' Army Group North Ukraine avoided the fate of Army Group Center, its XIII Corps was encircled and destroyed near Brody, and its remaining forces were severely shaken and had to be reinforced by troops transferred from Hungary. The cost of the operation to Konev was almost 300,000 casualties.

On July 18, after German defenses in Belorussia and around Lvov had become a shambles, Marshal K.K. Rokossovsky's 1st Belorussian Front's left wing unleashed a third major offensive thrust toward Lublin and the Vistula River. The *Stavka* had first considered such

Above: The Germans fought tenaciously to hold key cities such as Lvov in Poland but were overwhelmed in all aspects of fighting, such as this urban fighting near the station, by the increasingly capable Soviets.

an offensive in late May when it developed the larger concept for the summer offensive. Thereafter, Rokossovsky refined the concept while he planned and carried out the Bobruisk operation against the southern flank of German Army Group Center. On July 7, after completion of the Bobruisk encirclement and at a time when the center and right wing of the 1st Belorussian Front were advancing on a broad front toward Baranovichi and Minsk, Rokossovsky completed his planning. His orders were to cooperate with the right wing of the 1st Ukrainian Front, destroy the Lublin–Brest enemy group, and reach the Vistula River on a broad front.

Rokossovsky decided to launch his main attack from the Kovel area toward Lublin along the boundary between German Army Groups Center and North Ukraine. His *front*'s main force (three combined-arms armies and a tank army) would advance on the Vistula River and Brest to trap German forces withdrawing from southern Belorussia in a pincer, and destroy them.

Offensive preparations included a massive secret regrouping of forces within the left wing of the *front* and an equally massive influx of strategic reserves. Three armies and three mobile corps had to move from other *front* sectors together with numerous supporting units previously employed in 1st Belorussian Front's attack in Belorussia. The strategic regrouping encompassed 13 rifle divisions, three tank corps, two cavalry corps, and 18 artillery regiments. By the time of the attack, Rokossovsky had achieved force superiority.

On July 18, Rokossovsky's main assault force, led by 8th Guards Army, struck at German defenses west of Kovel. Within hours the German tactical defenses had been ripped apart, and on July 20, while rifle forces approached the Western Bug River, 2nd Tank Army moved forward and the next day began an operational exploitation which propelled it to the banks of the Vistula River. Soon 8th Guards Army arrived and breached the Vistula at Magnushev.

Complicating the German's situation on August 1, the Polish Home Army rose in Warsaw, seized large segments of the city, but failed to take the key Vistula bridges. The 2nd Tank Army, commanded by its chief of staff, Gen. A. I. Radzievsky, who had taken command after its commander had been wounded, raced northward from Magnushev to take advantage of the deteriorating German situation in Warsaw and reached the eastern suburbs of the city on July 29. Radzievsky swung his 3rd Tank Corps north in an attempt to outflank German defenders on the east bank of the Vistula, but between August 1 and 3 that corps ran into and was virtually destroyed by a German counterattack force (19th Panzer, Hermann Göring, and SS Viking Divisions) hastily assembled by the new Army Group Center commander, Field

Below: One of the Soviet's great strengths was their artillery, which was of excellent quality and available in large numbers. These are 152-mm field howitzers providing accurate fire to a range of 13,500 yds (12,150m).

Marshal Model. Radzievsky's badly damaged tank army held its positions east of Warsaw until reinforcements could arrive.

Throughout August, 1st Belorussian Front's forces struggled to hold their tenuous bridgehead over the Vistula at Magnushev against heavy German counterattacks, and to push German forces back toward the Narew River, north of Warsaw. This left the remnants of 2nd Tank Army and 47th Army covering the eastern approaches to Warsaw. Whether for political or military reasons, or both, the Soviets concentrated their attention on seizing bridgeheads across the Narew north of Warsaw rather than regrouping their forces for a direct assault on the city to aid the beleaguered Polish Home Army. Finally, on September 16–17, after the bulk of the eastern bank of the Vistula had been swept free of German forces, elements of 1st Polish Army – fighting with Soviet forces – assaulted across the Vistula, only to be thrown back across the river. By this time the Home Army had been virtually annihilated. Warsaw would not fall to Soviet forces until January 1945.

The five Soviet *fronts* which had smashed German strategic defenses between Vitebsk and the Carpathian Mountains, by early August struggled along an extended front from the Northern Dvina River to the upper Vistula River. The roster of cities reconquered by Soviet armies – Vitebsk, Mogilev, Bobruisk, Minsk, Vilnius, Grodno, Bialystok, Brest, Lublin, Lvov – bore mute testimony to the scale of the German disaster.

Soviet Fronts on the flanks now joined battle to capitalize on German collapse in the center. On the northern flank, the Baltic Fronts attacked German Army Group North in time-phased sequence from south to north in the so-called Baltic Strategic Offensive. The first to attack was the remainder of Marshal I. Kh. Bagramian's 1st Baltic Front, which went into action north of the Northern Dvina River on July 4. In short order, Marshal Eremenko's 2nd Baltic Front and Gen. Maslennikov's 3rd Baltic Front joined battle as the three *fronts* drove toward the Baltic coast and Riga, against heavy German resistance. This series of operations endured well into the fall – an unspectacular, slow, broad front advance measured in miles per week. Combined with the recent

Above: The schwerer Wurframen 40: six 280/320-mm rockets on a steel tube assembly fitted on the SdKfz 251 half-track: seen in the 1944 Warsaw fighting.

Below: Red Army shoulder board insignia. From the right: sergeant-major (starshina) of artillery; junior-sergeant (mladshiy serzhant) of the Air Force; junior-lieutenant (mladshiy leytenant) of infantry.
Imperial War Museum, London

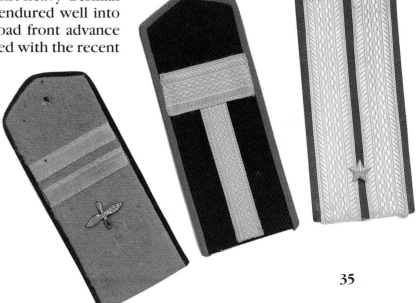

fighting in Belorussia and eastern Poland, however, it provided sufficient distraction for the Germans regarding what was about to occur in the south.

In the south, along the Romanian borders, the front had been relatively quiet since early May, when the Germans had considered it to be a prime location for a new major offensive. That offensive had not materialized. On the contrary, while the Germans waited expectantly for an attack, the Soviets had thinned out their front, dispatching army after army northward. Thereafter, as combat enveloped the Germans in Belorussia and Poland, the German High Command stripped its forces in Romania of its best mobile units and sent them north to stem the Soviet tide. The German command, however, remained confident that Army Group South Ukraine could avoid a disaster similar to those which befell every other German army group on the Eastern Front in the summer of 1944. Unknown to the Germans, however, the *Stavka* had chosen German forces in Romania as its final target in the fourth act of the summer strategic offensive.

Planning for the projected Soviet operation in Romania was complete by July 31, 1944. The *Stavka* ordered Marshals R. Ia. Malinovsky's and F. I. Tolbukhin's 2nd and 3rd Ukrainian Fronts, in cooperation with the Black Sea Fleet, to destroy enemy forces in the Iassy, Kishinev, and Bendery regions and subsequently to advance deep into Romania. The 2nd Ukrainian Front was to attack between the Tyrgu–Frumos and Iassy strongpoints of German Eighth Army, a region defended largely by Romanian troops, and 3rd Ukrainian Front south of Bendery at the junction of German Sixth and Romanian Third Armies. Mobile corps would then encircle the enemy force, and 6th Tank Army would begin a deep exploitation toward the Romanian capital Bucharest.

Massive secret internal regrouping was necessary to create required force concentrations, for the *Stavka* had few reserves available for use in the operation. During the 17 days of regrouping the two *fronts* had to redeploy 45 rifle divisions, 15 tank and mechanized brigades, and 96 artillery regiments a distance of between 12–68 miles (20–110km). In so doing, the Soviets built massive force superiorities over their opponents.

On August 20, the Soviet assault commenced, rapidly penetrating German and Romanian defenses in both sectors. By August 22, the breach in those defenses had become irreparable and was compounded by the surrender of many Romanian units. Within one week, Army Group South Ukraine had suffered a fate similar to that of Army Group Center – the destruction of Sixth Army and two Romanian armies and the utter collapse of the German front in Romania. German and allied losses exceeded another 400,000 men at a cost to the Soviets of

Below: Relaxed-looking Soviet infantry cruise into the Romanian town of Focsani on the decking of an American Sherman tank supplied to the USSR under the terms of the 1941 Lend-Lease Act.

about 67,000 casualties. An Axis retreat ensued which would not halt until Soviet forces had penetrated Bulgaria and swung west to enter the plains of Hungary.

During the successive strategic operations of the summer offensive, the Soviets destroyed three German army groups deployed on the central and southern portions of the Eastern Front and reached the eastern border of Germany and the Vistula River. Adroit Soviet use of diversionary offensives, secret strategic regroupment of forces, and strategic and operational deception permitted Soviet forces to achieve decisive force superiorities over the Germans. Faced with the growing Soviet force superiority of over two to one strategically, the Germans could ill afford to lose track of Soviet strategic reserves.

Soviet freedom to move their units with impunity and without German detection permitted the Soviets to create operational force superiority of up to five to one. The more serious German problem in 1944 was their inability to detect redeploying Soviet operational and tactical reserves. They did so adequately only in the single sector where they concentrated all their attention (Lvov) but failed to do so elsewhere. Consequently, the Soviets could convert operational superiorities of five to one into tactical superiorities of more than eight and ten to one with impunity. No defense could withstand such an onslaught, especially since each onslaught normally contained an armored nucleus which, after penetration of the tactical defenses, often went as far as its logistical umbilical permitted it to go. By the summer of 1944, this averaged a depth of 155 miles (250km).

The damage done to the German Army during the summer was staggering. German strength on the Eastern Front on November 1, had fallen to 2,030,000 men, plus 190,000 Allies, supported by 5,700 artillery pieces and 3,700 tanks and assault guns. Soviet strength had risen to 6,770,100 troops, almost 114,000 guns and mortars, and 8,300 tanks and SP guns. This Soviet superiority would spell further trouble for German defenders in 1945. To make matters worse, in July Hitler confounded a plot against his life which had severe repercussions in the Wehrmacht.

In late August 1944, the *Stavka* ordered its *Fronts* to consolidate their positions and occupy positions favorable for the launching of a new strategic offensive in the winter. This consolidation period was marked by bitter fighting for bridgeheads along the Narew and Vistula Rivers, where the Soviets strove to enlarge the bridgeheads against German armored thrusts designed to eliminate them. By mid-October, as if from sheer exhaustion, the lines in the central region stabilized with the bridgeheads still in Soviet hands. Now the attention of both sides shifted to the flanks where fighting flared anew, in reality a prelude to the forthcoming winter offensive.

Above: Officer's brass belt buckle, Red Army.
Imperial War Museum, London

V Three
The Reconquest
of the Philippines

Duncan Anderson

The war in the Pacific had reach a critical stage by the summer of 1944. The two major American drives, in the central and southwest Pacific were both making progress, but which was to be given priority in the advance towards Japan?

By the summer of 1944 Japan was reeling from a succession of disasters. The forces of Gen. Douglas MacArthur's Southwest Pacific Command had leap-frogged along the northern coast of New Guinea isolating Japanese garrisons; on July 30 the Americans occupied Sansapor on the northwestern tip of New Guinea's Vogelkop Peninsula, bringing them to within 800 miles (1,250km) of Mindanao, the southernmost island of the Philippines. Meanwhile Adm. Chester Nimitz's great battle fleets had swept through the central Pacific, sinking two Japanese aircraft carriers and destroying 450 Japanese carrier aircraft in the Battle of the Philippine Sea, while his amphibious task forces stormed ashore on Saipan and Guam in the Marianas in June and July. From here the Americans were only 1,000 miles (1,600km) due east of Luzon, the main island of the Philippines.

Saipan had been part of Japan's inner defensive perimeter and its loss meant that the Americans were now poised to cut off the heart of the co-prosperity sphere from its southern resources area, by driving on Luzon or Formosa. Rocked by this succession of disasters, on July 18 Japan's prime minister Gen. Tojo and his cabinet resigned. But the Japanese were very far from entertaining the possibility of defeat.

On July 21 planning staffs of the Japanese army and navy prepared schemes for a number of contingencies, the *Sho* (Victory) Plans, all of which were designed to impose a decisive battle on the Americans. Tokyo drew up four main plans, of which *Sho* 1, the blueprint of the battle Japan intended to fight for the Philippines, was considered the most likely. Several factors indicated that

Left: The USS *Pennsylvania* leads the USS *Colorado*, USS *Louisville*, USS *Portland* and USS *Columbia* in a battle line entering the Lingayen Gulf, prior to the US landings on the island of Luzon. The war in the Pacific would see the strategic influence of these great 'battle wagons' eclipsed by the spectacular success of naval air power and the aircraft carrier.

39

Above: American propaganda poster in Spanish; produced in 1942 for distribution in Central and South America. Below: Poster produced by/for General Motors Corporation for display in their factories.
War Memorial Museum of Virginia

the Philippines would be the Americans' next target.

Japan, therefore, began pouring reinforcements into the Philippines; by the fall 350,000 troops and some 2,500 front line aircraft were based in the islands. In addition, 70 warships of the Combined Fleet, stationed in anchorages as far apart as Singapore and Nagasaki, were ready to converge on the islands the moment American intentions became clear. Tokyo High Command believed it had converted the Philippines into a gigantic trap, one into which the Americans were sure to walk. Southern Area Commander, Gen. Terauchi, reported as almost euphoric at the prospect of the coming battle, transferred his headquarters from Singapore to Manila, in order to be near the scene of the action.

Tojo's resignation made possible some sweeping changes in command. Out went Tojo's appointee as commander in the Philippines, Lt. Gen. Juroda Shigenori, who had spent much of his time in Manila playing golf; in came Tojo's most bitter enemy, the 'Tiger of Malaya,' Lt. Gen. Yamashita.

The American High Command was, however, even more faction-riven than that of Japan. Adm. Chester Nimitz, the US commander in the Central Pacific, and Adm. Ernest J. King, Chief of Naval Operations and a powerful member of the Joint Chiefs of Staff, both disliked and feared Gen. MacArthur. The United States Navy had always regarded the Pacific as their preserve, and Adm. Nimitz did his best to turn the Southwest Pacific Area (SWPA) into a sideshow, but MacArthur outmaneuvered him at every turn. Now both forces were more or less equidistant from the Philippines.

Between July 26 and 29 1944 Roosevelt met with MacArthur and Nimitz in Hawaii, in order to determine the future direction of US strategy. Nimitz argued strongly for a Navy dominated offensive which would bypass Luzon and drive directly for Formosa and the coast of China. MacArthur was equally adamant that his forces should compose the main thrust, with Nimitz relegated to a supporting role. To the general it was inconceivable that America should bypass Luzon; he had given the Filipinos his personal promise – "I shall return" – and he was determined to keep his word. MacArthur presented the conference with a precise timetable – a landing on Morati Island halfway between New Guinea and Mindanao on September 8, followed by landings on Mindanao on October 25, Leyte on December 20, and Luzon on April 1, 1945. Roosevelt had no love for the general, but a landing on Mindanao on October 25 would help in the 1944 presidential election, due to be held in early November, and it seems this was the reason that Roosevelt now sided with MacArthur. The landings on Mindanao and Leyte were to go ahead.

Thanks to generally excellent signals intelligence and

to regular contact with Filipino guerrillas, SWPA head-quarters in Hollandia in West New Guinea had a fairly clear picture of the speed at which the Japanese were reinforcing the Philippines. MacArthur saw himself in a race with Terauchi and Yamashita; he had to get his forces to the island before the Japanese became so strong that the cost of a landing would be prohibitive.

On September 15, as MacArthur watched the landing of troops on Mortai from the bridge of the cruiser USS *Nashville*, carrier aircraft from Adm. William 'Bull' Halsey's Third Fleet operating off Leyte reported the complete absence of opposition. On the basis of these reports Halsey flashed a signal via Nimitz to the Joint Chiefs of Staff, urging the abandonment of the Mindanao and associated operations in favor of an immediate landing on Leyte. The Joint Chiefs of Staff flashed a signal back to SWPA HQ asking if it was possible to advance the Leyte landings by two months, from December 20 to October 20. MacArthur concurred and even tried to push for a simultaneous landing on Luzon, but even the most syco-phantic member of his staff argued strongly against this. The shipping was simply not available; and it was only by near super-human efforts that the invasion fleet could be assembled by mid-October.

MacArthur designated October 20 'A' Day, with 'A' standing for Assault. His former aide, Dwight D. Eisenhower, now Supreme Allied Commander in Europe, had already used 'D' Day as the designation for June 6, 1944. In later years, MacArthur claimed his A-Day as much bigger than Eisenhower's D-Day, and he was right. Although Normandy had involved a greater number of ships, Leyte involved a greater tonnage of shipping, and more troops and more warships. The landing force consisted of 738 transports and escorts, carrying 203,000 troops of Gen. Walter Krueger's Sixth Army, along with some two and a half million tons (tonnes) of supplies and equipment. Adm. Halsey's Third Fleet of 105 major warships, including 18 fleet aircraft carriers, cruised the Philippine Sea providing distant cover.

Leyte was a mountainous island, 115 miles (184km) long and between 15 and 45 miles (24 and 72km) wide. The only areas in which the construction or airfields and logistic bases on a large scale was feasible was in the Leyte Valley in the northeast of the island, and in the Ormoc Valley in the northwest. MacArthur's A-Day objectives lay on the northeast coast at the entrance to the valley – the city of Tacloban (population 30,000), and its nearby airfield. At dawn on October 20, warships and aircraft commenced a devastating bombardment of suspected Japanese positions along an 18-mile (29km) stretch of coast to the south of Tacloban. At 10:00 the bombardment lifted and four divisions of Krueger's Sixth Army began to land, the 1st Cavalry and 24th

Below: Japanese battle flag with honors, including from the left: Mindanao, Mindoro, Leyte, Panay, Hollandia and Goodenough Island. *Eugene C. Gibson Collection*

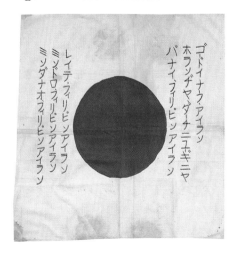

Infantry just south of Tacloban, and the 96th and 7th Infantry near Dulag, a town some 15 miles (24km) south of Tacloban. Resistance was negligible – during the entire day the Americans suffered only 49 men killed.

At about 13:30, a landing craft carrying MacArthur and other senior officers of SWPA staff to Leyte grounded off 24th division's beachhead, forcing the immaculately dressed supreme commander to wade ashore. MacArthur was furious; he prided himself on his appearance and was soaked to the waist. His annoyance quickly passed, though, for at 14:00, he broadcast from the back of a weapons carrier on the beach: "People of the Philippines, I have returned! By the grace of Almighty God, our forces stand again on Philippine soil . . . Rally to me!"

Between October 21 and 25 Sixth Army rapidly enlarged its beachhead against patchy Japanese resistance. Maj. Gen. Willoughby, MacArthur's intelligence chief, was certain that the Japanese were evacuating Leyte and that Sixth Army faced only a mopping-up operation. In fact the *Sho* Plan was already in operation. The Americans' preliminary reconnaissance on the east coast of Leyte on October 17 had given the Japanese 72 hours warning of the landings. Suzaki, aware that an American bombardment was likely to be very intense, pulled all but a light screening force back from the east coast, and concentrated his forces along the ridge which separated the Leyte and the Ormoc Valleys.

In the meantime the dispersed units of the Japanese Combined Fleet converged on the Philippines. The Northern Force, a fleet consisting of the four surviving aircraft carriers, two battleships, three cruisers and eight destroyers under Adm. Ozawa, steamed south from Japan. It looked powerful; but earlier battles had reduced its 450 aircraft to scarcely 100. Its real role was that of a decoy. Adm. Toyoda, commander of the Combined Fleet, told Ozawa that as soon as he had managed to attract American attention he was to put about and speed north, drawing the main part of the enemy fleet behind him.

On October 22, while Ozawa's ships ploughed south, the bulk of the Combined Fleet (seven battleships, thirteen cruisers and nineteen destroyers) rendezvoused in Brunei Bay on the north west coast of Borneo, some 700 miles (1,120km) from the Leyte beachhead. It now separated into two task forces. A Center Task Force under Adm. Kurita, comprising the super battleships *Yamato* and *Musashi*, three other battleships, twelve cruisers and fifteen destroyers, was to sail north along the western side of Palawan, and then turn due east, pass through the Sibuyan Sea and the San Bernadino Strait, to attack the American beachhead in Leyte Gulf from the north. At the same time a Southern Task Force commanded by Adm. Nishimura was to sail east across the

Below: US naval power was instrumental in the defeat of Japan. Seen here entering the lagoon of Ulithi Atoll after a strike on the Philippines in December 1944 are elements of Task Group 38.3 with the light carrier *Langley* followed by the fleet carrier *Ticonderoga*, the battleships *Washington, North Carolina* and *South Dakota*, the cruisers *Santa Fe, Biloxi* and *Mobile*, and the antiaircraft cruiser *Oakland*.

Sulu Sea, pass through the Surigao Strait, and strike the Leyte anchorage from the south. A fourth task force of three cruisers and four destroyers headed by Adm. Shima, coming south from the Ryukyus, was to follow Nishimura's Southern Task Force through the Surigao Strait, and deliver a follow-up attack on the beachhead.

Shortly after 01:00 on October 23 the US submarines *Darter* and *Dace* sighted Kurita's force off Palawan. Flashing the location to Halsey's Third Fleet, *Darter* and *Dace* launched full spreads of torpedos. Two cruisers exploded and a third, badly damaged, limped back to Brunei Bay. Through the night and the following day Kurita pressed on due east into the Sibuyan Sea while Halsey's fleet, responding to the submarines' signals, swept due west towards San Bernadino Strait. Halsey had divided Third Fleet into four mutually supporting task forces; by dawn on October 24 the westernmost of these, Rear Adm. Sherman's Task Group (TG) 38.3 had come within range of Japanese aircraft on Luzon. About 200 bombers, torpedo bombers, and fighters of Adm. Fukudome's airfleet flew towards Sherman's ships. US Navy Hellcat fighters brought most down, but one dive bomber managed to score a direct hit on the flight deck of the light carrier *Princeton*, which later sank.

While TG 38.3 fought off Fukudome's attack, aircraft from Rear Adm. Brogan's TG 38.2, sailing some 250 miles (400km) to the southwest of Sherman's ships, located Kurita's Center Force in the Sibuyan Sea. The Americans concentrated on Kurita's two super battleships, the *Yamato* and *Musashi*. *Yamato* fought off her attackers but *Masashi*, hit by bombs and torpedos, began to lose speed. All day long American aircraft pressed home their attacks, sending at least nineteen torpedos into her hull; shortly after 19:00 she rolled over and sank. By this time Kurita had reversed course, heading back to Palawan and the South China Sea.

Throughout the day the carriers of Ozawa's Northern Force had been sailing south, their radios broadcasting their positions to the Americans in clear language. The clarity of the message, ironically, proved counterproductive. US naval intelligence, overwhelmed by the amount of radio traffic, placed a low priority on translating clear messages. Ozawa, desperate to attract the US Navy's attention, ordered the *Ise* and *Hyuga*, two hybrid battleship-aircraft carriers, to steam straight at top speed for the nearest American task force. At about 16:00 reconnaissance aircraft from Sherman's Task Force spotted the battleships, and shortly thereafter located the four aircraft carriers. Halsey took the bait hook, line and sinker. He was now convinced that Kurita's force and the force under Nishimura which American reconnaissance aircraft had spotted earlier in the day, were diversionary. Within the hour virtually the entire Third

Above: A selection of Imperial Japanese Navy insignia and memorabilia. From the top: civilian paper parade flag bearing the IJN emblem; a dark blue wool junior officer's cap; naval belt buckle; seaman's insignia: the cherry blossom. Sleeve insignia of, from the left: ordinary seaman, leading seaman petty officer first class and chief petty officer.
US Marine Raider Museum, Richmond, Va

Below: A *kamikaze* bids farewell before departure on the one-way flight intended to cripple or sink an American warship. This tactic scored some considerable successes.

Fleet was speeding north in pursuit of Ozawa (who had now reversed course) for what the Americans believed would be the climatic battle of the Pacific War.

Adm. Kinkaid, commanding US Seventh Fleet off the Leyte beachhead, was far less convinced that Nishimura's task force was a diversion. On first receiving a report that Japanese battleships and cruisers were heading to the Surigao Straits, Kinkaid had sent Rear Adm. Jessie B. Oldendorf and virtually all Seventh Fleet's major warships steaming south at full speed to lay an ambush in the Surigao Straits. By dusk Oldendorf had stationed his battleships, cruisers, and destroyers at a point where the straits narrowed to only 12 miles (19km), while he sent his patrol-torpedo (PT) boats another 60 miles (96km) up the straits to act as a reconnaissance screen.

Shortly after midnight on October 25 Nishimura's warships ploughed through the line of Oldendorf's PT boats. At 03:00 American destroyer flotillas raced down the straits and came within 8,000 yards (7,200m) of the Japanese before launching successive spreads of torpedos. The battleship *Fuso* exploded, and shortly afterwards two Japanese destroyers were hit and went down. Nishimura, his Southern Task Force now reduced to his flagship the battleship *Yamashiro*, the cruiser *Mogami*, and two destroyers, pushed on towards the narrowest part of the strait. Just before 04:00 the American battleships and cruisers opened up, sending the *Yamashiro* with Nishimura aboard her, and another destroyer, to the bottom. The remnants of Southern Task Force, the *Mogami* and a single destroyer, put about and headed at full speed down the straits. At that very moment Adm. Shima's cruisers and destroyers, having just arrived from the Ryukyu Islands, were racing up the straits to join Nishimura. American PT boats dashed within range and crippled the cruiser *Ashigara*. A short time later Shima's force passed the blazing hulk of *Fuso* and then *Mogami* loomed out of the gloom and sliced into the stern of Shima's flagship, the heavy cruiser *Nachi*. That was enough for Shima; he too put about, leaving the crippled *Ashigara* and the badly damaged *Mogami* to be finished off by marauding American cruisers and destroyers after dawn.

As dawn broke over the Surigao Straits Oldendorf knew he had won a great victory. But a very different situation was developing only 200 miles (320km) to the north. During the night Kurita's Center Force had reversed course once more. With Halsey's fleet 400 miles (640km) to the north off Cape Engano in hot pursuit of Ozawa's aircraft carriers, Kurita's four battleships, six heavy cruisers and ten destroyers made an unimpeded passage of the San Bernadino Strait, then turned south down the east coast of Samar Island towards the Leyte beachhead. Only one American force — Taffy 3 — stood between beachhead and annihilation. Taffy 3 was a task force of seven destroyers and destroyer escorts, and six slow, unarmoured, escort carriers. Just before 07:00 the commander of Taffy 3, Rear Adm. Clifton T. Sprague, sighted Kurita's battleships. He immediately ordered his ships to steam at top speed for the south and sent his few dozen aircraft up to attack the Japanese ships. For his part, Kurita was convinced that the flat-topped silhouettes he saw in the far distance were in fact the aircraft carriers of Halsey's Third Fleet.

A fantastic two and a half hour running fight now developed. *Yamato* opened up at 35,000 yards (31km), her 18.1 inch shells falling amongst Sprague's ships, but a combination of American destroyer attacks and air strikes soon disabled two of Kurita's cruisers. Japanese battleships then bracketed and sank two American destroyers and the escort carrier *Gambier Bay*. By 07:30 other escort carrier groups had launched aircraft. But Kurita himself was also getting some welcome assistance. At 07:40 *kamikaze* suicide planes swept down on Taffy 1, an escort carrier task force whose aircraft had flown off to attack Kurita's ships, and plunged straight into the flightdeck of the escort carriers *Santee* and *Suwannee*, causing raging fires which badly damaged both ships. Shortly afterwards *kamikazes* hit Sprague's ships, sinking the escort carrier *St. Lo* and damaging the *Kalinin Bay*.

By 09:20 Kurita thought that victory was in his grasp. Off the Leyte beachhead transports were hurredly putting out to sea, steaming south to aid Kinkaid's battlefleet. But Kurita's ships could have overtaken most of them well before they reached Kinkaid. Since 07:00 Sprague had been sending desperate messages to Halsey, urging him to send the fast carriers of Rear Adm. Lee's Task Force 34 south to attack Kurita's battleships. Unfortunately Halsey had eyes only for Ozawa's aircraft carriers. By 10:00 the crisis off Samar had passed. Kurita had received reports of burning American carriers, but still American aircraft were attacking relentlessly. He thus came to the mistaken conclusion that he must be in the middle of Halsey's Third Fleet. Since he had already done it substantial damage, it was time for him to withdraw before Halsey brought overwhelming force to bear. At 09:23 Kurita ordered his fleet to put about and head back for the San Bernadino Strait. Had he but known it, real victory had been just within his grasp.

Meanwhile Halsey's aircraft had caught up with Ozawa. At about 08:00 180 aircraft from Rear Adm. Mitscher's fast carrier Task Force 38 located and sank the light carrier *Chitose*. During the morning two more massive strikes hit the carriers *Choyoda*, *Zuikaku* and *Zuiho* before, at 11:15, Task Forces 34 and 38 turned south to deal with Kurita. By the time Task Force 34

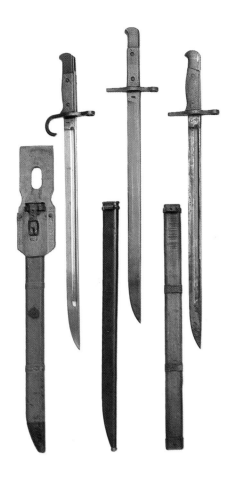

Far left and above: A selection of Japanese bayonets for the Arisaka 7.7mm rifle.
Salamander Books

reached the San Bernadino Strait at 01:00 on October 26 Kurita had long gone.

The Battle of Leyte Gulf, which entailed four naval actions spread over three days, was the largest and most complex naval battle in history. In all 282 ships were involved: 216 American, 2 Australian, and 64 Japanese. On the morning of October 23 Japan had still been a considerable naval power; by the evening of October 25 her navy was finished. She had lost four aircraft carriers, three battleships, ten cruisers and eleven destroyers, and virtually every other ship had been damaged, some very seriously. Yet the surviving Japanese admirals were unaware that it had been a defeat. Japanese losses had been grievous, but not (so Japanese intelligence claimed) as grievous as the losses they had inflicted on the Americans. The Japanese registered the burning *Princeton*, *Gambier Bay*, *St. Lo*, *Santee*, *Suwannee*, and *Kalinin Bay* as the destruction of major fleet aircraft-carriers. On October 27 Halsey pulled his carriers back to bases in the Central Pacific for refuelling and maintenance. By this stage even the sceptical Japanese High Army Command was convinced that the sudden disappearance of US carrier aircraft over Leyte could mean only one thing: their navy had won a great victory.

Gen. MacArthur accepted Halsey's decision on October 27 to withdraw his carriers to Central Pacific bases for maintenance and resupply, since on that day the first two squadrons of P-38s, his own South West Pacific Command airforce, flew into Tacloban airfield. On the same day, large numbers of Japanese reinforcements began to flow into Ormoc – the 1st and 26th Divisions, and the 68th Infantry Brigade, which would soon boost the 21,500 troops who had been on Leyte on October 20 to more than 65,000. Yamashita would still have preferred to have fought the decisive land battle on Luzon, but at Terauchi's urging he also came to believe that the Japanese Navy's 'victory' had changed the strategic situation.

Meanwhile, US Sixth Army forces advanced at an almost leisurely fashion along the north coast of Leyte, occupying the abandoned town of Carigara on November 2, convinced that the Japanese evacuation of Leyte must be almost complete. The following day, Krueger launched a double envelopment towards the port of Ormoc on the west coast of Leyte, which he believed was the last Japanese stronghold on the island. Maj. Gen. Irvine's 24th Division was to push southwest from Carigara across a ridge to the town of Limon and thence into the north of the Ormoc valley while the 7th Division, having crossed the narrowest part of the island and reached the west coast some 20 miles (32km) south of Ormoc, was to advance due north.

While Gen. Krueger had been occupying the north

Below: Propaganda poster produced in 1943 urging American workers to greater war production.
War Memorial Museum of Virginia

coast, the Japanese had moved large forces on to the ridge at the head of the Ormoc Valley. There they remained undisturbed for nearly two weeks while they built a complex series of fortifications. On November 5 they stopped the advancing US 24th Division in its tracks. Over the next nine days the 24th attacked up the ridge again and again, but to no avail. Looking for a scapegoat, Krueger relieved Irvine from command, withdrew 24th Division, and replaced it with the fresh 32nd Division. But the 32nd did little better. It advanced literally at a crawl. On November 22 the 32nd Division finally captured Limon on the reverse slope of the ridge. It had taken two divisions seventeen days to advance just two miles (3km) at a cost of 700 dead, across what Krueger's men now called Breakneck Ridge.

In the meantime, US 7th Division had slogged its way up the west. On November 23, only 13 miles (21km) south of Ormoc, it too was stopped dead while attempting to take a ridge held by Suzaki's 26th Division. The 7th Division later bitterly dubbed this particular conflict the battle of Shoestring Ridge.

In the early hours of November 27 the Japanese launched a complicated counter offensive designed to drive the Americans into the sea. Three transports attempted to crash-land onto the American airfield at Burauen, their objective the destruction of American land-based air power. They failed, and by December 10 artillery bombardments and airstrikes had forced the Japanese counteroffensive back to its start line.

By the end of the first week of December, the sheer weight of American manpower and material was beginning to swing the attritional slog in their favour. By this time 203,000 Americans had landed on Leyte, more than three times the number of Japanese. On December 7, 77th Division landed on the west coast only three miles (5km) south of Ormoc, a move which caught Suzaki by surprise; they then rapidly pushed north to meet the 24th Division and the 1st Cavalry Division at Libungao in the center of the Ormoc Valley on December 20. Suzaki's forces were now cut in half, and organized resistance ended on Christmas Day. The entire Japanese commitment to Leyte – 65,000 men plus another 10,000 who had been lost to American airstrikes and submarines in transit – had become casualties. The American loss – 16,000 – was lighter, but still a very high price to pay for what had been seen as a mopping-up operation.

As the fighting on Leyte dragged on, MacArthur reluctantly postponed the invasion of Luzon from December 20 to the first week of January 1945. The Allies' lack of land-based aircraft had been a problem on Leyte. It was likely to do so again on Luzon. MacArthur therefore intended to construct airbases on the island of Mindoro to the southwest of Luzon. The landing force sent to the

Below: Bosun's Mate 1st Class John E. Landau of the US Navy, raises the Stars and Stripes over the beachhead on Leyte in the Philippines during the first stages of the US invasion starting on October 20, 1944.

island was relatively small – roughly 20,000 men, most of whom were engineers and construction troops. The force which escorted them was, however, formidable: three battleships, three escort carriers, and six cruisers. But it was not formidable enough to withstand *kamikaze* assaults. On December 13 as they approached Mindoro the *kamikazes* struck, sinking two transports and damaging many other ships. The actual landing at San Jose on the eastern coast of Mindoro on December 15 met little opposition. Engineers immediately started work, finishing the first airstrip an astonishing five days later. It was just in time. On Christmas Day, a Japanese task force of two cruisers and six destroyers raced across the South China Sea from Indo-China and headed straight for Mindoro. They reached San Jose after dark on December 26, shelled the airfield and sank a transport and a PT boat. But other PT boats were able to sink one Japanese destroyer and force the rest of the task force to withdraw.

By the beginning of January, US air attacks on Luzon airfields had reduced Japanese air strength to just 600 machines. The US Air Force had meanwhile been trying to mislead the Japanese into believing that the landing on Luzon would take place in the extreme south of the island. It was a vain hope. Yamashita knew that the coast of Luzon offered only two possible landing points for large forces: the now heavily-defended Manila Bay, and Lingayen Gulf. Lingayen was the obvious choice. MacArthur planned to land more than 200,000 men of Krueger's Sixth Army, who would then advance on Manila (120 miles – 192km – to the south). This operation would be followed by landings at the neck of the Bataan Peninsula, to seize the entrance of Manila Bay, and to the south of Manila.

On January 2 an immense assault force set sail from Leyte Gulf. It covered about 500 square miles (1,250km^2) of ocean, and incorporated Adm. Oldendorf's support fleet of 160 battleships, escort carriers, cruisers and destroyers followed by Adm. Barbey's 750 transports and escorting warships. The *kamikazes*, now flying low to avoid radar and US fighter patrols, began their attacks on January 4, and kept them up for the next nine days. They concentrated at first on Oldendorf's fleet, sinking the escort carrier *Ommaney Bay*, and damaging six others.

Barbey's fleet proved just as vulnerable. The *kamikazes* sank 20 transports and escorts and damaged another 22. And on the night of January 9-10, when the fleet was inside Lingayen Gulf, 70 Japanese motor boats, heavily laden with explosives, attempted to ram the long columns of ships. They managed to sink or damage nine. In all, the approach to Luzon cost the Allies 91 ships sunk or damaged and 3,000 casualties, including 1,230 dead.

Below: The main landing on Luzon was carried out on January 9, 1945 in the Lingayen Gulf. This is a view of part of the beachhead created by the US Sixth Army as a first step in an advance to capture Manila.

At 10:00 on January 9, the first of Sixth Army's 200,000 troops went ashore at Lingayen, meeting with very little resistance. Four hours later MacArthur and his staff approached the beach. Since the beginning of January MacArthur's intelligence services had been convinced that Yamashita now had only about 150,000 men left on Luzon. Shortly after the landing, intelligence picked up signals that the Japanese were evacuating Manila. When he met with Sixth Army commander Gen. Krueger on January 12, MacArthur urged an immediate dash for the capital. But Krueger had other ideas.

Sixth Army intelligence had concluded that Japanese forces on Luzon were far stronger than MacArthur himself believed. Krueger surmised that Yamashita had at least 250,000 troops left. Thus the apparent ease with which the Americans had landed at Lingayen could only be deceptive. Krueger rejected MacArthur's plans for a headlong dash for the capital, insisting on waiting until his forces were fully established. After two weeks at loggerheads, the tension between the supreme commander and the commander of Sixth Army was palpable. Neither, however, had any real idea of Yamashita's strength or his intentions. In fact the Japanese garrison on Luzon numbered some 275,000 – reasonably close to Krueger's estimate. But MacArthur was right in one respect; Yamashita had indeed ordered the abandonment of Manila, though Rear Adm. Sanji Iwabuchi, the commander of a 20,000 strong Japanese naval force in the city, was disposed to disregard the orders.

Yamashita's plan was quite simple. The best he could achieve was to keep enough of his own forces in the field to tie down the largest possible number of American troops for as long as possible. He therefore had no intention of allowing MacArthur to trap his forces in the Manila Bay area. The 5,200 strong garrison of the fortress island of Corregidor was to hold out for as long as possible to deny the Americans Manila's port facilities. The remainder of his forces were to be deployed in three groups. Shimbu Group, 80,000 strong, was to dig in in the mountains directly east of Manila. The 30,000 strong Kembu Group was deployed about 40 miles (64km) north of Manila, and 80 miles (128km) south of Lingayen, to deny MacArthur the vast 200 square mile (500km^2) complex of airstrips and bases known as Clark Field. But the bulk of Japanese forces, some 152,000 troops along with virtually all the armor, formed Shobu Group which was under Yamashita's direct command. These he deployed in the rugged north east of Luzon, from where they could harrass any American advance from Lingayen to Manila.

After the landing, Krueger's 43rd and 25th divisions had rapidly advanced to the northeast and were soon heavily engaged with part of Shobu Group. This only

Above: Members of the crew of a US Navy PT boat pause to rescue a survivor from one of the many Japanese ships, including two battleships, sunk during a vain attempt to force the Surigao Strait on October 24, 1944.

Above: The sword of Lt. Gen. Tomoyuki Yamashita which he surrendered to US forces on September 2, 1945 when Japanese forces on Luzon finally capitulated.
West Point Museum, NY

confirmed Krueger's apprehension that if he were to advance on Manila, the Japanese to the northeast would advance across his lines of communication and cut him off from Lingayen. And then on January 23, 40th Division, advancing cautiously to the southwest, ran into Kembu Group just to the north of Clark Field. A fierce battle developed. Krueger was now convinced he was advancing into a trap; once he was close to Manila, the jaws of a Japanese pincer would spring shut behind him. For MacArthur the prevarication was too much. On January 30 he commanded the 1st Cavalry Division to make a drive on the city.

This was to be achieved by flying columns each composed of a company of tanks, towed field guns, and lorry loads of infantry. These were sent dashing down Highway 5, far ahead of the rest of the division. The cavalrymen covered nearly 100 miles (160km) in just two days. The speed of the advance overcame what opposition the Japanese attempted to offer. At 18:00 on February 3, 1st Cavalry sped down Rizal Avenue in northern Manila and drove to Santo Tomas University, where they quickly overwhelmed Japanese guards and liberated nearly 4,000 American and Allied civilian internees. Soon other units of 1st Cavalry reached the Malacanan Palace overlooking the Pasig River. The division had liberated the northern suburbs of Manila with scarcely a shot fired. To the south, across the Pasig, lay the administrative and commercial heart of the city; at its center stood the old walled Spanish city of Intramuros.

Meanwhile on January 31, US 11th Airborne Division had come ashore south of Manila Bay at Nasugbu, a town 40 miles (64km) southwest of Manila. The 11th Division quickly moved up Highway 17 towards Manila. By the morning of February 4 the paratroops had reached the Paranaque River, only six miles (10km) south of the 1st Cavalry at the Malacanan Palace. Japanese resistance over the next 48 hours increased. In the south, 11th Airborne were able to advance only about one mile (1.6km) to Nichols Field, while 1st Cavalry units consolidating on the northern side of the Pasig came under increasing heavy fire from the south side of the river.

Meanwhile MacArthur's intelligence chief, Gen. Willoughby, had intercepted signals from the area still controlled by the Japanese notifying High Command that they were destroying their code books. Willoughby interpreted this as a sure sign that the Japanese intended to withdraw from the city. He could not imagine the awful truth. Iwabuchi and his 26,000 naval troops had no intention of withdrawing from Manila; if necessary, they would die there. Disregarding Yamashita's orders, Iwabuchi had transformed every modern concrete building in the city center and the old city of Intramuros, whose stone walls were 40 feet (12m) thick, into fortresses.

On February 7 US 37th Division, which had just reached the city, launched assaults across the Pasig. Most of them ran into heavy Japanese fire and were soon pinned down. MacArthur turned down the divisional commander's request for airstrikes but eventually allowed artillery to fire in support. In the meantime, 11th Airborne was still battering its way north.

Though MacArthur still refused to authorize airstrikes, more and more artillery was employed. One by one the familiar landmarks of Manila were obliterated. By February 17 the converging attacks of 11th and 37th Divisions had pushed the Japanese back into Intramuros. For the next six days massed American artillery pulverized the old city, eventually producing breeches in the thick walls. The 37th Division's troops went in with flame throwers, fighting from building to building and room to room. Finally on March 3 all but a handful of the defenders were dead. The battle for Manila was officially over. About 1,200 Americans had been killed in action, and the Americans recovered 16,665 Japanese bodies. The real losers were the Filipino civilians, of whom at least 100,000 died.

From a strategic viewpoint the capture of Manila remained pointless since her harbor could not be used while the Japanese held Corregidor. The Japanese defences were formidable and manned by more than 5,000 troops. A conventional amphibious assault was likely to incur large casualties. On February 16, while the fighting in the capital raged, the 503rd Airborne regiment parachuted from C-47s only a few hundred feet above the island onto the small golf course and parade ground on Topside. Surprise was complete. Japanese resistance, though tenacious as ever, soon became disorganized. The paratroopers held the surface of the island but the Japanese fought back from tunnels underground. When they finally ran short of small arms ammunition they blew themselves apart by detonating the main underground magazines.

But the recapture of Corregidor was of far more than symbolic importance. By March 16 the first Allied convoys were making their way past the island into Manila harbor. And by the end of March the city was coming back to life. American engineers restored water supplies, electricity, and a public transport system while logisticians distributed 380,000 tons of supplies each month to Filipino civilians on Luzon. While the campaign against the residue of Yamashita's forces dragged on, Manila was transformed into the base from which MacArthur intended to lead the invasion of the Japanese Home Islands. It didn't work out that way but the reconstruction of Manila provided US forces with very useful experience. They would soon face a very similar task when they got to the Home Islands, just five months later.

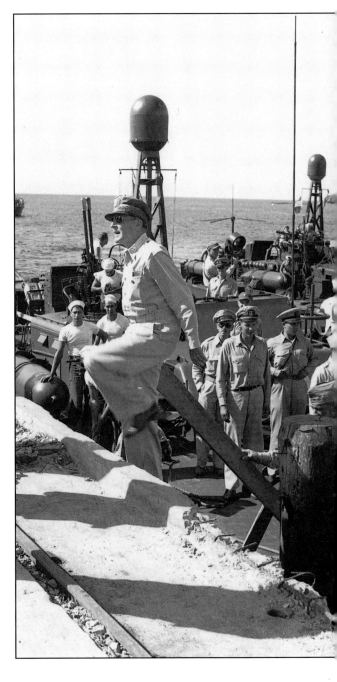

Above: Gen. Douglas MacArthur leads members of his staff from the PT Boats that had ferried the party to Corregidor island, whose recapture in February 1945 finally opened Manila Bay to US ships.

V Four

Drive to the Rhine

Roger Cirillo

As the summer of 1944 came to an end, German forces in western Europe had been crushed in the Normandy fighting and driven from France. However, a crisis in logistics and a series of strategic debates were soon to slow the Allied advance.

Supreme Headquarters, Allied Expeditionary Force (Forward) opened on September 1 at Jullouville, south of Granville at the base of the Cotentin Peninsula in Normandy. With its establishment, Gen. Eisenhower assumed operational control of Montgomery's 21st and Bradley's 12th Army Groups. In two weeks time, when the forces advancing from the southern France invasion beaches linked with Patton's army, Devers' 6th Army Group would be added to SHAEF's order of battle. Controversy, however, accompanied the change. Two arguments sprang up which were to persist for the rest of the war. One concerned overall battle strategy. The other, command of Allied ground forces.

The catalyst for both arguments was Sir Bernard L. Montgomery. Promoted to Field Marshal the same day Eisenhower assumed direct control of the four Allied armies edging toward Germany, Montgomery had just overseen the great Allied ground victory in Normandy. Though a hero to his own soldiers and the British people, Montgomery seemed unable to understand that America was not a junior partner in the coalition, and that command of her soldiers and her generals was not his perquisite.

Eisenhower had devised his strategy against Germany a month before D-Day. Planning a "broad front" advance with the main Allied attack being made north of the Ardennes through Aachen, and with a secondary effort going towards the Saar through Metz, he planned to keep the entire front active by shifting forces to meet opportunities or to concentrate for major attacks. After destroying the German army west of the Rhine, he planned a

Left: A patrol of British paratroopers picks its way through the rubble of the town of Oosterbeek west of Arnhem; the strain of seven days continuous combat etched into their faces. Part of an Allied airborne force meant to seize the bridges over the Lower Rhine prior to the arrival of reinforcements, these men instead quickly found themselves besieged by German forces.

53

massive double envelopment of the great industrial region of the Ruhr, to precede a final drive toward Berlin.

Nearly two weeks before SHAEF's move, Montgomery proposed that his own Anglo-Canadian 21st Army Group and Bradley's 12th, stay "together as a solid mass of forty divisions . . . secure bridgeheads over the Rhine before winter began . . . and seize the Ruhr quickly." Outwardly looking like the 1914 German Schlieffen Plan in reverse, Montgomery counted on Gen. Jacob Devers' newly operational 6th Army Group in southern France to move on Nancy and the Saar, thus threatening any German move to strike the Allied left flank. If the Ruhr could be taken, Hitler's industrial base would be halved, and most of his population dominated. German collapse would be inevitable. Montgomery offered himself as commander-in-chief of the ground forces.

Bradley originally planned to send both his First and Third Armies to the Rhine between Mannheim and Strasberg. Considering that Montgomery's Army Group was too small to maintain an attack on the rest of the front, Monty's forces would essentially become a flank guard, a supporting attack. Bradley, whose forces would link up with Devers' Army Group, would command the main Allied effort.

Eisenhower rejected both plans. His logistics planners warned that rather than being able to pursue the remnants of Hitler's armies, an impending supply famine loomed in the coming weeks. The tenacious German forward defense in Normandy had prevented the phased buildup needed to support a general advance beyond the Seine. Unable to stock supplies forward due to the small lodgement area eked out during the campaign's first two months, Allied transport companies now struggled to supply Bradley's rapidly moving armies. Because Allied airpower and the retreating Germans had destroyed France's railroads, only motor transport remained. Supplies existed, but truck companies were in short supply.

Serviceable ports were also a problem. With impending bad winter weather, over-the-beach unloading would have to cease, and Cherbourg's which was still yet to be opened, could not handle adequate tonnages. Most importantly, Cherbourg was now hundreds of miles behind the front. One of Montgomery's armies, the Canadian First, commanded by Gen. Crerar, was tasked to clear the channel ports to provide closer supply bases for 21st Army Group. Patton's Third Army, whose original mission to seize the Brittany ports had been handed to a weakened stay behind force, by rapidly pursuing the enemy, now posed the greatest supply burden for the Americans. The lack of either of these groups of ports – planned as part of a gradual buildup – the

Below: A wounded soldier of the British 49th Infantry Division is brought back for evacuation in a Universal Carrier. The Allies placed great emphasis on the speedy and effective treatment of the wounded.

additional burden of supporting Allied air force squadrons deploying to the continent, and the sustenance of Paris, made logistics the final arbiter of any strategy.

Eisenhower simply could not select one of the two courses of action proposed by his army group commanders. Both seemed doomed to be halted by transport problems, and he intended to link the three army groups in a coherent front before logistics stopped their advance.

Unfortunately, the command issue poisoned the strategic argument. With American divisions rapidly rising in numbers while British divisions were being broken up to sustain Dempsey's British Second Army, Eisenhower viewed Monty's ascendancy as the single ground commander as unreasonable, especially since Monty intended to retain personal command of 21st Army Group while also controlling Bradley and Devers. Instead, Ike would direct operations of the three army groups.

Though the Americans seemed the only ground gainers in late summer, that would soon change. Monty's own crossing of the Seine at August's end soon became a rapid pursuit, with Lt. Gen. Brian Horrocks' XXX Corps dashing 250 miles (400km) in six days. Brussels was liberated on September 3, and the great plum, the port of Antwerp, was captured by Maj. Gen. G. P. B. "Pip" Roberts' 11th Armoured Division on the 4th. Montgomery had been advised by Adm. Sir Bertram Ramsay that the port, located at the head of a 60-mile (96km) channel, required the crucial Scheldt Estuary to be cleared, a mission never passed on to Horrocks or Roberts.

Where fortune had smiled, providing a guide to bypass the German defenses and cross canals on smaller bridges to gain the port, no such savior appeared to advise Roberts of the Resistance fighters attempting to

Below: A selection of dress daggers, knives and bayonets worn by the German armed forces, police and Nazi party officials.
Salamander Books

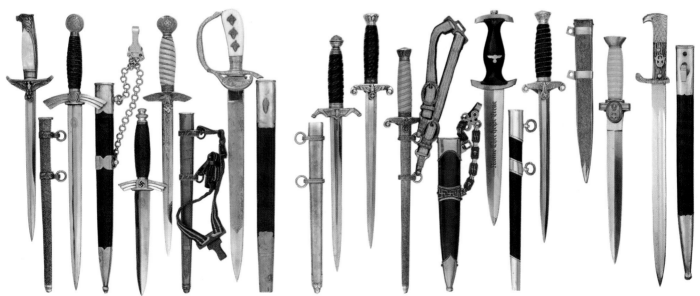

Above: Lt. Gen. B.G. Horrocks proved a highly capable commander of the British XXX Corps in the last stages of the Normandy fighting and then in the Allied pursuit across northern France and into Belgium.

hold a crucial bridge over the canal north of the town or to correct Roberts' mistaken knowledge of the bridge based on a faulty map. Concerning himself primarily with capturing the garrison in town which netted 6,000 prisoners, 11th Armoured lunged too late. The gallant Belgians lost their battle and the bridge, with the result that the Germans barred the way to the crucial neck of the estuary. With Montgomery and Dempsey eyeing the east flank, hoping to rush forces into Germany before von Runstedt could build units for the defense, the Scheldt problem gained prominence too late.

But the loss of the port's usage was not the entire problem. Though the German Fifteenth Army in Belgium and Holland appeared to be pocketed, most of its 100,000 men made use of ferries to cross the estuary to escape to the Walcheren and Beveland islands and then north, eventually pulling some 82,000 men out of the trap.

Montgomery's tenacity in trying to revive a "full-blooded thrust" straight into the Ruhr coupled with the single ground command job to ensure its support, muddied the waters. Content that the channel ports could support his own move, he pressed Eisenhower to support his "narrow front plan," naming Berlin as his final objective, in the same message in which he reported the capture of Antwerp's docks. Intending to keep Dempsey's Second Army moving eastward at any expense, he also wanted the entire US First Army to press through the vital Liège-Aachen corridor, both armies moving directly on the Ruhr. Crerar's six divisions would clear the channel ports and the Scheldt. Though Monty had already begun this move, the size of the front and the rapidly hardening German defense meant that 21st Army Group couldn't do it alone. It was a decision for the "land forces commander."

Meanwhile, Eisenhower's intelligence staff (G-2) reported opportunities which he could not ignore. SHAEF's first estimate delivered at Jullouville called the retreating Germans "no longer a cohesive force but a number of fugitive battle groups, disorganized and even demoralized, short of equipment and arms." By September 10, SHAEF counted about 15 division equivalents for the entire German "West Wall" defensive line – or "Siegfried Line" – providing stray units were equipped and organized. G-2 claimed that no more than 20 divisions could be in shape to fight by the end of September. Fifteenth Army was rated as a skeleton without formed units and trapped against the sea; Seventh Army in front of Bradley had but three divisions with its southern 70 miles (112km) covered by only seven battalions. *Ultra* decrypts reported the armor status of the entire German forces in the west at 100 operational tanks.

In effect, however, Eisenhower had already weighted

his effort to a Rhine thrust, with the addition of the First Allied Airborne Army on Monty's planning boards. Consisting of six airborne or airportable divisions and the combined RAF and American troop carrier aircraft, Lt. Gen. Lewis H. Brereton's newly formed command had been hastily planning operations since mid-August, most in support of 21st Army Group. All had been cancelled or had been made obsolete by ground advance.

During the five days following Antwerp's liberation, the fifteenth of these operations was being readied. *Comet* was designed to seize the bridges across the Rhine between Arnhem and Wesel using the British 1st Airborne Division and the Polish Airborne Brigade, but evolved into only capturing the bridges in the Nijmegen-Arnhem area. Delayed by weather and finally cancelled, *Comet*'s replacement, (plan sixteen), targeted the same bridges and others. Codenamed *Market*, it spearheaded the Allies' first attempt to cross Germany's great natural land barrier.

September 10 was a critical day for Allied strategy. Prompted by news that V2 rockets hitting London were launched from western Holland, Montgomery dropped Dempsey's attack toward Wesel for an outflanking move around the West Wall through the Rhine delta. Meeting the same day with an injured Eisenhower who had been bedridden for a week, Montgomery repeated his command and strategy argument which had been conducted via fouled communications links during the previous week.

Below: A British Daimler Dingo scout car. This two-man armored car was introduced in 1940 and served the British and Canadian forces throughout the war. This example bears the black boar insignia of the British XXX Corps.
Memorial Museum, Bayeux

Above: The shoulder insignia of the 82nd Airborne Division 'All American' (top): 101st Airborne Division 'Screaming Eagles' (center); 1st Allied Airborne Army (bottom). This last patch is of British manufacture.
Salamander Books

Failing to convince Eisenhower of a major change, he did secure backing for Operation *Market Garden*, an expanded plan including a three corps ground advance: *Garden*. This combined operation was designed to eradicate the Fifteenth Army, the V2 problem, and outflank the Ruhr. Ike agreed to accept a delay in opening the Scheldt Estuary, but refused to stop Patton's movement in favor of a strong supporting attack by Gen. Hodges' US First Army.

Market was meant to lay an "airborne carpet," dropping the US 101st and 82nd Airborne Divisions between Eindhoven and Nijmegen, and the British 1st Airborne Division north of the Lower Rhine near Arnhem. Reinforcements of the Polish Airborne Brigade and the airportable 52nd Lowland Division would follow. While the 35,000 men of Lt. Gen. F. A. M. Browning's 1st Airborne Corps seized six bridges and controlled the 64 mile (102km) long corridor to the Rhine, Dempsey's Second Army, with Horrocks' XXX Corps on a single road spearheading the attack, would move north on the "carpet," cross the Rhine, and end on the Zuider Zee, 99 miles (158km) from the start point. Called *Garden*, the ground plan would seal Holland off, the Fifteenth Army would be fatally trapped, and the Ruhr outflanked.

First Allied Airborne Army's rendering of *Market* distinctly failed to satisfy Montgomery's intent. Despite Brereton's dramatic preface to the plans conference saying that his troops would "grab the bridges with thunderclap surprise," the airmen ruling supreme in drop zone selection abandoned the *coup de main* design which had been part of *Comet*. Watching the ominous buildup of flak positions throughout the *Market* target area, they ruled that aircraft routing, not the objectives, were the controlling factor. Both the 82nd and British 1st Airborne Division would find themselves dropped about eight miles (12 km) from the key bridges at Nijmegen and Arnhem. Moreover, having insufficient airlift for a simultaneous drop of the three airborne divisions, priority was granted from "bottom to top" to ensure XXX Corps' speedy progress. Therefore, each division's lift would only carry a portion of their force. Nor would the troop carrier commander permit two lifts per day as had been planned in *Comet* to place the maximum force on the objectives in the shortest time. Therefore, each of the three divisions would have to rely on subsequent lifts on succeeding days, lifts which bad weather in England or Holland could delay or cancel. The three-day dropping schedule necessitated holding airheads and diverting troops needed to seize objectives and control the road to the tasks of holding drop zones and glider landing zones. Additionally, Brereton's headquarters prohibited fighter bombers tasked to provide close support from flying while the troop carriers were in the air.

Second Army's *Garden* plan, likewise, became a patchwork unable to fulfill Monty's concept. Promised a 1,000 tons (1,016 tonnes) extra daily supply from US sources to release transport for moving grounded British divisions from the Seine, no tonnage appeared in Brussels until September 16, the day before the attack was scheduled to advance. Dempsey's lack of transport meant that the critical flank support needed for Horrocks' rush for the Rhine would be committed late, and piecemeal.

By the 15th, intelligence indicators, from *Ultra*, low-grade signals, photo reconnaissance, and the Dutch Resistance, all indicated that the II SS Panzer Corps was refitting north of the Rhine near Arnhem. Its two divisions had been virtually destroyed in Normandy. Were they still shells as most German divisions in the West Wall had been assessed, with perhaps only a company of tanks and several battalions of troops? Second Army assessed the corps' strength at about double this. Montgomery felt the risk justified and ordered the attack to proceed before the Germans could strengthen their defenses.

On Sunday, September 17, the sky train divided into 90 mile (144km) long northern and southern routes to accommodate the 1,500 planes and 500 gliders needed for the first lift. Some 2,600 bomber and fighter sorties had been flown against selected targets, including 117 flak positions along the route. More than 1,000 fighters covered the transport's flight to the target area. On the

Above left: American airborne equipment and uniforms. These uniforms carry the insignia of the 82nd Airborne Division. The Stars and Stripes brassards are of the type used during the D-Day landings. The M1A1 30 caliber carbine features the folding wire stock developed for airborne forces.
Tony Stamatelos Collection

Above: The leaping pegasus insignia of the British 6th Airborne Division. *Memorial Museum, Bayeux*

Below: Men of the British 1st Airborne Division give their equipment a final check before departing for Arnhem. Behind them are the converted Stirling bombers used as tugs for Horsa assault gliders.

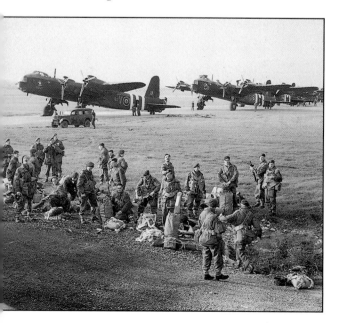

ground, Horrocks' corps from "teeth to tail" numbered over 20,000 vehicles and 100,000 men.

The drops which began at 13:00 were parade ground perfect. Within 70 minutes, over 20,000 men floated to the ground or landed by glider. But with surprise rapidly fading, the plan began to unravel. A key objective of Maj. Gen. Maxwell Taylor's 101st Airborne, the Wilhelmina canal bridge at Son, was blown by preset charges as was the alternative bridge at Best the next day.

To the north, Brig. Gen. James Gavin's 82nd Airborne landed well. Grabbing the 1,800-foot (540m) Grave bridge over the Maas River, its luck held with its capture of the bridge at Heuman. With orders to seize and hold the eight mile (13km) long Groesbeek ridge dominating his division sector, Gavin's attention was focused south of Nijmegen. No attempt was made until after dark, about eight hours, to send troops toward Nijmegen's 1,960 foot (588m) bridge.

Maj. Gen. R. E. "Roy" Urquhart's 1st Airborne landed two brigades about 8 miles (13km) west of Arnhem. Urquhart planned to send a jeep-mounted reconnaissance squadron ahead to seize the Rhine bridge at Arnhem while three parachute battalions followed on separate roads leading east to the town. The airlanding brigade remained to hold drop zones for the subsequent lifts. The squadron was soon ambushed, and two of the battalions found themselves blocked by a German kampfgruppe quartered in nearby Wolfheze. Lt. Col. John Frost's 2nd Parachute Battalion, taking the river road skirting Oosterbeek, arrived too late to prevent the demolition of a rail bridge, but managed to arrive at the road bridge near dark. Counterattacked from the bridge's southern end by Germans who had crossed earlier, Frost's force totaling about 600 men and a few antitank guns, held, and established a perimeter around the north end of the bridge awaiting the rest of the division. Urquhart who had moved forward to his blocked battalions, found his division divided and without working communications.

German reaction was rapid. Field Marshal Model in Osterbeek and Gen. Kurt Student commanding First Parachute Army reacted quickly, possibly helped by a complete plan for *Market* found in a crashed glider. Model drew in units from throughout Holland and the German border. Arriving in increasing numbers, this buildup of scratch forces placed under local command was to prove fatal. Student, located west of the 101st's drop, sent units of his First Parachute Army against British Second Army's west flank and spearhead, while forming a tank and infantry attack against the 101st for the next day. Model, now north of Arnhem, sent Kampfgruppe "Frundsberg" south across the Arnhem bridge to Nijmegen, and Kampfgruppe "Hohenstaufen" toward the drop zones west of Arnhem. By nightfall, forces held the Nijmegen bridge and essentially blocked the Arnhem bridge from the north and south.

Maj. Gen. Alan Adair's Guards Armoured Division spearheaded Horrocks' attack. Following a 350-gun rolling barrage at 14:35, and supported by 100 rocket-firing Typhoon aircraft, its lead element, the Irish Guards met with early resistance losing nine tanks and over 200 of its supporting infantry. After breaching the line, they cleared woods south of Valkenswaard where they leaguered for the night. In support of XXX Corps' advance, the XII Corps "flank attack" floundered, and VIII Corps was yet to cross its start line. Linking with 101st at midday, Adair's tankmen waited while a new bridge was built at Son during the night of the 18th.

The 18th saw bad weather in England, delaying second air lifts until afternoon and essentially shutting off effective air support. The 1st Airborne received Hackett's 4th Parachute Brigade, but with the division commander cut off and a preoccupation with Arnhem bridge, the crucial Heavedorp ferry and its controlling hill mass behind it were ignored. The Germans began ferrying tanks east of Arnhem to evade Frost's band, realizing the battle would be decided by holding the advance south of the Waal River.

Starting movement at 06:45 on the 19th, Guards Armoured moved 22 miles (35km) arriving at the Grave bridge about 08:20. Taylor's 101st fended off tanks at the Son bridge later on the 19th, the first of a series of attacks which raged from flank to flank over days while the Americans fought to hold open Horrocks' lifeline more appropriately called by the GIs, "Hell's Highway." The VIII Corps, who now joined the fight by receiving a XXX Corps division unable to join the queue, moved up on the east.

Above: The bridge over the Rhine was the primary objective of the Arnhem operation, but the British paratroops captured and held only its northern end. This dead German lies on one of the approach roads.

Below: Trained not to rely on paradropped supplies, the British paratroops made extensive use of expedients, such as this shell crater turned into a foxhole by lightly armed men of the 1st Parachute Battalion.

Above: Uniforms and insignia of German armored units. The field gray uniform is that of a self-propelled gun crew's NCO. The vehicle pennant is that of a general officer. The camouflage uniform is of the pea pattern worn by panzer crews of the Waffen-SS. The divisional cuff titles (far right) are those of Waffen-SS panzer units which served in western Europe. From the top: 17th SS Panzer Grenadiers; 10th SS Panzer; 1st SS Panzer; 2nd SS Panzer; 12th SS Panzer; 9th SS Panzer; 1st SS Regiment, part of the 2nd SS Panzer. *Memorial Museum, Bayeux*

While Nijmegen's bridge was still to be attacked, Urquhart's 1st Airborne was pushed back into a thumb-shaped perimeter at Oosterbeek ringed by two brigade-strength forces. Though Urquhart had returned, he had no reinforcements, and with the loss of his drop zones and poor communications, no resupply.

Assault boats needed to cross the Waal were held up by ambush and traffic jams. Finally, on the afternoon of the 20th, an assault in canvas boats by an American parachute battalion began attempts to take Nijmegen bridge from the rear. While fighting raged at Wyler and Mook east of the vital Groesbeek Ridge, British tanks and American infantry fought to clear a path to the south end of the bridge. At 19:10, Guards Armoured crossed its first tanks, 35 hours after its linkup at Grave. The huge bridge, saved by the failure of its own detonating charges, was only about ten miles (16km) south of Arnhem. Perhaps three German battalions and a dozen tanks held the "island" between Nijmegen and Arnhem. Lacking infantry to go forward and unwilling to advance the tanks at night, the British armor halted while the Germans reinforced their defenses.

Most of the 21st was spent trying to clear the bridgehead, with no forward moves attempted until late. The continuing battle along Hell's Highway paralyzed movement. Unknown to XXX Corps, on the same day, Frost's battalion, out of ammunition and out of hope, was overrun at the bridge. Maj. Gen. Sosabowski's Poles finally jumped on the 21st, not near the bridge as planned, but on a new drop zone near Driel, across the river from the Red Devil's perimeter. Weather had delayed them three days, and poor visibility permitted only half the brigade, about 750 men, to arrive, Sosabowski's men attempted crossings on two successive nights, both under heavy fire from the crucial Westerbouwing heights which the Germans seized on the 21st. Urquhart's beleaguered force received perhaps 200 reinforcements from the Poles. Failing to break through German armor south of the town, Horrocks shifted 43rd Wessex Division to take up the battle but with little result. An abortive reinforcement attempt on the night of the 24th probably convinced commanders that a full division assault would be needed.

With battles raging in both the 101st and 82nd Airborne sectors, little solace received from the flank corps, and the prospect of Urquhart's men being overrun before an effective assault could be mounted, Dempsey ordered Urquhart to withdraw.

During a heavy rain on the night of September 25/26, 1st Airborne's survivors withdrew while XXX Corps laid down artillery supporting fire. Only 2,500 of Urquhart's original force of 10,300, escaped. *Market Garden* cost over 16,000 Allied casualties, nearly 12,000 among the airborne, nearly half, from 1st Airborne Division. Urquhart's final words in his report on the action were, "We have no regrets."

SHAEF's planners identified four major avenues to enter Germany: Flanders, Maubeuge-Liège-Aachen, the Ardennes, and Metz-Saarbrücken. By September, Bradley's Army Group spanned them all except Flanders. The joint planners saw Liège-Aachen and Metz-Saarbrücken as the two most decisive and the two with the heaviest defenses. Montgomery's demand for one thrust included the Aachen approach, and Bradley, perhaps seeing First Army coopted, leaned heavily toward the Metz Gap. Despite Eisenhower's directives stressing priority on the left, supplies were almost equally apportioned and one of First Army's corps was directed through the Ardennes to cover Patton's north flank.

Bradley resented Montgomery's insistence on First Army covering his flank, despite the fact that VII Corps' dash north toward Mons netted 25,000 Germans escaping the failed Falaise trap. *Market Garden*, however, added more frontage to Hodges' army as Dempsey swung north, further dissipating Bradley's attacks. Like Dempsey, Hodges had temporarily grounded a corps to keep his other two corps moving. First Army soon

Above: Dropping into an area where two SS Panzer divisions were refitting, the British 1st Airborne Division landed in a hornet's nest of opposition amounting to more than 6,000 men including these infantrymen.

crossed the Meuse River throughout the length of Belgium, liberated Liège and Luxembourg, and by September 11, had small forces inside the German border though it had little concentrated force to smash a determined defense.

Patton after losing five days to an enforced halt, refused to be stopped by logistics. Instead of defending on the Meuse as expected, his army strained to make an additional 30 miles (48km) and then seized bridgeheads on the Moselle River south of Metz. Receiving bare minimums of gasoline, using captured stores and fuel, and constantly juggling artillery and gasoline tonnages to eke out further advances, Patton began simultaneous encircling moves toward Nancy and north and south of Metz, while still moving forces to link with Patch's US Seventh Army west of Dijon on the same day that Hodges put patrols into Germany. Eisenhower's broad, continuous front was now realized, but the days of pursuit were over. Von Rundstedt's "miracle in the west," the rapidly building defense along the German border, was becoming reality.

The Emperor Charlemagne's former capital, Aachen, stood out as the key entry on both Eisenhower's and von Rundstedt's maps. First Army kicked off attacks against the West Wall on September 12 to capture it, but met only with progress with its northern XIX Corps, while "Lightning Joe" Collins' VII Corps, which was to advance into the Stolberg corridor leading to Aachen from the south, ran into increasingly heavy resistance. Collins intended to use separate divisions to encircle the city from the south, to drive deeply into the corridor, and to move east to clear the wooded flank, the Hürtgen Forest. Hodges directed XIX Corps to complete the encirclement from the north.

Field Marshal Model was able to rush in a full division as the remnants of the German Seventh Army, destroyed in France, fought viciously against First Army. Bad weather stripped Collins of his air support and hidden

Below: Urban fighting was a discipline in which many German units excelled and which Allied units soon learned. This is a machine gun team of the US 26th Infantry Regiment in the Aachen fighting of October 15, 1944.

Above left: Colt M1911A1 .45 caliber automatic pistol. Above: Thompson M1 .45 caliber submachine gun with 20 round clip.
Salamander Books

antitank guns stopped his armored assaults. US V Corps, whose advance into the Ardennes had been unopposed, made little progress at its far end against the Eifel region and by month's end, operations halted while VIII Corps transferred from Brittany to take over the long Ardennes front.

Bitter fighting north and south of Aachen raged where XIX and VII Corps finally closed the ring on October 16 after beating off determined counterattacks. Hitler ordered the city to be defended to the last, bringing on a bloody house-to-house battle that saw tanks, and artillery as large as 155mm, being used as direct fire support against ancient stonewalled buildings. Captured on the 19th, Aachen was the first major German city to fall.

The Hürtgen, however, proved even more difficult. Under skies which now were either overcast or raining, Collins' troops moved to finish clearing the woods and seize the ridgeline and town of Schmidt, a key road juncture along the approach to Düren and the Rur River, whose flood waters were controlled by the dams and tributaries behind the town.

The veteran 9th Infantry Division suffered more than 4,500 casualties during its unsuccessful attempts to gain the ridge against increasing resistance. Hodges shifted corps boundaries to give V Corps Schmidt as an objective, while Collins' VII retained the main effort to the Rur River. The new offensive would begin in early November.

To the south, Patton drew the enemy's first attempt to regain the initiative. Intending to take Patton in the flank, prevent Third Army's juncture with Allied troops driving up the Rhône valley, and hold open an escape route for German forces being pursued from southern France, Hitler's plan targeted Maj. Gen. Manton Eddy's XII Corps then holding bridgeheads north and south of Nancy. The Americans fought off these attacks during bitter fighting at Dieulouard, Gremecey Forest, and Pont-à-Mousson. During the course of the largest German attack, Combat Command A, 4th Armored Division, destroyed two separate panzer brigades which attacked it during a week long battle near the town of Arracourt. Nearly 150 German tanks were destroyed for the loss of less than two dozen American, most of the enemy being defeated by the tank battalion commanded by Lt. Col. Creighton

W. Abrams, later the American commander in Vietnam.

Knowing that Metz, Gen. Pershing's unfulfilled offensive of the Great War, stood in his path, Patton was eager to seize the famous fortress system on his way to the Rhine. Fighting through fields made famous in the Franco-Prussian War of 1870, regiments soon were being chewed up by an enemy deep in concrete fortifications, some dating to the last century. The 5th Division making the first attacks, soon suffered more than 5,000 casualties in its attempt to assault the fortress city.

While fuel and transport generally stopped Third Army until November, Patton responded by aggressive patrolling and using captured howitzers and ammunition to fire on the Germans. Heavy rains, however, washed out valuable bridging and tanks found themselves mired as well as low on fuel.

Often forgotten, but nevertheless critical, Lt. Gen. Jacob L. Devers' 6th Army Group, which was activated on September 15, had by mid-October, sealed the fate of the remaining Germans in France. Driving up the Rhône Valley from its Riviera landing grounds, the infantry-heavy force nearly trapped the German Nineteenth Army, but more importantly, it captured the critical ports of Marseille and Toulon. For a loss of approximately 10,000 casualties, the "Dragoon Forces" had moved more than 300 miles (480km) in 26 days, had killed or wounded nearly 30,000 Germans, and had isolated or captured more than 130,000.

Further north, *Market Garden*'s failure shifted priorities to Crerar's First Canadian Army. With six Allied divisions immobilized and the effect of improvised supply breaking down, a large port close to the front was needed to sustain any further advance. Antwerp became 21st Army Group's top priority,

Monty started prodding Crerar toward the Scheldt Estuary even before *Market Garden*, but Crerar had already begun to reduce each channel port in turn, saving Antwerp for last. On September 12, when Montgomery began stressing Antwerp's importance, most of Crerar's forces were already committed elsewhere, thus delaying a shift of forces which was not accomplished until the 16th. The 1st Polish Armoured Division rapidly cleared over 20 miles (32km) of the estuary west of Antwerp while British I Corps controlled by Crerar, moved across the Albert Canal north and east of Antwerp. The 4th Canadian Armoured Division deployed its few infantry in canvas boats, but amid the flooded polderland, little could be accomplished until more infantry from the coastal sector could move up.

To open Antwerp, two major battles had to be fought. South of the West Scheldt, the Germans held positions north of the Leopold Canal from Zeebrugge to Antwerp. The Poles had cleared the open areas. The first battle

Below: The landing of the US Seventh Army on the French south coast between Hyêres and Cannes met only limited opposition, and the Americans soon moved inland leaving swelling numbers of prisoners behind their lines.

would be for the "Breskens Pocket," a group of defenses surrounded by flooded areas and held by an entire German division. The second battle would be sought for the northern coast, and the crucial South Beveland and Walcheren Islands dominating the West Scheldt from the north. Protected by flooded areas blocking entrance to a thin neck of land, frontal assault by canvas boat or through the narrow avenue were the only attack options against the separate enemy divisions holding both the South Beveland and Walcheren Islands. Moreover, with 30,000 of the enemy invested on the channel coast in his rear, Crerar had to fight in multiple directions.

Crerar's men took Dieppe without a fight, but stopped to parade in honor of their dead there from 1942. While Roberts' 11th Armoured Division was entering Antwerp, Crerar's army was moving on Boulogne which did not fall until September 22. Calais was reduced in a five-day battle ending on October 1. Freeing Antwerp would not be as rapid, and with army commander Crerar evacuated sick to England, Lt. Gen. Guy Simonds stepped in to take command only to find Montgomery angling part of I Corps to the northeast to close up on the Maas.

The Scheldt operations matched the Hürtgen and Metz in ferocity but were actually conducted under worse conditions. Fought over innumerable waterways and flooded areas which channelized advances onto prepared defenses, Simonds' II Corps launched a short amphibious hook to take the Breskens Pocket from the rear. In brutal fighting reminiscent of their fathers' actions in the World War I, Canadian soldiers fought for three weeks to clear the pocket. On October 10, the battle for South Beveland began with a frontal assault via the narrow neck approach. Failing to get Brereton's approval for an airborne drop on Walcheren, plans were made to "sink" that island by bombing its dikes and drainage system. Boat assaults by commando and special service brigades would be launched after South Beveland was captured.

Launched on November 1, the final assault took eight days to clear the nearly inundated Walcheren Island of its casemated guns, many by attacks launched in boats or amphibious "buffaloes." Minesweepers needed three weeks to remove 267 naval mines from the West Scheldt permitting ships to enter the port on November 28.

Clearing the Scheldt cost over 13,000 British and Canadian casualties, but it was not the only campaign waged after *Market Garden*. British Second Army, which now included both the US 7th Armored and 104th Infantry Divisions, cleared the area between Antwerp and the *Market Garden* corridor. Fending off a two-division attack from Venlo through the Peel Marshes at the end of October, heavy fighting still lay ahead before 21st Army Group could turn back towards the Rhine.

Above: The US and French forces invading the south of France intended a rapid advance up the River Rhône using forces with equipment such as this tank destroyer with a powerful gun in a light turret on a tank chassis.

Replacing Collins' battered 9th Division for the Rur Dams attack, V Corps' 28th Division, which had paraded for photographers on the Champs Elysées in Paris, was ticketed to take Schmidt while Collins' corps broke out of both the Stolberg corridor and the Hürtgen. Delayed almost two weeks until clear weather for air support, VII Corps watched as the 28th Division tackled Schmidt alone on November 2.

Launching a three-pronged attack to clear its flanks as well as the ridge leading to the objective, disaster struck the 28th immediately as both flanking attacks ran into heavy resistance. Still, one battalion took Schmidt and then endured heavy counterattacks while fruitless flank attacks were launched to free its rear. Finally giving up its toehold at Schmidt, the 28th held onto the lower ridge at Vossenack, a 2-mile (3km) finger-like gain after a week of fighting for a cost of 6,184 casualties, the American's bloodiest single division action of the campaign.

US VII Corps attacked on November 16, finally breaking clear of both the Hürtgen and the Stolberg by the end of the month, but Schmidt was yet to fall. Five American divisions and six German were battered in an area which observer-participant, Ernest Hemingway called, "Passchendaele with tree bursts." The Hürtgen had claimed more than 30,000 US casualties.

Farther north, Bradley moved Lt. Gen. William Simpson's Ninth US Army into the line taking over XIX Corps and the northern half of the Aachen corridor. Simpson provided flank support for British VIII Corps in the Peel Marshes while continuing forward to keep pressure on the Aachen corridor.

On November 8, in heavy rain, Patton's renewed offensive began on Eddy's XII Corps front and was heralded by 42 battalions of guns firing more than 20,000 shells. The next day, Maj. Gen. Walton Walker's XX Corps silently crossed the Moselle River north of Metz. Swirling floodwaters destroyed Walker's bridging but finally armor got across and Metz soon found three divisions systematically reducing its strongpoints in a concentric attack. Encircled by November 19, the garrison finally surrendered on the 21st. Patton proudly claimed to be its first conqueror since AD 451.

By early December, Patton had toeholds on the German border and began to reduce Saarlautern, which like Aachen, degenerated into a house-to-house battle. Patton's front had moved 60 miles (96km) at its farthest point by mid-December. Third Army had suffered more than 50,000 casualties in its march since September. Events would conspire to put the upcoming Saar offensive on hold.

On November 14, Montgomery turned Dempsey's VIII and XII Corps eastwards to clear the intervening

Below: A selection of shoulder patches worn by official US war correspondents.
Tony Stamatelos Collection

Left: One of the greatest commanders of World War II, Lt. Gen. George S. Patton rose to prominence in Northwest Africa and Sicily but is best remembered as commander of the US Third Army in France.

ground to the Maas River and its confluence with the Rur. Wet ground, mines, and prepared defenses slowed the attack which was joined in the south by US Ninth Army's XIX Corps attack toward Jülich and Linnich on the Rur. Both attacks would halt by December 3.

To the south Lt. Gen. Devers' 6th Army Group, launched its own offensive in mid-November. Devers sent Lt. Gen. Alexander Patch's Seventh Army toward Strasbourg while Gen. Jean de Lattre de Tassigny's French First Army attacked toward the Rhine through the Belfort Gap. Though the Germans managed to hold a salient around the town of Colmar, Devers' offensive which suffered 28,000 casualties in two weeks, achieved the goal of every Allied general on the front. On November 20, near the Swiss border, 1st French Corps reached the Rhine. Turning north to Mulhouse, the French moved to clear the west bank while Patch's forces were directed both northward toward the Saar and east to the Rhine. The quiet Patch beat the obstreperous Patton, both to the Rhine, and into Germany. But, Devers' drive was relegated to a supporting role and Patch's desire to put a corps across the Rhine was ignored.

By mid-December, Bradley intended to renew Pattons' attacks in a week and First Army and 21st Army Group looked toward major offensives in the Rhineland after New Year. Hitler, however, had other plans.

V
Five
The Strategic Bombing Offensive

"NO ENEMY PLANE WILL FLY OVER THE REICH TERRITORY"

HERMAN GOERING

Bernard Nalty

By December 1944, as Allied troops entered Germany and closed on the Rhine River, the battle for the heartland of the Reich was already being fought by men of the Allied air forces.

The Royal Air Force and the United States Army Air Forces went to war confident that the heavy bomber, attacking in daylight, could bludgeon Germany into surrender. By September 1939, the British had built a fleet of fast twin-engine bombers, some of them featuring one or more power-operated turrets, each turret with as many as four .303-caliber machine guns. The best of these aircraft, the Blenheims and Wellingtons of RAF Bomber Command, proved no match for Germany's Messerschmitt fighters, the single-engine Bf 109 and the twin-engine Bf 110. After the fall of France in the summer of 1940, the bomber, though driven from the daytime skies, remained the only weapon capable of carrying the war to Hitler's Germany. The RAF had no choice but to keep on bombing, attacking targets like oil refineries or factories believed large enough to be hit at night.

An investigation of night bombing revealed, however, that the average navigator could not find these targets in darkness, the average bombardier could not hit them, and the weight of bombs dropped on the average mission could not destroy them. As a result, the RAF invested scarce resources on four-engine bombers capable of carrying perhaps twice the load of the Wellingtons – aircraft such as the unsuccessful Short Stirling, the improved Handley Page Halifax, and the magnificent Avro Lancaster. In addition, British science developed electronic beams for nighttime navigation and airborne radar for bomb aiming. Finally, Bomber Command chose a target easier to locate and attack than an individual factory: the homes of workers and the other structures that made up the heart of an industrial city. Under the

Left: Seen in May 1944, S-for-Sugar (a Lancaster heavy bomber of No. 467 Squadron, Royal Australian Air Force) reveals an impressive tally of missions flown and the award of two DFCs to members of its crew.

71

aloof and relentless leadership of Air Chief Marshal Sir Arthur Harris, Bomber Command made devastating use of its new equipment, sending highly trained pathfinders to drop incendiary bombs or flares and create an aiming point for a rain of incendiaries and high explosive that could destroy the center of a city. Harris, for example, massed almost a thousand bombers, ranging from new Lancasters to Wellingtons that verged on obsolescence, some of them manned by crews still in training, and obliterated Cologne on the night of May 30, 1942. The RAF Bomber Command, having discovered that its pre-war tactical doctrine did not work, developed tactics and weapons that did.

The US Army Air Forces went to war in 1941 believing that self-defending formations of Boeing B-17 Flying Fortresses and Consolidated B-24 Liberators could fight their way in daylight to any target within range and bomb accurately enough from high altitude to destroy a specific factory. Before the United States entered the conflict, the RAF tested a few export versions of the B-17 but pronounced them too lightly armed to penetrate German fighter defenses, finding them fit only for coastal patrol. Power-operated turrets mounting twin .50-caliber machine guns replaced some of the hand-manipulated weapons and seemed to remedy the short-coming of which the British had complained. Erroneous reports by air crews of sinking Japanese warships in the Philippines and during the Battle of Midway reinforced the mood of confidence in the deadly accuracy of the strategic bomber attacking by daylight from an altitude

Below: From left to right, this impressive bevy of air commanders includes Air Marshal Sir John Slessor, Air Chief Marshal Sir Arthur Harris, Air Chief Marshal Sir Trafford Leigh-Mallory and Lt. Gen. Ira C. Eaker.

of five miles (8km), using the secret optical bombsight invented by Carl Norden.

Maj. Gen. Carl Spaatz took on the assignment of directing the newly-created American Eighth Air Force against Germany. The prewar American–British Conversations at Washington DC, (the ABC talks) had produced an agreement that, in the event of war, an American would command the American bombers operating from Britain. The aerial campaign started slowly, however. Crews arrived from the United States only partially trained, aircraft production had still to gather momentum, and the available men and aircraft wasted their efforts against the German submarine pens on the coast of France, a target impervious to bombs of the size the Americans used. The invasion of French Northwest Africa in November 1942 required a diversion of American air power from Britain, and during December, Spaatz reported for duty in North Africa, leaving Maj. Gen. Ira Eaker in command of the Eighth Air Force, which had yet to drop a bomb on Germany.

In contrast, RAF Bomber Command had intensified its nighttime bombing, setting fire to towns as distant as Rostock and Lubeck, on the Baltic; as Harris undertook a systematic attack on German industry, not by attacking individual factories but by bombing cities where they were located and "dehousing" and demoralizing the workers. The tonnage of bombs devoted to this purpose rapidly mounted, especially in repeated attacks on the industrialized Ruhr. While the Americans restricted their bombing to Nazi-occupied Europe, the British hammered the Third Reich itself.

When President Franklin D. Roosevelt, Prime Minister Winston Churchill, and their military advisers conferred at Casablanca in January 1943, pressure was mounting to combine the American and British bombing campaigns. Eaker, Spaatz, and Lt. Gen. Henry H. Arnold, the Commanding General, US Army Air Forces, recoiled from the prospect of a unified command, for they feared that Harris, whose airmen had set fire to a succession of German cities, would take charge and use his influence with Churchill to shift the American bombardment groups from daylight to nighttime attack. Called upon to defend the VIII Bomber Command, Eaker ignored its lack of accomplishment – his aircraft did not attack their first target in Germany, the port of Wilhelmshaven, until January 27, and the strike force numbered only 53 B-17s – and conjured up instead an exciting vision of American bombers darkening the skies by day and the British continuing the attack after sunset. Skeptical at first, but eager to batter Germany, Churchill agreed, for the present at least, to a separate American daylight campaign that would complement the efforts of the British by night and "bomb the devils 'round the clock."

Above: The shoulder insignia of the USAAF Eighth Air Force which was based in Britain.
Salamander Books

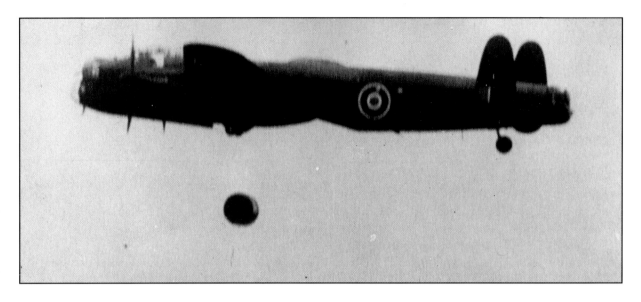

Above: A Lancaster B.Mk I bomber of No. 617 Squadron unloads a 'bouncing bomb' during trials of this weapon designed to skip across water and then roll down the face of a dam before exploding under the water.

Below: Two of Germany's major dams were breached in the RAF's daring Operation *Jericho*. This is the scene at the Möhne Dam during the morning after the courageous but costly raid.

The Casablanca Conference thus launched the Combined Bomber Offensive, which was confirmed by the *Pointblank* Directive, drafted by Eaker's staff and approved by the Anglo–American Combined Chiefs of Staff in May 1943. *Pointblank* established an initial order of priorities, though the Americans and British might modify them as desired. The directive did not establish an agency capable of enforcing priorities or designating targets, so that two loosely coordinating bombing offensives, one British and the other American, emerged in the aftermath of the meeting at Casablanca. While the RAF Bomber Command attacked industrial cities by night, the Eighth Air Force hit factories by day.

Harris maintained the pace of nighttime bombardment during 1943, fighting the aerial Battle of the Ruhr, in which Essen took an especially savage battering. He destroyed the city of Hamburg in four attacks between July 24 and August 2; his crews flew 3,095 sorties and dropped 9,000 tons (8,820 tonnes) of bombs, about evenly divided between high explosive and incendiary, killing at least 30,000 people, injuring roughly the same number, and driving perhaps a million from homes destroyed in a firestorm that consumed the heart of the city. At Hamburg, everything worked exactly as Harris planned. A clearly defined radar return enabled the pathfinders to mark the target precisely and the subsequent streams of bombers inflicted maximum damage. *Window* – strips of metal foil dropped by the attackers – reflected radar waves, masking the approach of the aircraft and confusing the controllers on the ground, who mistook *Window* for actual bombers and shifted the night fighters accordingly. Although surprised and confused by *Window*, the defenders managed to shoot down 86 bombers during the series of raids; this amounted, however, to a loss rate of 2.8 percent, a far lower price than Harris was willing to pay to achieve such devastation.

On occasion, Harris would employ his bombers by day, rather than by night, or against precision rather than area targets. By night, Lancasters led by Wing Commander Guy Gibson used special bombs, designed by Barnes Wallis, a celebrated aeronautical engineer, to breach the Möhne and Eder dams on May 16, 1943, causing local floods and disrupting the supply of power to war industries. On the night of August 17 of that year, more than 500 heavy bombers damaged the rocket research center at Peenemünde. By day, small numbers of Lancasters made a costly low-altitude attack on a diesel-engine factory at Augsburg in May 1942, and during November 1944 sank the battleship *Tirpitz* at anchor in a Norwegian fjord.

City-busting by night dominated Bomber Command's agenda, however, and on November 18, 1943, Harris launched the Battle of Berlin. He vowed to destroy the German capital "from end to end" and hoped that the Americans would join in the campaign; but by the time the attacks on Berlin had begun, the Eighth Air Force had suffered a stunning reverse. The doctrine of the Army Air Forces maintained that the bomber could gain air superiority by shooting down German fighters and destroying the factories that built them. Convinced of the soundness of doctrine and the invincibility of the bomber, Arnold, Spaatz, and their peers had seen no need before the war to develop a long-range escort fighter. Arnold, in particular, objected to installing fittings on fighters to accommodate disposable fuel tanks because doing so would exact a penalty in performance. The Americans did, however, experiment with substituting machine guns and ammunition for bombs in some B-17s and B-24s intending to reinforce the defensive firepower of the bomber formation.

To deal with enemy fighters, Eaker's principal subordinates, Maj. Gen. Curtis E. LeMay and Brig. Gen. Frederick L. Anderson, developed the combat box, a massive formation of 54 bombers – three 18-plane groups, each

Above: The 12,000-lb 'Tallboy' bomb, the weapon which sank the Tirpitz. Tallboy was designed for high-altitude release, its streamlined shape ensuring a high-velocity impact and then deep ground or water penetration before detonation and massive concussion.

Below: With the B-24 Liberator, the B-17 Flying Fortress was one of the two 'workhorses' for the USAAF's daylight penetration missions over Europe for the precision bombing of strategically important targets.

of three squadrons – stacked to direct firepower in every direction. Mutual protection depended upon the integrity of the formation; individual aircraft could not maneuver independently either to avoid antiaircraft fire or to aim bombs. One bombardier aimed for the formation – whether the 54-plane box or the smaller ones used later in the war – with the others releasing their bombs on his signal. The result tended to be area bombing in all but the name.

Eaker put Army Air Forces' doctrine to the test in the summer and fall of 1943, when he attempted to attack the aircraft industry by bombing ball-bearing and airframe factories. On August 17, he dispatched two raids, one against the Messerschmitt fighter plant at Regensburg and the other against the ball-bearing factories at Schweinfurt. Plans called for the Regensburg force to take off first, stir up a hornet's nest of interceptors, but minimize its vulnerability by continuing on to North Africa instead of doubling back to England. Before the German fighters could rearm and refuel, the Schweinfurt group would bomb its target and return to Britain. The escorting P-47s could fly no farther than Aachen on Germany's western border, so success depended on timing. Unfortunately, fog delayed the Schweinfurt bombers, enabling the Luftwaffe to mass its fighters against each force in succession. In a single day, VIII Bomber Command lost 601 crewmen killed, captured, or interned in a neutral country, 60 bombers destroyed, and 27 others badly damaged.

Eaker took heart from the results, especially the destruction visited upon factory buildings at Regensburg. The airframe industry proved resilient, however, and under the direction of Albert Speer, Hitler's Minister for Armaments and Munitions, production would actually increase despite Anglo–American bombing. Ball-bearing manufacture might have proved Germany's Achilles' heel, had the Combined Bomber Offensive singled it out

Right: Daylight raids over Germany ran into determined and frequently effective opposition from the fighter and AA arms: many bombers were lost, but others such as this B-17G struggled home before crash-landing.

for destruction. Harris, however, had an abiding distrust of what he termed "panacea targets" and refused to be diverted from attacking cities. Nor could Eaker press the attack on ball-bearing manufacture, since he was forced to regroup after the August attack.

The American aircraft industry replaced the bombers the Eighth Air Force had lost, and the efficient training establishment sent new crews that Eaker melded into his depleted squadrons. Within a month, his bombers were again boring deep into Germany, without escort and with further losses – 45 bombers shot down in an attack on Stuttgart in September, and 148 lost in a single week in October that ended with a second attack on Schweinfurt. The October raid on Schweinfurt temporarily reduced ball-bearing production by 67 percent, but at the price of 60 of the 291 bombers launched that morning. American bombers, although flying in large formations to mass their defensive firepower, had failed to gain control of the daytime skies over Germany. Eaker could not follow up the advantage gained by the October attack on Schweinfurt.

Above: Allied high altitude/winter flying gear. On the left are the fleece lined flying jacket and trousers worn by the RAF and Commonwealth flight crews, while on the right is a Shearling flight suit of the type worn by bomber crews of the USAAF.
Memorial Museum, Bayeux (left)
West Point Museum, NY (right)

Above: A USAAF Type A6 flying helmet with an A14 oxygen mask. The mask and helmet feature an incorporated radio mike and headset.
Salamander Books

The unrelenting attrition throughout the summer and fall of 1943 forced Eaker to rebuild the VIII Bomber Command, resting weary survivors, repairing airplanes, and absorbing new bombers and replacement crews. Weeks passed, and he could not resume the campaign against German industry. Arnold who had never in his long career commanded a unit in combat, lost patience, blamed Eaker for the delay, and in January 1944 replaced him with Maj. Gen. James H. Doolittle, who had commanded the Twelfth Air Force in North Africa. Eaker assumed command of the Mediterranean Allied Air Forces, replacing Air Chief Marshal Sir Arthur Tedder as the senior airman in that theater, (Tedder becoming Gen. Eisenhower's deputy for the *Overlord* operation). At the same time, Spaatz returned to Britain and took over the newly created US Strategic Air Forces in Europe, consisting of the Eighth Air Force in Great Britain and the Fifteenth in Italy.

Spaatz and Doolittle arrived in time to take advantage of three technical developments: a radar bombsight invented by the British for night attack; large jettisonable fuel tanks for the P-47, that were pressurized for high-altitude use; and a new long-range fighter, the North American P-51B Mustang. Radar enabled American bombers to attack by daylight through the cloud cover prevalent over western Europe in the winter, though at a sacrifice in accuracy. Under clear skies, a bombardier using the Norden optical sight could place 90 percent of his bombs in a circle a mile (1.6km) across; radar bombardment proved about half as accurate through cloud.

The other two developments — new external fuel tanks and the P-51 — made it possible for the US VIII and XV Fighter Commands to escort bombers on every daylight mission. The 75-gallon (337 liter) tanks slung under the wings of the P-47, and the 108-gallon (486 liter) type under the fuselage, converted the airplane into a true escort fighter; which became increasingly effective as the internal fuel capacity grew greater in subsequent models. Like the Republic P-47 Thunderbolt, the P-51 Mustang evolved into a deadly escort fighter. Initially, an American-designed Allison engine, without a supercharger, restricted the Mustang's effectiveness to low and medium altitude. A British Rolls-Royce Merlin engine, with a two-stage mechanical supercharger, substituted for the Allison at the urging of Thomas Hitchcock, the American air attaché in London, enabled the P-51 to fight at an altitude of 30,000 feet (9,000m). Because of its large internal fuel capacity, supplemented by disposable tanks, the P-51B and later versions could escort bombers to Berlin and beyond.

With the earliest P-47s, a lack of fuel capacity kept the Thunderbolts tied to the bomber formation until they had to turn back. Now the fighters could range ahead,

attacking the enemy wherever they found him, shooting up his airfields and destroying his interceptors in aerial combat. However effective these forays might prove, bomber crews preferred to have the escort close at hand. The African–American 332nd Fighter Group made a practice of satisfying that desire, staying with the bombers and raising morale while providing protection.

While the Eighth Air Force gathered strength, the German day-fighter force declined rapidly in effectiveness. Since 1939, the Luftwaffe had been in constant combat from Britain to the Soviet Union and from North Africa to Norway. Since Hitler and Hermann Göring, the

Above: One of the keys to the success of US daylight bombing was the escort fighter, such as this P-51B Mustang which could successfully engage German fighters at virtually the full range of the escorted bombers.

commander of the Luftwaffe, had not anticipated a long war, the training base proved woefully inadequate. By 1944, many of the veteran pilots were dead, and their hurriedly trained replacements lacked the skill to survive long enough to make full use of the fighters that German industry was producing. During the first six months of 1944, for instance, 2,200 German fighter pilots died in combat; the life expectancy of a pilot fresh from training did not exceed 30 days.

When the Eighth Air Force, now under Doolittle's command, returned to the skies over Germany, the Combined Bomber Offensive remained two loosely coordinated campaigns. The Americans, bombing by day, went after the German aircraft industry, hitting factories throughout the Third Reich and paying another destructive visit to the ball-bearing plants at Schweinfurt. In a rare example of collaboration, Harris conducted night attacks on five cities already bombed by the Americans. During the so-called Big Week,

Below: A dress jacket with lanyard and iron cross of a captain (hauptmann) of a Luftwaffe construction unit.
Salamander Books

February 20–25, 1944, the bomber commands of the US Eighth and Fifteenth Air Forces dispatched some 4,000 sorties and suffered losses of 6 percent, compared to a toll as high as 20 percent during the summer and fall of 1943.

Speer feared a sustained attack on the ball-bearing industry, but none came. His program of decentralized aircraft production in difficult-to-locate shops frustrated that aspect of the Combined Bomber Offensive. He could not apply the same principle, on a similar scale, to ball-bearing manufacture, but he began dispersing the delicate equipment, inasmuch as he could, and practiced conservation by using precisely-ground bearings only where absolutely necessary.

In the late winter of 1943–44 RAF Bomber Command continued to fight the Battle of Berlin, launched the previous November. During the first raid of the campaign, 444 heavy bombers attacked the German capital at the cost of nine aircraft. Fifteen attacks followed, totaling more than 9,000 sorties, almost 80 percent of them by Lancasters; damage mounted, but so did losses – 492 aircraft failed to return, another 95 crashed trying to land, and another 859 sustained some degree of damage.

American participation in the attacks on Berlin had to await the coming of the escorting fighter and the offensive against the aircraft industry. On March 4, 1944, some two dozen bombers failed to receive a recall order and dropped their bombs through heavy cloud; but 600 attacked on March 6, 500 on the 8th, and 600 on the 22nd. The combined bombing, in which the British dropped the heavier tonnage of munitions and suffered the greater share of losses, did not bring the victory that

Above: Radar equipment such as this Reise Würzburg were used by the Germans to track incoming streams of British nocturnal bombers so that night-fighters could be vectored into position for an interception.

Below: Though looking clumsy as a result of their external antennae, whose drag also degraded outright flight performance, night-fighters such as this Bf 110G with SN-2 interception radar proved effective weapons.

Harris had envisioned. The people of Berlin absorbed the punishment, and Hitler still ruled.

As the British losses during the Battle of Berlin indicated, Germany's nighttime defenses remained dangerous. *Window* no longer surprised radar operators at control centers on the ground, and radar-equipped fighters proved deadly. Even the day fighters that the Luftwaffe pressed into service by night could claim victims, especially in bright moonlight. Moreover, the practice of dispatching streams of bombers gave the defenders repeated opportunities to locate and intercept some of the aircraft. An attack against Nuremberg on the night of March 30, 1944, under a full moon, inflicted only moderate damage — the target lay beyond the range of the radio beam used at the time for precise navigation — at the cost of 95 bombers destroyed out of 782, 743 crewmen killed or wounded, and 159 captured. The casualties suffered over Nuremberg reinforced the impact of the losses sustained in the indecisive Battle of Berlin and shook the morale of Bomber Command.

Early in April, Harris advised the Air Ministry that:

The strength of German defenses would in time reach a point at which night-bombing attacks by existing methods and types of heavy bombers would involve percentage casualty rates that cannot in the long run be sustained ... We have not yet reached that point, but tactical innovations which have so far postponed it are now practically exhausted ...

Below: Known to its designers as the A-4 but to the Nazi leadership and also to the Allies as the V-2, this ballistic missile had great psychological impact and was a true portent of the military future.

He realized that he might require fighter cover by night, much as the Americans needed escort by day. Fortunately, the approach of D-Day resulted in shifting the focus of the Combined Bomber Offensive from the cities and factories of Germany to targets directly related to the invasion, thus providing Harris with the opportunity to regroup.

When the Allies invaded Normandy on June 6, 1944, bombers of the US Strategic Air Forces were conducting an experiment in shuttle bombing, taking off from Britain or Italy, hitting targets in the Third Reich, continuing to airfields in the Ukraine from which the aircraft conducted further attacks in eastern Europe, and then returning to their bases, delivering yet another strike en route. On June 21, a German reconnaissance plane followed a force destined from Britain to Poltava. Luftwaffe bombers struck the Ukrainian airfield that very night, destroying 43 B-17s and 15 P-51s. The shuttle bombing continued despite this setback, only to come to an end in September when the Soviet Union refused to cooperate with the Anglo–American allies in using the Ukrainian bases to supply noncommunist Polish resistance forces fighting the Nazis in Warsaw.

To help prepare for the landings in France, the heavy bombers attacked the French transportation network to disrupt the movement of German supplies and reinforcements. The strategic bombing forces also went after the launch sites for the V-1 flying bombs and V-2 rockets that Hitler had begun launching at Britain, an air campaign that continued after the invasion. These operations, and other diversions to support Allied ground troops or local resistance forces, troubled Spaatz, who believed that bombing could subdue Germany, if given enough time, and feared, as late as the spring of 1944, that any land invasion might fail. The American airman firmly believed that one industry, oil production, held the key to the German war effort, and that its destruction would doom the Third Reich.

To demonstrate the importance of oil, Spaatz arranged with Eaker to send the Fifteenth Air Force, not directly involved in the preparations for D-Day, against the vast refineries at Ploesti, Romania, which had not been bombed since August 1943. That attack, delivered at rooftop altitude, inflicted superficial damage at a cost of 54 bombers destroyed and more than 500 crew members killed or captured. Three successful raids by the XV Bomber Command on April 5, 15, and 24, 1944, served as prelude to a deluge of high explosive and incendiary bombs from both the American strategic air forces and ultimately from RAF Bomber Command.

Spaatz persuaded Gen. Eisenhower, who had taken over responsibility for air operations in preparation for the invasion, to allow the Eighth Air Force to join in the

Above: Luftwaffe qualification badges in original presentation cases. From the top: ex-flight crew commemorative badge; pilot's badge; observer's badge. *George Fistrovich Collection*

oil offensive, and on May 12, 800 of Doolittle's bombers attacked eight synthetic oil plants, losing 46 bombers and ten fighters. To Speer, the May 12 raids represented "a new era in air warfare" that eventually deprived the Nazi war machine of the oil upon which it depended.

Except for the May 12 raids, and an occasional attack as part of the shuttle bombing, the Eighth Air Force concentrated during the spring of 1944 on targets related to D-Day or the V-weapons, leaving the Fifteenth Air Force to bear the brunt of the oil offensive. Within months, however, the Allied advance from Normandy, and after August 15 from the French Riviera coast, enabled VIII Bomber Command to join in systematic attacks against oil production. Soon, British *Ultra* intelligence revealed the impact of the resulting shortage of fuel; decoded message traffic reported, among other things, that the Luftwaffe was cutting back on pilot training and that draft animals were pulling trucks on the Italian front, as Germany tried desperately to conserve gasoline.

At the time the oil campaign began, the Luftwaffe introduced the revolutionary Messerschmitt Me 262, the world's first operational jet fighter, which made its combat debut in April 1944 and saw increasing service during the summer and fall. The new German fighter outperformed the P-51, the Americans would not have a successful jet until the spring of 1945, and the Royal Air Force had only a handful of its Gloster Meteor jets. The Me 262 might well have challenged Allied air supremacy, had it appeared in large numbers, but German industry could produce only 1,500 of these airplanes. The pace of development slowed because Hitler could not make up his mind whether the jet should be an interceptor or a bomber, but the greatest obstacle to a successful program proved to be the inability of German manufacturers, beset by shortages of raw materials, to turn out a reliable engine. Moreover, once attrition had

Below: The Liberator was built in larger numbers than any other US warplane of World War II for a number of major roles, but was most important in its heavy bomber role with the designation B-24.

depleted the initial group of jet pilots, trained replacements could not be found, in part a result of the fuel shortage. The scarcity of pilots also prevented the Germans from making full use of another advanced fighter, the rocket-powered Messerschmitt Me 163 interceptor, an extremely demanding aircraft to fly. Like the Me 262, it appeared late in the war and in limited numbers.

Harris, despite his contempt for panacea targets, joined in the oil offensive. "I still do not think," he wrote after the war, "it was reasonable at the time to expect that the campaign would succeed," but succeed it did; the Allies, he conceded, had bet on a long shot, "an outsider" that "happened to win."

The RAF Bomber Command, because of the heavier loads its aircraft could carry, dropped some 40 percent of the bomb tonnage directed at the oil industry after the campaign began at Ploesti in April 1944. Most of the British bombs fell after November, when *Ultra* already indicated a worsening fuel shortage. Soviet troops contributed to the oil crisis by overruning the Ploesti refineries in August 1944, but the compact synthetic fuel plants proved hard to destroy. Not only were they difficult to find and hit, but some 350,000 workers struggled full-time to operate and repair them. The production effort and the stringent program of conservation provided fuel enough for Germany to launch not only an ill-fated attack from the concealment of the Ardennes, triggering the Battle of the Bulge, but also a fruitless series of air strikes on New Year's Day 1945 against eleven Allied airfields in northern France, Belgium, and Holland. Although these actions accomplished nothing strategically, they sustained the illusion that Germany remained a truly formidable enemy.

Despite the German counterattacks in the West, Allied air power dominated the skies. Strategic bombers continued the oil offensive, helped attack the German transportation network, and carried the war to cities thus far untouched by war. By the time the roads, canals, and railways came under systematic attack, the shortage of fuel had so crippled the Luftwaffe that it could send up interceptors only in defense of Berlin. While the heavy bombers – along with fighter-bombers and other tactical aircraft based in Europe – battered transportation targets, Soviet troops under Marshal I.S. Konev broke through on the Eastern Front and advanced into Germany. Refugees from Konev's advance and German reinforcements trying to blunt the Soviet thrust passed through the railyards at Dresden, a large industrial city scarcely harmed by aerial attack. Earlier in the war, bombing Dresden would have required a long flight through heavily defended air space, but those defenses had now crumbled. Industrial cities more important than Dresden already lay in ruins, and almost by default,

Above: The intensity of the day and night bombing campaign against Germany demanded the creation of huge bomb dumps, the American ordnance all having to be carried across the Atlantic in valuable shipping.

Dresden moved toward the top of the target list.

Konev's offensive focused a spotlight on Dresden. Harris hoped to disrupt German efforts to oppose the advance by attacking that city and two other rail centers, Chemnitz and Leipzig. Spaatz doubted, however, that bombing the three targets would accomplish much until the Soviets had advanced farther and increased the strain on the transportation system. Air Chief Marshal Sir Charles Portal, the Royal Air Force Chief of Staff, sided with Spaatz, but Prime Minister Churchill, preparing to meet Stalin and Roosevelt at Yalta in the Crimea, would not tolerate delay. Churchill demanded action that would aid and encourage Konev and demonstrate to Stalin that the British and Americans were actively aiding his armies. The Prime Minister prodded his military leaders to prepare, in time for the Yalta Conference, a plan for "blasting the Germans in their retreat from Breslau," now Wroclaw in Poland, east of Dresden.

At Yalta early in February 1945, the British military delegation advocated bombing Berlin and the rail centers of eastern Germany. Gen. Alexsey Antonev, serving as Stalin's chief of staff, agreed that Anglo–American strategic bombers could aid the Soviet offensive by "paralyzing the junctions of Berlin and Leipzig." Berlin, however, was already scheduled for sustained attack, and Dresden, due more to circumstances than to its inherent military value, had risen to the top of the Allied target list.

Below: Up to World War II, Dresden had been one of the architectural, cultural and intellectual jewels of eastern Germany, and lacked the overt military features that would have invited Allied attack.

On the night of February 13, 1944, immediately after the Yalta Conference adjourned, Harris dispatched a typical night attack against the heart of Dresden, setting blazes that merged into a huge firestorm that consumed entire blocks and killed most of the 35,000 or more persons who perished during three days of bombing. The Americans followed up on the 14th and 15th with daylight strikes on the railyards, but cloud cover and the use of radar resulted in scattered damage. Indeed, the railroad bridge that served as aiming point escaped unscathed. The defenses of Dresden proved feeble; fighters lacked fuel, the advancing Allied armies had overrun the early warning radar sites, and antiaircraft batteries had redeployed to protect more important targets. Less than one percent of the 1,200 Anglo–American bombers that pounded Dresden fell victim to flak or fighters.

While the fate of Dresden was being decided, Harris launched Operation *Thunderclap*, a campaign against

Above: Believed in 1945 to be a major communication center serving the German armies seeking to check the Soviet armies, Dresden was destroyed by Allied bombers, and as late as 1949 was still a mass of rubble.

Berlin designed to bomb the already battered Nazi regime into submission. Spaatz agreed to cooperate in *Thunderclap*, but he hoped rather than believed that it would end the war. He continued to draw a distinction between his own bombing of military targets and Harris' area attacks, intended to drive people from their homes and create intolerable burdens for the government, but in this last campaign against Berlin, the difference vanished. On at least one occasion, American bombardiers simply aimed for parts of the city, and at other times, the designated military target lay submerged in the urban mass. For example, when more than a thousand B-17s raided Berlin on February 3, residential areas and government offices sustained severe damage, along with the rail stations and marshaling yards earmarked for destruction. Despite visual aiming with the Norden sight, accuracy proved abysmal, with some bombardment groups missing entirely a city that encompassed 833 square miles ($2,082km^2$). The scattered bombing resulted from intense antiaircraft fire that encouraged pilots to attempt evasive maneuvers, now possible

Below right: Major targets such as Berlin were defended by multi-gun flak towers whose excellent fields of fire were ideal for potent weapons such as this Flakzwilling 40 mounting carrying two 128-mm AA guns.

Below: A plan of one of the massive concrete flak towers which were built around Berlin. Construction began in 1940 on Hitler's personal order. Although six were originally planned only three were built. Each took six months to construct and stood 130ft (39m) high. They also served as civilian air raid shelters and could accommodate up to 18,000 people on lower floors.

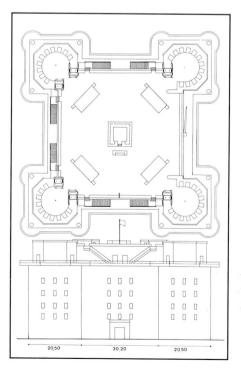

because of smaller formations and an absence of fighter opposition that would have forced the bombers to maintain a tight formation and mass their defensive firepower.

Subsequent American precision attacks on the German capital also resembled the British area attacks in results. On February 26, for instance, the use of radar to attack railroad stations within the city, along with bomb loads of more than 40 percent incendiaries, resulted in widespread damage and set fires that still blazed when British Mosquito bombers delivered a harassing attack that night.

Strikes against the oil industry continued during the bombing of Berlin, and the Allies also had the aerial resources to paralyze the German railways, disrupting the movement of coal, raw materials, refugees, and reinforcements. Although *Ultra* intelligence did not immediately discern the effects of the transportation campaign, by February 1945 decoded message traffic clearly revealed that coal and ore were piling up at the mines, as

Above: Considerable loss of life as well as devastation was caused by the Allied bombing campaign. Here the bodies of civilians killed in a raid have been laid out for identification in a Berlin gymnasium decorated for the Christmas of 1943.

Above: A long-exposure photograph reveals the strange patterns of fires and antiaircraft fire over Hamburg on January 30, 1943 when the city received its 94th British raid. A Lancaster is silhouetted against the ground.

Below: The Luftwaffe qualification badge for antiaircraft (flak) personnel. *George Fistrovich Collection*

factories that had survived the bombing fell silent and the manufacture of weapons declined sharply. The most spectacular of the attacks on transportation, Operation *Clarion*, consisted of strikes by every type of American fighter and bomber, including the B-17s and B-24s, against railyards, tracks, bridges, and rolling stock. On February 22 and 23, 1945, more than 8,000 fighters and bombers attacked from low and medium altitude, temporarily throwing the rail net into utter confusion.

During the Combined Bomber Offensive, B-17s and B-24s of the Eighth and Fifteenth Air Forces dropped slightly more than a million tons (980,000 tonnes) of bombs, 28 percent of them directed against transportation targets, mainly marshaling yards and rail stations in urban areas, 18 percent against elements of the aircraft industry, and 13 percent against oil production. RAF Bomber Command dropped a slightly greater weight of bombs over a longer period, September 1939 to the German surrender in May 1945. Anglo–American strategic bombing killed at least 250,000 persons and forced another 7.5 million from their homes, thus redeeming Churchill's pledge to "bomb the devils 'round the clock", the Americans by day and the British at night.

Although the bombing enthusiasts of the 1920s and 1930s, airmen like the American Billy Mitchell and the British Hugh "Boom" Trenchard, had envisioned air power as a bolt from the blue capable of sudden and decisive results, the air war over Europe became a battle

of attrition. During the fall of 1943, the Luftwaffe controlled the daylight skies, and briefly in the following spring, it exercised air superiority by night. Air battles in Europe and North Africa had already eroded the strength of the German air force, which could not resist the tide of Allied men and machines. True, the Combined Bomber Offensive crippled the oil industry and the transportation system, but doing so took time. The Allies had to train the manpower, acquire the necessary aircraft in sufficient numbers, and gain control of the air before attacking these truly decisive targets. Consequently, before the German war machine suffered the full impact of the Combined Bomber Offensive, Allied ground forces had reached the borders of Germany, enabling even fighter-bombers to scourge the Third Reich.

Above: The night bombing campaign was really an imperial rather than a purely British effort: this Lancaster's seven-man crew included men from countries as far distant as New Zealand and Canada.

V Six

War in Italy: The Final Year

David Hogan

In 1944 the invasion of France
relegated the strategic importance of
the Italian war. But as the eyes of
the world focused on Northwest Europe,
the soldiers in Italy continued
their own bloody campaign.

On the morning of June 5, 1944, Rome witnessed a celebration on a scale seldom, if ever, equalled in modern times. The day before, patrols of the Allied Fifth Army had infiltrated into the city from the south and east, and were followed by task forces racing to seize key bridges over the Tiber River. Now, as Allied troops, tanks and vehicles made their way through the streets of the Eternal City, joyful crowds waved flags, embraced soldiers, offered fruit and bottles of wine, and placed flowers in the muzzles of rifles and tank guns. As they basked in the adulation of the Roman populace, those troops could take great pride in a long, rugged campaign which had begun the previous September on the beaches of Calabria and Salerno, continued through the epic battles at Cassino and Anzio, and had now achieved its greatest triumph yet, with the occupation of the first Axis capital to fall to the Allies.

Within a day, news of the invasion of Normandy thrust the fall of Rome and the Italian campaign into the background, a status that it would hold for the rest of the war. American strategists had always been suspicious of operations in Italy as a distraction from the decisive front in Northwest Europe. Only with the greatest reluctance had they agreed to an invasion of the Italian mainland to knock Italy out of the war. Once established on the mainland, the Allies were soon shipping divisions from Italy to Britain for the cross-channel attack, and Allied staffs were planning to use troops from the Mediterranean theater for an invasion of southern France in support of the Normandy landings. Shortages of landing craft caused planners to postpone the

Left: British troops take cover amongst the sand dunes of the Anzio beachhead. The landings at Anzio in May 1944 were just one of many Allied attempts to outflank the German defensive lines that crossed Italy's mountainous interior.

Above: The Italy Star. Awarded to British and Commonwealth personnel for service in the Italian theater – including Greece and the Mediterranean islands – June 11, 1944 to May 8, 1945.
Salamander Books

invasion of southern France, codenamed *Anvil*, until mid-August, but Allied commanders in Italy still faced the prospect of losing large numbers of their best troops to the "main front." As for the front in Italy, American planners could see little use for it other than to tie down large numbers of German troops.

British goals for the Italian campaign were more ambitious. The attachment of British leaders to a Mediterranean strategy reflected a combination of national interests, personal predilections, and the memory of Britain's heavy losses in France during World War I. A drive through Italy and the Alps into Austria and the Danube basin would maintain British influence and forestall Soviet inroads in the region, and it would also be on the scale of a limited land offensive in which relatively meager British resources, drained by almost five years of war, could still exert at least an unequal influence to those of the United States and the Soviet Union. British strategists, therefore, opposed *Anvil* and favored the diversion of more resources to the Italian theater, arguing, among other things, that the Italian option would provide the Allies with the flexibility to emphasize whichever front offered the most opportunities. Often heated, the debate would reach new levels of intensity in the postwar era when Mediterranean advocates, arguing with the benefit of Cold War hindsight, would castigate American wartime *naiveté* toward the spread of Communism.

Actually, any drive up the Italian boot, part of what Churchill liked to call "the soft underbelly" of Axis-controlled Europe, faced formidable obstacles. The coastal plains of the Italian peninsula extended only a few miles inland. Beyond these plains, an advancing army would have to contend with rolling hills, which, in turn, gave way to range after range of mountains, crossed only by an occasional, easily blocked road or trail. Adding to the miseries of Allied troops, the weather in "sunny Italy" could be quite bitter. In summer, the climate turned hot, dry, and dusty. In winter, frequent rains transformed roads into quagmires of mud, while, at higher elevations, snow and extreme cold added to the already imposing obstacles facing an attacking force. The rugged terrain and inhospitable climate posed major challenges not only for combat units but also for supply officers, who had to support large forces in nearly inaccessible locations at the end of inadequate transportation networks. Too often, optimistic plans of Allied commanders would founder on the rock of logistics.

Of these commanders, two stand out as the dominant figures in the campaign: Field Marshal Sir Harold Alexander and Lt. Gen. Mark W. Clark. In a theater bringing together soldiers of 16 Allied nations, political skills in a commander were essential, and no one possessed those skills to a greater degree than Alexander, chief of 15th Army Group and, after December 1944, commander-in-chief, Mediterranean. Ever the picture of an English gentleman, the calm, polished, supremely self-confident Alexander has been dismissed by some as an unimaginative strategist and lightweight who allowed his subordinates too much discretion, but, like his friend Gen. Eisenhower, he had the ability to make officers of many nationalities work together in a common cause. Among those subordinates, Clark, leader of Fifth Army and later Alexander's successor at 15th Army Group, has emerged as one of the most controversial figures of World War II. Although lacking experience in high command prior to the Italian campaign, the tall, hawk-nosed, hard-driving American possessed definite qualities of leadership and learned quickly on the job. In person, he could be charming and unaffected, but he was also intense, ambitious, a little Anglophobic, and so conscious of his image that one British officer, paraphrasing Clausewitz, described his view of war as "an extension of publicity by other means."

In Field Marshal Alfred Kesselring commander-in-chief of the Germans' Army Group C, Alexander and Clark would face a formidable foe. A former Luftwaffe commander, "smiling Alfred" had already won the respect of observers for his skill as a defensive tactician in the campaign south of Rome. His persuasive abilities had been largely responsible for a skeptical Hitler's decision to fight there rather than withdraw his troops to the Northern Apennines or the Alps following the Italian surrender in September 1943.

Although such a strategy left the Germans in southern Italy exposed to amphibious landings behind their positions, Kesselring could point to several benefits from holding in the south, including the greater distance of Allied forces and bomber bases from Germany, additional time to fortify the mountains to the north, and control of the Po Valley, Italy's agricultural and industrial heartland and the center of Mussolini's rump Fascist Republic. Over time, however, the German strategy to hold as much Italian terrain as possible stemmed less from these factors than from Hitler's stiff opposition to any, even local, withdrawals.

With the collapse of the Cassino front and the fall of Rome, however, the Germans had to limit their immediate goals to saving their army. Noting the enemy's disarray in the wake of the fall of Rome, a jubilant Alexander ordered an all-out pursuit, hoping to breach the Apennines and enter the Po Valley before the Germans could recover. Along the Tyrrhenian coast in the west, Clark sent Maj. Gen. Lucian K. Truscott, Jr.'s US VI Corps up the coastal road to Civitavecchia, where it captured the "Anzio Express," two huge railway guns that

Above: Commanding the US Fifth Army, Lt. Gen. Mark W. Clark was one of the most important commanders in Italy, where a polyglot Allied army faced problems of national rivalry as well as the Germans.

Above: German Army Infantry Assault Badge in its presentation box. *George Fistrovich Collection*

Below: As in other theaters, the German 88-mm gun proved itself a superb weapon in Italy: in its primary flak role it was an effective antiaircraft gun, and in its secondary antitank role it was a potent armor killer.

had made life miserable on the Anzio beaches. From there, Maj. Gen. Willis D. Crittenberger's US IV Corps continued the pursuit along the coast to Montepescali, while élite mountain troops of Gen. Alphonse Juin's French Expeditionary Corps drove through the ranges on IV Corps' right and French colonial troops occupied the island of Elba, Napoleon's first place of exile. To the east, Lt. Gen. Sydney C. Kirkman's XIII Corps led the British Eighth Army's pursuit through rolling farmland to Lake Trasimene, while Lt. Gen. Sir Richard L. McCreery's British X Corps covered XIII Corps' right to Perugia and Lt. Gen. Wladyslaw Anders's Polish II Corps pursued the Germans to within 25 miles (40km) of the key Adriatic port of Ancona. Except for occasional stands by rear guards, the Germans were too disorganized to offer much resistance, and Allied pursuers found roads littered with the wrecks of German armor and other vehicles.

Several factors combined to save the Germans from complete destruction. Even before the Allies decided to mount *Anvil*, the uncertainty was having an impact on morale, notably among French troops eager to liberate their homeland, and on Alexander's planners, who could not be sure which troops would be available. Finally, on June 14, the Allied theater chief, Gen. Henry M. Wilson, Supreme Allied Commander, Mediterranean, directed Alexander to withdraw US VI Corps, along with three American and two French divisions from the front, and, three weeks later, he passed on the final decision to launch *Anvil*. The loss of so many fine troops at such a critical point in the campaign had a damaging effect, but the advance was already starting to bog down by the fourth week in June. Heavy rains, more rugged terrain, and the wear on men and vehicles were beginning to take a toll. As communications lengthened, Allied logisticians were hard-pressed to keep frontline units supplied with ammunition, gasoline, and other critical items. Given even a slight respite, the Germans could carry out a thorough job of mining roads, blowing bridges, and demolishing culverts. Through skillful demolitions and rear guard actions, Kesselring was able to buy enough time to bring up several new divisions and rally his troops along a line centering on Lake Trasimene and covering the key ports of Leghorn and Ancona.

For the rest of June and July, the Allies slugged their way toward the Arno River, as Kesselring sought to delay his foe long enough for fall rains and new fortifications to make the Northern Apennines impassable. The Germans resisted with special tenacity in the east, where Lt. Gen. Sir Oliver Leese of Eighth Army sent XIII Corps up the west side of Lake Trasimene in an attempt to outflank the Germans resisting X Corps on the other side of the lake.

After ten days of hard fighting, Kesselring withdrew to a new line from Ancona through the Arezzo area to the Tyrrhenian coast just north of Cecina, where the 16th SS Panzer Grenadier Division 'Reichsführer SS' had inflicted heavy losses on IV Corps' advance. The German commander held his new line just long enough to force the Allied corps to deploy and mount a series of coordinated attacks before again slipping away to the north, where he intended to make a stand along the Arno. As usual, the Germans used successive rear guards and a promiscuous array of mines, obstacles, and blown bridges to slow the Allied advance. Ancona fell on July 18, Leghorn the next day, and Pisa on July 23. On August 4, the Germans evacuated Florence and withdrew across the Arno, blowing all bridges except for the historic Ponte Vecchio. While preserving his army group, Kesselring had also managed to wear down the Allies and waste seven weeks of summer weather.

More weeks would pass before the Allies could continue their offensive. The *Anvil* contingent was now on its way to southern France, and the remaining units would need considerable rest before they would be ready to assume the advance. Clark had already inserted Maj. Gen. Geoffrey Keyes' US II Corps into the front on the right of IV Corps, and XIII Corps had taken over the sector vacated by the French. To his depleted army, Clark added the 92nd US Infantry Division and the division-sized Brazilian Expeditionary Force. At the same time, logisticians were replenishing supplies and bringing forward depots and communications left behind by the advance. The Germans had done their best to make Leghorn unusable, destroying port facilities, blocking the harbor with sunken ships, and scattering over 25,000 booby traps through the ruins of the city. Engineers estimated that it would take two months to restore Leghorn to full operating capacity, but, by various expedients, two Liberty ships were able to dock there within five weeks. Meanwhile, Eighth Army extended its supply lines to Arezzo, where it installed a major railhead. While the Allies reorganized their logistics, in July Alexander had authorized Allied air forces to bomb the Po bridges, implicitly admitting that 15th Army Group faced a tough battle to breach the Northern Apennines.

The Germans had won another month to complete the 'Gothic Line,' their system of fortifications in the Northern Apennines. Located about 155 miles (248km) north of Rome, these mountains extend from the Ligurian Alps north of Genoa southeast across the peninsula, almost as far as the Adriatic coast south of Rimini, and then turn south to become the Central Apennines, Italy's backbone. On their southern face, the Northern Apennines rise sharply above the Arno plain, reaching an average height of 3,000–3,600 feet (900–1,080m), with

Above: Many of the irreplaceable historical and artistic beauties of Italy were lost in the war, but a large number did survive: one of these was the Ponte Vecchio, seen here in the midst of rubble-strewn Florence.

97

Above: The Iron Cross, Second Class with ribbon and presentation box. *George Fistrovich Collection*

Below: The Nashorn (later the Hornisse) was one of Germany's better tank destroyers, and was a modified PzKpfw IV chassis with a rear fighting compartment that was too lightly armored. The armament was one 88-mm gun.

some peaks in the west as high as 6,000 feet (1,800m) before sloping more gently to the north toward the Po Valley. The Germans took full advantage of this ground in constructing the Gothic Line. Begun in the spring of 1944, this defensive system was largely complete in the western sector by August, but the Germans still had not finished most of the rest of the line, especially in the eastern sector where they relied on a series of defensive positions along the rivers which flowed from the mountains down to the Adriatic. Tenth Army had the task of defending this sector, while Fourteenth Army guarded most of the rest of the Gothic Line. Still concerned about an amphibious flanking movement, Kesselring positioned two Italian divisions to guard his Tyrrhenian flank.

Observing these German dispositions, Alexander decided on a change in strategy. He had intended to deliver his main thrust up the center of the German line toward Bologna, but, in early August, Lt. Gen. Leese came to 15th Army Group to argue against the idea. Lacking mountain troops, Leese felt that he could better use Eighth Army's firepower and mobility, and better exploit any success, in a drive along the Adriatic coast. He also thought an Adriatic advance would catch the Germans by surprise. The change appealed to Alexander, largely because it would enable him to use his two armies like the two fists of a boxer to keep the Germans off balance, and, after meeting with Leese and Clark, he issued orders for the attack, codenamed Operation *Olive*. According to the plan, Eighth Army would send 11 divisions through the narrow gap between the mountains and the sea and drive north into the Romagna Plain to Bologna and Ferrara. Within five days of Eighth Army's attack, US Fifth Army would strike north from Florence through the Apennines to Bologna, where it would link up with Eighth Army's columns and trap the German Tenth Army. To guard his right flank in this move, Clark took British XIII Corps under his command. Through mid-August, Eighth Army shifted its strength to the east, while Polish II Corps advanced along the coast to screen the move from German reconnaissance.

The Poles did their work well, for, when Eighth Army launched *Olive* on the night of August 25, it caught the Germans by surprise. Lt. Gen. E. L. M. Burns' Canadian I Corps and Lt. Gen. Charles F. Keightley's British V Corps advanced rapidly, V Corps encountering more problems from traffic control than from real resistance. By September 1, the Allies had overrun 20 miles (32km) of the Gothic Line, occupying unmanned works and minefields that were still carefully marked. Over the next few days, however, poor weather, mechanical problems, Allied fatigue, fumbling of the exploitation by V Corps, and stiffening enemy resistance combined to slow the drive, and the Germans managed to regroup on Coriano Ridge, the last major hill feature before the Romagna Plain. The Allies took the ridge on September 13, but another week of desperate fighting, featuring battles between German Panther and British Churchill and Sherman tanks, would pass before the Greek brigade entered the demolished port of Rimini, gateway to the Romagna Plain. In 26 days, Eighth Army had covered 30 miles (48km) and reached the Romagna Plain but at a heavy cost in tanks and infantry. The general frustration over the botched breakthrough was not eased by the realization that Eighth Army now faced a series of river lines which, swelled by fall rains, would prove as much of an obstacle as mountains.

The Allies now focused their hopes on Fifth Army's drive north from Florence. Fortunately for Fifth Army, the terrain, upon closer examination, was not as imposing as it first appeared. Several north–south highways connected the Arno and Po Valleys, and most followed the valleys of the numerous spurs branching off from the main spine of the Apennine chain. Also, to consolidate his position and free reserves for the Adriatic front, Kesselring had decided not to contest Fifth Army's crossing of the Arno and had withdrawn his troops to the Gothic Line in the mountains. Knowing from *Ultra* intelligence that the Germans thought the main thrust would come at Futa Pass, Clark feinted toward Futa and sent the US 91st and 85th Infantry Divisions of II Corps against Il Giogo Pass. For three days, the two divisions worked their way up to the pass, driving through forests and brush, gun pits, and concrete bunkers, to reach the summit. Fortunately for the attackers, the Germans had stationed only one regiment of the 4th Parachute Division to guard the pass, giving the Americans a three to one advantage. By September 15, troops of the two divisions held high ground on either side of the pass at the crest of the Northern Apennine range. From there, they began their long descent toward the Po, against strong opposition from the Germans at Radicosa Pass and Battle Mountain. From Monghidoro on October 5, Clark could see the Po Valley and, in the distance, the Alps.

As October wore on, however, it became increasingly clear, even to the hard-driving Clark, that the Allies would not be able to achieve a decisive victory in Italy before the end of the year. Kesselring was again using a skillful defense in depth, and a series of delaying actions to ensure that the Allies would remain in the mountains for the winter. At the Livergnano escarpment, the Germans held US II Corps at bay until small patrols found gaps in the cliffs which enabled their regiments to outflank the position. Through a supreme effort, the US 88th Infantry Division overran Monte Grande, but its attempt to exploit its penetration fizzled when three companies

Above: The Tiger I was a potent tank offering excellent protection and firepower, but its mobility and mechanical reliability were both too limited to allow the vehicle to realize its true potential.

Above: After linking up in the fall of 1944, the forces of the Red Army and the People's Liberation Army of Yugoslavia undertook a joint offensive to liberate Belgrade during October 1944.

Below: In 1944, when civil war broke out in Greece after the German withdrawal, British troops moved in to support the Royalist government against the communist ELIAS organization. Here a Sherman tank provides cover for paratroops as they probe the ruins of a demolished house during December.

were wiped out by a German counterattack at Vedriano. As October waned, heavy rains and fierce German resistance had stopped Fifth Army's advance four miles (6km) from the Po, and Eighth Army could do little better. McCreery, who had replaced Leese when the latter left for Southeast Asia, attempted to put more impetus into his attack by relieving X Corps on his left with Polish II Corps and sending the Poles and British V Corps through the hill country above the flooded Adriatic coastal plains toward the Ronca river. By the end of the October, however, when Wilson directed Alexander to halt the offensive, Eighth Army had reached a standstill on a 30-mile (18km) front, eight miles (13km) short of Ravenna and ten miles (16km) from Faenza.

Despite the disappointment of not reaching the Po Valley, the Allied High Command was pleased with the campaign's progress. When Allied leaders met at Quebec in September, the great initial gains achieved by *Olive* led them to consider options for exploiting the success, including a trans-Adriatic amphibious operation to link up with the Yugoslav partisan leader Tito and, in conjunction with a Fifth Army offensive in Italy, drive north to the Ljubljana Gap, gateway to Austria and southern Germany. With victory on the horizon in the early fall of 1944, Churchill was increasingly concerned about postwar arrangements, and he pushed for a trans-Adriatic operation to offset growing Soviet influence in the Balkans. By November, however, the Allied drive to Bologna and Ravenna had stalled. The Canadian I Corps was leaving for Northwest Europe, and the British were shifting X Corps to Greece, which was on the verge of civil war. These factors, along with Roosevelt's refusal of a British request for three divisions for Italy, Tito's increasing opposition to a landing in Yugoslavia, and Eisenhower's support for a continued Italian offensive to draw German divisions, eventually caused the Allies to shelve the trans-Adriatic project and focus on their basic goal of tying the enemy in Italy.

Not until spring, however, would the Allies be able to launch another full-scale offensive in Italy. The grinding, incessant advance through rugged mountains and muddy coastal plains had taken a toll on the Allied divisions, few of whom could claim any lengthy rest out of the line since the start of the campaign. Eighth Army experienced serious desertion problems, and, in the US 34th Infantry Division, commanders faced a near-mutiny among troops who grumbled that over two years of combat was enough and demanded rotation home to the United States. What is more, the Poles were incensed over what they considered to be a betrayal by Allied leaders at Yalta and could only with difficulty be persuaded to resume their place in the line. Both Fifth and Eighth Armies needed replacements, to the point that the British had to break up their 1st Armoured Division and reorganize some other units to find fillers, and Clark had to appeal to his old friend Eisenhower for 3,000 replacements for his army. In both armies, artillery ammunition was in especially short supply, and both instituted severe restrictions on the use of artillery to build up their reserves. Except for some limited objective offensives, notably in the east where Eighth Army finally took Faenza and Ravenna, the Allies settled for a long lull to rest troops, bring forward their supply depots, and welcome new units, notably the 10th Mountain Division from the United States.

In their baptism of fire, the new divisions had different experiences. Since its arrival in August, American commanders had been concerned about the 92nd Infantry Division's poor training and morale; problems that stemmed from the inferior education of its black enlisted men and mutual antagonism between them and their mostly white officers. Despite efforts to ease the 92nd into a quiet sector of the front along the Tyrrhenian coast, the division performed so poorly that the Allies eventually needed to use the 8th Indian Division to backstop the 92nd. The Brazilian Expeditionary Force's experience proved more positive. The Brazilians had come to Italy lacking everything from training in mountain warfare to winter clothing. After showing their inexperience in their initial clashes with the Germans, they performed well in capturing Monte Castello in February. On the Brazilians left, the 10th Mountain Division showed its mettle in its first engagement. Built around members of the US National Ski Patrol, the division included several ski racers, ski instructors, and mountain climbers. Just after dark on February 18, climbing teams led a regiment of the 10th Mountain up a 1,500 foot (450m) cliff to take Riva Ridge. The capture of that peak and nearby Monte della Torracia and Monte della Spe by the 10th Mountain gave IV Corps excellent staging positions for the spring offensive.

The success of the Brazilian Expeditionary Force and 10th Mountain Division underlined the desperation of the German situation as winter came to an end. With its relatively high morale, rested troops, and unbroken front, Army Group C may have been in the best condition of the Wehrmacht's remaining forces, but Generaloberst Heinrich von Vietinghoff, who succeeded Kesselring in March 1945, could not view his situation with anything but discouragement. By March, Army Group C had lost four divisions to other fronts, leaving him with only 26 understrength divisions. His new line, incorporating the western sector of the Gothic Line and relying on a series of rivers in the east, enjoyed nowhere near the strength of the lines farther down the peninsula and ironically forced von Vietinghoff to

Above: The shoulder insignia of the 10th Mountain Division. Below: The 10th was the only specifically-trained mountain division in the US Army. *Salamander Books*

Above: The flat Po Valley demanded different techniques of the Allies: seem in April 1945, this is a long pontoon bridge over the Po beside the original bridge destroyed by bombing or blown by the Germans.

defend a longer front than he would have held if the Allies had succeeded in forcing him back to the Alps. Thanks to Allied bombers, his communications were in poor condition, despite skillful improvisation by his engineers, who, to deceive planes, would build bridges a few inches underwater or use bridge spans that could be removed by day and placed over water at night. Von Vietinghoff would have liked to have retreated at least to the line of the Po, but Hitler had refused all withdrawals except under pressure of a major Allied offensive. The new commander could only rearrange his units and hope that, when the inevitable breakthrough came, he would have time to save his forces.

On the Allied side, a new command team was working to ensure that the next campaign in Italy would be the last. With Wilson's departure to head the British Joint Staff in Washington, Alexander assumed the theater command, Clark moved up to 15th Army Group, and Truscott, now a lieutenant general, returned from France to direct Fifth Army. Still regarding the British as too cautious, Clark arranged for Fifth Army to have the main attack in the coming offensive, even though the Eighth was the stronger of the two armies. McCreery, nevertheless, was in no mood to play second fiddle, and his plan ensured a sizable role for Eighth Army. The plan called for amphibious operations over Lake Comacchio in the north to outflank the German positions, while V Corps sent three divisions across the Senio River toward Bastia Bridge, key to the heavily fortified Argenta Gap which provided the only dry route through the flooded lowlands. On the left, Polish II Corps would support V Corps' flank with a drive up Highway 9 to Bologna. Four days after Eighth Army's attack, IV Corps, followed by II Corps, would launch the main attack toward the Po, bypassing Bologna which would fall of its own accord. Having broken through, the two armies would encircle as many Germans as possible south of the Po and then cross the river, Fifth Army driving north for Lake Garda, and Eighth Army turning northeast toward Istria.

After a diversionary attack by a reorganized 92nd Division on the west coast, Eighth Army launched its spring drive on April 10. British commandos, units of the Special Boat Service, and troops of the British 56th (London) Division in amphibious landing craft had already secured the northern flank by clearing Lake Comacchio. On April 9, Allied air units began the heaviest air preparation of the campaign as over 1,600 heavy bombers carpeted target areas between the Senio and Santerno Rivers and over 620 medium bombers hit enemy defenses and troop concentrations opposite V Corps and Polish II Corps. As the sun set on April 10, the two corps began their attack. By the following morning, the 2nd New Zealand Division and the 8th Indian

Division of V Corps had established bridgeheads over the Senio, and, the next day, they had crossed the Santerno. McCreery now turned the British 78th Infantry Division toward Bastia Bridge, which fell on April 14. Having already deployed his only mobile reserve division to guard against a landing in the Gulf of Venice, von Vietinghoff now desperately shifted I Parachute Corps from Fifth Army's front, but too late to stop the British advance, which was gaining momentum. After the fall of Argenta on April 17, V Corps drove toward Ferrara, while Polish II Corps reached Bologna on April 21.

At Bologna, the Poles met units of Fifth Army, which had finally broken through to the Po Valley. Truscott had originally set D-Day for April 12 but postponed it for two days when fog closed in Allied airfields. The morning of April 14 dawned cloudy but soon cleared enough for the air assault, followed by a bombardment by 2,000 artillery pieces. On IV Corps' front, the 10th Mountain Division and 1st US Armored Division spearheaded the attack and, by the night of April 18, had almost reached the mountains overlooking Highway 9. Von Vietinghoff sent the 90th Panzer Grenadier Division to plug the widening gap in his line, but again the Germans had reacted with too little too late. Meanwhile, on April 15, II Corps had begun its assault with the 6th South African Armored Division and 88th Infantry Division, followed by the 91st and 34th Infantry Divisions the next day. The advance proceeded slowly at first in the face of fierce German resistance, but, under pressure all along the line and with its flanks threatened by Allied advances, the German front began to buckle. Truscott sensed that a breakthrough was at hand and shifted II and IV Corps west of Highway 65, leaving only the Italian Legnano Combat Group to the east of the route. On April 18, Fifth Army renewed the attack. On April 19, the German front collapsed, and, two days later, the 34th Division entered Bologna.

The race to the Po had begun. Aided by close air support, the Allies were engaged in a general pursuit all along the front. Even without authorization from Hitler,

Below: A German motorcycle of the Victoria KR 35 type. Used in signals and reconnaissance work, these motorcycles formed an important communications link in German mobile units. By 1944, each panzer regiment, on paper, was operating over 50 of both these machines and the larger Zundapp KS 750 motorcycle and sidecar combination.
Memorial Museum, Bayeux

von Vietinghoff put into effect his plan for a general withdrawal behind the Po in an effort to save what remained of his forces. Events, however, were moving far past his ability to control them. The open terrain and superb road net of the Po Valley enabled the mobile Allied forces to bypass and cut off pockets of resistance. Allied engineers were performing prodigious feats; in one day, Eighth Army sappers built 29 separate bridges, using 1,500 tons (1,524 tonnes) of equipment. In the west, Task Force Duff of the 10th Mountain Division had reached San Benedetto on the Po by the evening of April 11, while the rest of IV Corps and the lead elements of II Corps closed up to the river the next day – in the process trapping thousands of Germans waiting to cross. Further east, Eighth Army's advance met the 6th South African Armored Division at aptly-named Finale on April 23, trapping most of what remained of I Parachute Corps before continuing on to the Po. With his command trapped between the Allies, Po, and Adriatic, the LXXVI Panzer Corps's commander Gen. von Schwerin told his troops to abandon their equipment and swim the Po. He himself surrendered to the British on April 25.

With the collapse of German resistance, the Allies threw aside their elaborate plans for a forced crossing of the Po and took the river on the run on their way to the Alps. Using bridges, captured assault boats, amphibious vehicles, and anything else handy, Allied troops crossed the Po on April 23–24 against almost no opposition.

The pursuit now turned toward the Alps, using what Truscott later called, "controlled dispersion." While the 92nd Division moved along the coastal road to Genoa and Turin, the US 1st Armored Division raced to Lake Como to cut off exits from the Po Valley into the northern lake country. The rest of the IV Corps headed north for Lake Garda and the Brenner Pass, while Keyes' II Corps captured Verona and turned northeast into the Dolomite Mountains. Meanwhile, Eighth Army's V and XIII Corps had reached the Adige by the evening of April 26 and crossed the river the next day. Because of lengthy communications and lack of transport, McCreery could send only two divisions past the Adige, but those two turned out to be more than enough. The British 56th (London) Division occupied Venice on April 29, while the 2nd New Zealand Division sped along the coastal route to Trieste, entering that port on May 2. Wherever they went, the Allies met Italian partisans who had harassed enemy columns, saved installations from demolition by the Germans, and often liberated towns and regions prior to the arrival of Allied troops. Over 145,000 Germans had surrendered since the start of the spring offensive, and the remainder were heading for the Alpine passes to Austria and southern Germany.

By May 1945, the surrender of all German troops in

Below: The British Eighth Army, pursuing the German Fourteenth Army, reached the border between Italy and Austria at the Brenner Pass on May 6, 1945 and immediately instituted strict border controls.

Italy was at hand. Secret negotiations had been underway since February between Gen. Karl Wolff, the SS officer responsible for internal security in German-occupied northern Italy, and Allen Dulles, head of the American intelligence office in Berne, Switzerland. The Germans sought an honorable capitulation and permission to withdraw into Germany, but the Allies demanded unconditional surrender. Suspicious, with some reason, that the Germans were playing for time, the Combined Chiefs of Staff ordered a cutoff of negotiations on April 20, but Dulles reopened the discussions a few days later when a representative from von Vietinghoff joined the talks. On April 28, Italian dictator Benito Mussolini was executed by partisans, and on April 29, two German representatives signed a surrender agreement at Alexander's headquarters in Caserta. Due to poor communications with von Vietinghoff's headquarters, dissension among the German officers, and the arrival of a new commander for Army Group C, confirmation of the agreement was delayed. Finally, the army chiefs convinced the new commander that they had nothing left with which to fight, and on May 1, as the Allied deadline was running out, the Germans agreed to execute the agreement. With the announcement of the cease fire on May 2, the war in Italy came to a close.

Notwithstanding the fondest hopes of Churchill, Alexander, Clark, and other Mediterranean advocates, the campaign in Italy during the final year of the war was a mere sideshow. In the end, the war against Germany was decided on the plains of Northwest Europe or, perhaps more accurately, the Russian steppes, not the mountains of the Italian peninsula. For their efforts in Italy, the Allies could claim some measurable political benefits, not least an appreciably better chance of a non-Communist Italy in the postwar period, but the main justification for the Italian campaign had always been diversion of German troops from the decisive theaters. Whether in fact, it achieved that objective has been hotly debated ever since the war, and can probably never be settled conclusively. Nevertheless, it is worth noting that, if the campaign did cause the Germans to shift several divisions to Italy that they needed elsewhere, it happened as much because of faulty Axis strategy as because of anything the Allies did. The Germans could have withdrawn to the easily defensible Alps, but instead elected to battle the Allied advance up the peninsula. Nevertheless, if, as seems likely, the Allies caused the Germans to divert substantial numbers of troops to Italy and away from the decisive theaters in Russia and Northwest Europe, then the Allied troops who served in the campaign, as well as 312,000 Allied casualties, could have been said to have suffered and died for a purpose.

Above: The bodies of Benito Mussolini, his mistress Clara Petacci and other Fascists, all shot by the partisans on April 28, were mutilated and hung by their feet on public display in the Piazzale Loretto in Milan.

V
Seven
The Ardennes
Counteroffensive

Steven Dietrich

**As 1944 drew to a close,
the Allies in Northwest Europe thought
they could expect a quiet winter.
Hitler, however, had brought together
his last reserves in the west
and had other plans.**

By mid-December 1944, Eisenhower's broad-advance strategy had nearly exhausted his forces. At the end of an overextended supply line they had stalled, their front lines uneven. Eisenhower planned to resume the offensive at the end of the year to rupture Hitler's vaunted Siegfried Line, the "Westwall," and thrust into the heart of Germany. Keeping up supplies from the newly opened Belgian port of Antwerp, Eisenhower planned to shift priority to Field Marshal Montgomery's 21st Army Group on the Maas River north of Aachen. With one Canadian, one British and one American army Montgomery would strike into the Ruhr, the industrial region vital to German war production.

To Montgomery's south, Gen. Bradley's 12th Army Group straddled Belgium's Ardennes region. The Ardennes runs 80 miles (128km) along the Belgian/German border from near Eupen in the north to the vicinity of Luxembourg city. A western extension of the high plateau of Germany's Eifel region, the Ardennes stretches 60 miles (96 km) westward across the Meuse River. Heavy forests and mountainous terrain along the Ardennes' eastern boundary make military operations difficult. Sloping gradually westward, the ground becomes less rugged, and more easily traveled. Combined with the difficult terrain, heavy winter rains, snow, and fog further impede military operations, keeping forces essentially road-bound and requiring the control of major road junctions for any rapid maneuver — notably the junctions at St. Vith, Bastogne, Malmedy, and Houffalize.

The Losheim Gap, between the Elsenborn Ridge in the

Left: German troops double over a Belgian road amidst the wreckage of an American column. The opening phases of the Ardennes battle would see this sight repeated time and again as the American lines crumbled in the face of German assaults.

107

north and the high Schnee Eifel ridge in the center of the region, beckoned westbound invaders. German forces attacked through the Ardennes with stunning success in 1914 and again in 1940. During World War I, the Germans built rail lines to several towns where the Eifel's dense woods could conceal troop concentrations across the border from the Ardennes.

Bradley concentrated his three US armies in the north and south of his sector. On the left, north of the Ardennes, Lt. Gen. William H. Simpson's Ninth Army protected Montgomery's right flank. To Simpson's right, Lt. Gen. Courtney Hodges' First Army, recovering from 33,000 casualties sustained in two months of heavy fighting, occupied the Ardennes.

Holding the north of First Army's sector, Maj. Gen. Leonard T. Gerow's V Corps covered a 20-mile (32 km) front from Monschau to Losheimergraben. On V Corps' right, the 99th Division, newly arrived from the United States, sat on the excellent defensive terrain of Elsenborn Ridge. Gerow's seasoned 2nd and fresh 78th Divisions were moving through the 99th to seize the Roer River dams.

To Gerow's right, in the middle of the Ardennes, lay Maj. Gen. Troy Middleton's VIII Corps. Expecting little enemy activity in the Ardennes, since September Bradley had used Middleton's quiet sector to ease new units into the theater and to mend battle-worn ones. On the left, one squadron of the 14th Cavalry Group guarded the Losheim Gap, a division-sized sector, with the

Below: Hardly a typical Christmas scene, but the M4 Sherman tanks of US armored units could not have been a more welcome sight to the hard-pressed infantry that were holding the Germans' Ardennes offensive.

reserve squadron 20 miles (32km) behind. East of St. Vith, the untested 106th Division secured the Schnee Eifel on the cavalry group's right. Farther south, the 28th Division, battered in the Hürtgen Forest, rested along the Our River, a combat command of the untried 9th Armored Division on its right. The 4th Division, also licking its wounds after the Hürtgen Forest held the corps' southern flank around Echternach.

Below the Ardennes, Lt. Gen. George S. Patton's Third Army prepared to attack the Saar River. South of Patton, Gen. Jacob L. Devers' 6th Army Group touched the Rhine.

Adolf Hitler began considering an Ardennes offensive in August 1944, even as his army retreated. He decided to hold the Siegfried Line and prepare to attack along the Western Front in November when bad weather would ground the Allies' superior air forces. On September 1, Hitler recalled Field Marshal Gerd von Rundstedt as Commander-in-Chief West.

Hitler had secretly begun massing forces for a major counteroffensive. Despite heavy losses and dwindling reserves, he still had ten million men in uniform, three quarters of them in the army. He would expand that arm another 750,000 by extending the draft age to include 16 and 60 year olds, ending deferments, and converting sailors and airmen into ersatz soldiers.

Despite Allied bombing, German industry peaked in the fall of 1944. Hitler collected over 2,100 tanks and assault guns and 1,900 artillery pieces for his offensive, but only about 1,000 aircraft. A successful operation would gain production time for Hitler's secret wonder weapons – jet-powered fighter planes, rocket propelled robot bombs, and improved submarines. By tapping Germany's last resources, Hitler staked the Reich's survival on the outcome of one final offensive.

On September 16, still scarred from the July assassination attempt, Hitler unveiled a momentous decision. "I shall," he declared, "go over to the offensive ... [through] the Ardennes, with the objective, Antwerp!" He planned to cut off Montgomery, Hodges, and Simpson from their supply sources, destroy 25 or more Allied divisions, and capture or destroy stockpiled equipment and supplies. With the western enemy so weakened, Hitler hoped to turn his full might against Soviet forces in the east. He thought a major victory would force the western Allies to drop demands for "unconditional surrender" and eventually agree to a negotiated peace.

By October 22, the plan took shape. Four armies comprising Field Marshal Walter Model's Army Group B would attack Blitzkriegstyle on November 25 along a 60-mile (96km) front between Monschau and Echternach. Model's forces would be upgraded to 30 full-strength divisions – 12 panzer or panzergrenadier and 18

Above: The shoulder insignia of the three US Army divisions which were among the first to bear the brunt of the German attack on the Ardennes. From the top: 4th Infantry Division; 28th Infantry Division; 106th Infantry Division.
Salamander Books

Above: German officers' greatcoats. The fur-lined winter coat on the right was formerly owned by SS Oberstgruppenfuhrer 'Sepp' Dietrich. *West Point Museum, NY*

volksgrenadier (peoples' infantry) divisions. Inexperience and fuel and motor transport shortages, however, degraded Model's potential combat power.

Two panzer armies in the center of Army Group B would make the main effort while two armies on the flanks supported. Hitler's Nazi crony, SS Oberstgruppenführer Josef 'Sepp' Dietrich, would lead his Sixth SS Panzer Army of nine divisions (four panzer) – comprising roughly 550 tanks and assault guns – in the main attack in the north through the Hürtgen Forest, cross the Meuse River in 48 hours, capture Liège, control the Albert Canal, and seize Antwerp, thus dividing US and British forces and separating them from the bulk of their supplies. General der Panzertruppen Hasso von Manteuffel's Fifth Panzer Army of seven divisions – 450 tanks and assault guns – would make the secondary attack on Dietrich's left through St. Vith, cross the Meuse at Namur, and orient on Brussels and Antwerp. General der Panzertruppen Erich Brandenberger's Seventh Army of four infantry divisions and 40 assault guns would protect the southern flank from counterattacks by Patton. Fifteenth Army would attack with six divisions and 700 tanks to exploit Dietrich's breakthrough in the north. Hitler held six divisions and two elite mechanized brigades in OKW (High Command) reserve with 450 tanks and assault guns.

Keeping operational control to himself, Hitler shrouded the operation in secrecy and deception. Even the plan's name, *Wacht Am Rhein* (Watch on the Rhine), was misleading. Distrustful of his own officers since the assassination attempt, Hitler informed his generals of the plan only when necessary, making them swear silence or death. Even von Rundstedt, the nominal commander, first learned of the plan in late October. Hitler forbade discussion of the operation – even encoded – on wireless, telephone, or telegraph for fear of Allied intercept. Officer couriers trailed by Gestapo agents hand-carried all information. Headquarters assumed bogus titles, missions, and dispositions. Attack forces moved into the Eifel by night and hid in the forests by day.

Senior commanders believed the plan too ambitious and proposed limited alternatives. If the attackers reached Antwerp, which was doubtful, they could themselves be encircled and destroyed. Adequate logistical support was unlikely. Furthermore, German units would be at the mercy of Allied air forces once the weather cleared. Finally, too little time remained for proper planning. The generals advised stopping at the Meuse. Even Sepp Dietrich complained that the "impossible" attack was planned for "the worst time of the year through the Ardennes where the snow is waist deep and there isn't room to deploy four tanks abreast let alone armored divisions! Where it doesn't get light until eight and it's dark again at [five] and with re-formed divisions made up chiefly of kids and sick old men – and at Christmas!"

Hitler, however, ruled the operation "unalterable in every detail" but postponed the attack until mid-December when poor weather was expected to ground Allied planes for ten straight days. He also changed the code name to *Herbstnebel* (Autumn Mist). Poor weather, of course, would also impede the German advance and restrict vehicles to the Ardennes' limited roads, forcing commanders to fight through roadblocks and capture road junctions, violating their doctrine of bypassing strong points. A defender could stall a larger attacking force under these conditions. In the end, ironically, the weather favored the Americans.

Misreading signs of the coming attack, Allied commanders remained ignorant of Hitler's intentions. American cryptanalysts decoded messages to Japan from the Japanese ambassador in Berlin. This so-called *Magic* intelligence announced German plans for a November "large-scale offensive in the West." Prisoners of war described German troop buildups and attack plans. Intelligence officers watched headquarters and other units appear across the lines. But Allied commanders remained unconvinced that the Wehrmacht was capable of a major offensive, especially in the Ardennes. Patton was the sole exception to this delusion.

Below: 'Sepp' Dietrich was the SS officer who commanded the Sixth SS Panzer Army entrusted with the task of punching through the US First Army's VIII Corps and then pushing through to Antwerp and all its supplies.

By November 24, Patton feared Middleton's quiet sector invited attack. He analyzed the Ardennes' terrain and sent reconnaissance planes over German staging areas to Middleton's front. Using *Ultra* decryptions of German railroad communications, Patton tracked the influx of German units. A week before the attack he observed nine battle-ready divisions opposite VIII Corps and ordered "limited outline planning begin at once to meet the threat to the north," later directing his staff to study countering a breakthrough in the Ardennes. On the eve of the attack, Patton's G-2 surmised the enemy was massing his armor "for a large-scale counteroffensive."

When German forces advanced under radio silence on December 16, Patton ordered his staff to plan "pulling the Third Army out of its eastward attack, change the

Below: Heavily armed and apparently well equipped, German soldiers pose with US cigarettes captured during their lightning advance in the Ardennes. Behind them is a knocked-out American M8 light armored car.

direction ninety degrees, moving to Luxembourg and attacking north." Patton's contingency plan was brilliantly prophetic.

On December 16, all hell broke loose. The 20-division, 200,000-man attack completely surprised the 82,260 American soldiers in its path. Following a 45-minute artillery preparation that began at 05:30 and cut communications to forward posts, German infantrymen moved through the darkness and fog to cut gaps for the panzers. Isolated from their headquarters, many US units spent the day fighting confusing small-unit actions, often unable to see their enemy. Some units held, others were overrun.

The main thrust hit the weakest point, Col. Mark Devine's 14th Cavalry Group in the Losheim Gap. By dawn the 18th Volksgrenadier Division had destroyed one of Devine's troops on the main attack at Roth. In the afternoon German units crossed the Our River. Elements of both panzer armies had penetrated through Devine's sector.

The situation was worse for the 106th Division. Although two regiments on the Schnee Eifel held throughout the day, the collapse of the Losheim Gap left the division's northern flank exposed. By midnight the 18th Volksgrenadier Division had encircled the two regiments and continued westward meeting with little resistance.

To the south, the Fifth Panzer and Seventh Army boundary bisected the 28th Division's porous defensive

Above: German infantrymen advance past a burning vehicle. The soldier at the rear is armed with a captured US M3 carbine, a version of the M1 with provision for automatic fire and an infrared night sight.

line of company strongpoints. By the end of the day elements of five divisions had attacked, bypassed, and isolated 28th Division's 110th Regiment, outnumbered ten to one. Few escaped.

Two divisions held on the flanks of the evolving penetration. In the north the 99th Division and other V Corps elements stood firm against Sixth SS Panzer Army's main drives against Monschau and the Elsenborn Ridge. In fierce fighting, the division gained time for the corps to send the 2nd Division to their aid and reposition units to keep the Germans from widening their penetration.

Units of the 4th Division and 9th Armored Division refused to yield to two of the Seventh Army's divisions in the south. Wedged between the 28th and 4th Divisions, the 60th Armored Infantry Battalion fought off the entire 276th Volksgrenadier Division. To the right, the 12th Infantry, 4th Division, aided by a tank company, stopped the 212th Volksgrenadier Division cold.

Though vastly outnumbered and unprepared for such a strong attack, battle-weary or inexperienced American forces generally held their ground on December 16, allowing only minor penetrations of two or three miles (3–5km), most dangerously in the Losheim Gap. The Germans had not achieved their goal of collapsing the entire front on the first day. But now the panzers were coming.

After that first day, the lines on US situation maps showed a front in danger of collapse. Allied commanders

Below: Short of high-quality equipment, the Germans stripped the bodies of the Allied dead. Here a German infantryman adjusts the boots he has just taken from one of the four US soldiers lying face-down in the mud.

reacted sharply. Montgomery returned from a golf outing and sent liaison officers throughout First Army, soon learning more about the situation than even Hodges and Bradley, and consequently moving British XXX Corps to block along the Meuse River. Many of Hodges' deputies, relaxing in Britain and Paris, hurriedly returned to the embattled headquarters and First Army began evacuating logistics bases and requesting reinforcements. Eisenhower rushed two uncommitted tank divisions to Middleton's aid — Patton's 10th to reinforce the stubborn 4th Division and Simpson's 7th to Bastogne.

Hitler picked Obersturmbannführer Joachim Peiper, ruthless and competent, to spearhead Dietrich's main attack. Making up nearly half of 1st SS Panzer Division's strength, Kampfgruppe (battle group) Peiper was a powerful 4,000-man unit consisting of 119 medium and heavy tanks, a panzergrenadier battalion, a towed artillery battalion, and combat support units. Dietrich's failure at Elsenborn Ridge on the first day forced Peiper to reroute through the 3rd Parachute Division at Lanzerath. Massive traffic jams behind the stalled advance delayed Peiper's 19-mile (30km) column for four hours. Early on December 17, Peiper sidestepped the 99th Division and dashed toward the Meuse.

There was nothing holy about that sabbath day for scores of Americans in Peiper's way. Not wanting to be burdened with prisoners and perhaps seeking vengeance for Allied bombing raids against German civilians, Peiper's men executed prisoners and murdered civilian witnesses. In Honsfeld, the victims exceeded a hundred. Near Malmedy, Peiper's panzergrenadiers executed 86 soldiers of the 7th Armored Division in what came to be known as the Malmedy Massacre. In a dozen separate incidents, Peiper's men murdered 111 Belgian civilians and 353 US soldiers. News of the murders quickly spread throughout American ranks. In its first bloody day, Kampfgruppe Peiper had moved 25 miles (40km) through the lines to Stavelot, losing less than a dozen armored vehicles.

Above: A German MG42; a 7.92mm aircooled machine gun. This example is mounted on a tripod for its heavy machine gun role and includes its original optical sight: a Zielfernrohr 40. *US Army Ordnance Museum, Aberdeen, Md.*

Over the next days the Americans expended considerable effort against the rampaging Kampfgruppe, using combat power that was needed elsewhere. By the 20th they had surrounded and smashed Peiper with overwhelming ground forces. Fighter-bombers had delayed the forces Peiper thought were following. Decimated and out of fuel, on December 23, the remnants of the Kampfgruppe escaped on foot.

Peiper's operation did more good than harm to the Americans. His initial moves shocked US commanders into decisive action. Peiper lost nearly a quarter of the tanks in Hitler's main attack without achieving even his initial objectives. The units the Americans moved against Peiper formed a strong defensive line along the northern flank of the German penetration. The Americans had seized the initiative from Dietrich, denying him freedom to turn north towards Antwerp.

Two other special German operations also miscarried. An airborne assault behind enemy lines scheduled for the night of December 15/16 (Operation *Stösser*) totally failed. Unable to assemble in time, the 1,200 paratroopers were hopelessly scattered by inexperienced pilots a night late. The airborne commander, Col. Graf Friedrich August von der Heydte, managed to gather only a quarter of his force near Belle Croix behind Monschau. Twenty-one Jagdtigers – 82 ton (83 tonne) Tiger tanks mounting a 128mm antiaircraft gun – scheduled to link up with the paratroopers to hold open the northern shoulder, were bombed at their railhead. The lightly armed paratroopers watched helplessly as the US 1st Infantry and 7th Armored Divisions streamed south.

Below: One of the most potent of Germany's fighting vehicles was the Jagdtiger tank destroyer, which was the chassis and hull of the Tiger II surmounted by a well armored barbette carrying a 128mm gun.

After dark on December 20, von der Heydte fled toward friendly lines, but surrendered the following night.

Obersturmbannführer Otto Skorzeny, leader of the daring airborne rescue of Mussolini in September 1943, formed a group of American-uniformed, English-speaking commandos to infiltrate the lines, confuse the enemy, and seize Meuse River bridges. The Americans learned of Skorzeny's ruse, Operation *Greif*, and special search parties quickly rounded up most of the thirty-some teams that had infiltrated the lines in American vehicles on the nights of December 16 and 17. For violating the rules of war by posing as Americans, the commandos were treated as spies and promptly executed by firing squad.

On December 17, Eisenhower sent his reserves, the XVIII Airborne Corps comprising the 82nd and 101st Airborne Divisions, to bolster Bradley. When Middleton warned that Bastogne was in danger of encirclement and recommended it be held, Bradley wished to move the entire airborne corps there. SHAEF, however, diverted the 82nd Airborne to plug the line near Malmedy. Late on the 18th, the 101st Airborne joined two combat commands from the 9th and 10th Armored Divisions and the 705th Tank Destroyer Battalion to defend Bastogne. Brig. Gen. Anthony C. McAuliffe, temporarily commanding the division, took charge. Meanwhile, Gen. der Panzertruppen Heinrich Freiherr von Luttwitz, commanding von Manteuffel's XLVII Panzer Corps, learned of the intended reinforcement of Bastogne from an intercepted message and rushed two panzer divisions there. Meanwhile, Middleton redirected the 7th Armored Division to St. Vith.

Brig. Gen. Bruce C. Clarke, commanding 7th Armored Division's Combat Command B, arrived in St. Vith ahead

Above: US longarms and equipment. On the top is the M1930A3 rifle with its pattern bayonet and scabbard. The M1930A3 was largely obsolete by 1944/45. It had been replaced by the M1 Garand (seen with its rifle grenade attachments). By the end of the war over four million Garands had been manufactured.
Russ Pritchard Collection

Above: Infantrymen attached to the US 4th Armored Division fire on German soldiers during this formation's push north for the relief of the US 101st Airborne Division holding out in beleaguered Bastogne.

of the division. The 106th Division commander, having lost all but a fraction of his outfit, relinquished command of the town's defense to Clarke. When Brig. Gen. Robert W. Hasbrouck, 7th Armored Division commander, later arrived, he left Clarke to defend the town itself while he directed the forces around the town. Because of his division's late arrival, Hasbrouck had to postpone counter-attack plans to save the two 106th Division regiments on the Schnee Eifel.

By midnight on the 18th, Clarke's units, strung out 60 miles (96km) on icy roads congested with advancing Germans, fleeing Americans, and refugees, began to arrive in St. Vith. They soon repulsed the first of many attacks. On the 19th, Hasbrouck formed a horseshoe-shaped line ten miles (16km) around St Vith using a combat command of the 9th Armored Division and two battered regiments surviving from the 106th and 28th Divisions. Later that day the marooned American regiments on the Schnee Eifel surrendered, freeing more German units to join the 62nd Volksgrenadier Division attacking St. Vith.

December 19 and 20 were days of decision for the opposing forces. On the 18th, Bradley and Patton had discussed Patton's plan for Maj. Gen. John Millikin's III Corps to attack the penetration's southern flank. Patton would send Maj. Gen. Manton Eddy's XII Corps on Millikin's right if Devers shifted north to fill Eddy's lines. Bradley obtained Eisenhower's tentative approval, transferred VIII Corps to Patton, and ordered Millikin's

4th Armored and 80th Divisions to move north immediately. Within minutes both divisions headed northward toward attack positions. Patton became responsible for both the defense and relief of Bastogne.

Eisenhower met with his commanders and staff the following morning in Verdun, the 19th, and coordinated Patton's counterattack and Devers' shift. Patton would attack toward Bastogne on December 22 and continue on to Houffalize, now abandoned.

Bradley had visited neither Hodges nor any First Army units since the battle began. Bradley's headquarters in Luxembourg was remote, communications were tenuous, and the German penetration threatened to isolate him from his northern armies. Believing that Montgomery was better positioned, on December 20, Eisenhower transferred command of the battle north of the Prum–Givet line to him, as well as Bradley's Ninth and First Armies. Bradley would control the southern portion, with only Patton to command.

Montgomery arrived at Hodges' headquarters within hours of the command change. Simpson had already transferred Maj. Gen. J. Lawton Collins' VII Corps to Hodges who had established blocking positions and was preparing counterattacks. Montgomery began "tidying" the lines, forming reserves, and cancelling counterattacks.

Hitler also made a major change on the 20th. While more US divisions arrived, German divisions sat in traffic jams, and as casualties mounted, German superiority declined. With Dietrich hopelessly stalled, Hitler grudgingly shifted the main attack to von Manteuffel, releasing to him OKW reserves and some of Dietrich's units to exploit breakthroughs. The capture of St. Vith became critical because it controlled movement through the northern portion of von Manteuffel's area.

On December 22, von Manteuffel increased pressure on St. Vith, attacking with elements of two SS panzer divisions while two other panzer divisions bypassed the town to north and south. Facing overwhelming odds, Clarke abandoned St. Vith during the night of December 21/22 and defended on high ground 760 yards (700m) to the rear, withdrawing on frost-hardened ground on December 23.

The Germans had needed St. Vith on the first day and could not make up the week of lost time. Hasbrouck's force had halted an entire corps, jammed a main route with supplies, troops, and equipment needed by two German armies, and stranded Peiper. By December 23, resolute defenses at Elsenborn Ridge and St. Vith had stymied Hitler's plan, though Model could not convince him to amend it.

Von Manteuffel wanted Bastogne taken by day three – his main routes to Namur and Dinant ran through it – but

Below: American infantrymen laboriously dig foxholes for themselves in snow-covered hard ground as German artillery opens fire on them near Berismenil in Belgium.

Above: An American soldier inspects a C-47 transport that made a successful crash landing after being hit by German antiaircraft fire. It had dropped supplies to the US airborne soldiers holding Bastogne.

the Americans beat von Luttwitz in the race to control the town. Remnants of 28th Division's 110th Regiment, combat commands of the 9th and 10th Armored divisions, and separate engineer battalions, succeeded in slowing the German advance until the 101st Airborne Division arrived. By December 19, they formed a defensive belt around Bastogne and awaited rescue by Patton. Von Luttwitz arrived a day behind schedule.

Early on December 19, the vanguard of the Panzer Lehr Division failed to penetrate Bastogne's defenses. Restricted to roads by soft ground, Panzer Lehr and 26th Volksgrenadier Division attacks later in the day also failed, though they did destroy part of the 10th Armored Division at Longvilly.

Von Manteuffel ordered the 26th Volksgrenadier and elements of Panzer Lehr Divisions to besiege Bastogne and sent von Luttwitz's other divisions onward. On December 20, 2nd Panzer Division bypassed Bastogne to the north and broke for the Meuse while the bulk of Panzer Lehr slipped around the south of Bastogne toward Sibret and the Meuse.

Combat Command B, 4th Armored Division, traveling 161 miles (257km) in 22 hours, arrived near Bastogne around midnight on December 20/21. McAuliffe moved a task force to Sibret, but Patton withdrew the entire combat command to Arlon so the division could attack intact on the 22nd.

The siege of Bastogne began on December 21 by more than four German regiments after the 2nd Panzer Division cut communications to the north. Elements of the Panzer Lehr Division, joined by Fifth Army's 5th Parachute Division cut communications to the south and prepared to meet the US 4th Armored Division whose progress von Manteuffel tracked through radio and wire intercepts. It is improbable that the division's combat command could have prevented Bastogne's encirclement or significantly aided its defense.

On the 22nd, McAuliffe's feisty response, "NUTS!," to a demand for Bastogne's unconditional surrender, steeled American resolve to rescue the defenders.

Patton attacked on schedule, but the waiting Germans slowed 4th Armored Division's advance to a bloody crawl. Fortunately, Patton's prayer for good weather was answered on December 23 and the US Army Air Forces dropped over 144 tons (146 tonnes) of supplies to the defenders and pounded the besiegers. The 15th Panzer Grenadier Division joined the siege. Finally, at 16:50 on December 26, after taking over 50 percent casualties in the five-day attack, the lead battalion of the 4th Armored Division broke through the German blocking positions and linked up with McAuliffe. Bastogne's fate now depended on which side could reinforce more quickly.

December 26 marked the high tide of the German counteroffensive. Bastogne was relieved. Patton's XII Corps pushed back Brandenberger's left flank and hardened the southern shoulder. In Montgomery's sector, the US 2nd Armored Division and British 29th Armoured Brigade crushed the fuel-starved, western-most German units, 2nd Panzer Division and the bulk of

Below: The Germans committed virtually all their available first-line strength to the Ardennes operation, but its failure led to the loss of advanced equipment such as this Tiger II tank knocked out near Houffalize.

Above: A camouflaged M4 Sherman tank of the US First Army's 2nd Armored Division moves up to the attack on the north side of the German advance's extreme westward tip, which was checked just short of Dinant.

Panzer Lehr Division, within sight of the Meuse near Dinant. Meanwhile, VII Corps stopped the 116th Panzer Division east of Marche. Hitler had not received his ten days of bad weather and more than 30,000 tons (30,500 tonnes) of Allied bombs had marked the roads from Bastogne and St. Vith east to the West Wall with flaming vehicles, dashing any hope of supplying forward German units. Allied air had crippled the Luftwaffe on Christmas Day, making forward German units even more vulnerable. Dietrich's failure and supply problems had forced Hitler to cancel Fifteenth Army's attack. By day's end the German spearhead was shattered and the initiative passed to the Allies.

On December 28, Eisenhower asked Montgomery to counterattack the stalled enemy with VII Corps from the north to link up with Patton. Montgomery, however, expecting another German attack, was pulling VII Corps from the line to form a reserve despite Collins' and Hodges' objections. Moreover, Montgomery did not want to risk his British reserves, preferring to keep them fresh for their upcoming battle of the Rhine. Eisenhower acquiesced but demanded that if the Germans did not renew their attack, Montgomery counterattack on January 3 to meet Patton at Houffalize.

Meanwhile, von Rundstedt urged Hitler to suspend the offensive and defend from St. Vith to Wiltz. Still wanting Antwerp, Hitler ordered von Rundstedt to hold his ground, regroup to continue the attack, and take Bastogne. Hitler had scheduled Operation *Nordwind*, a strike by nine under-strength divisions of Army Group G against Devers in Alsace, for New Year's Eve. *Nordwind*, Hitler surmised, would force Patton to abandon his Ardennes counterattack to deal with the new threat, freeing Model to regain the initiative.

Fighting around Bastogne intensified during December 27–31. The Germans moved the Führer Begleit Brigade, 3rd Panzergrenadier Division, Führer Grenadier Brigade, 9th and 12th SS Panzer Divisions, 340th and 167th Volksgrenadier divisions, and remains of the 1st Panzer Division to Bastogne. Eisenhower matched the Germans by releasing the newly arrived 11th Armored and 87th Infantry Divisions to Patton. Each side employed eight divisions before the fighting at Bastogne ebbed.

Below: The American M1A1 rocket launcher, more commonly known as the 'bazooka.' This electrically-operated weapon fired a 2.36-inch armor-piercing projectile. The bazooka came into service in 1942.
US Army Ordnance Museum, Aberdeen, Md.

January 1 was another fateful day for the Germans. The Luftwaffe reserve of 1,035 planes struck toward Allied airfields, hoping the Allies would be less alert after New Year's Eve, and again surprised the Allies. But the Germans destroyed only 206 planes at a cost of 277 planes and 253 irreplaceable pilots. The commander of the fighter arm called this heavy loss the Luftwaffe's "death blow". Farther south, *Nordwind* utterly failed. Using *Ultra*, Devers had detailed the German buildup, pinpointed the attack, and brought it almost to a halt by January 2. *Nordwind* provided little relief for the Ardennes and, by January 25, was over.

Patton attacked around Bastogne's western edge toward Houffalize on December 30. The inexperienced 11th Armored and 87th Divisions smacked into the Führer Begleit Brigade and 3rd Panzergrenadier Division, attacking the Bastogne corridor from the west. Patton's divisions and artillery halted the badly crippled German units. Meanwhile, a Kampfgruppe of the 1st SS Panzer Division, the 14th Parachute Regiment, a Panzer Lehr regiment, and the full-strength 167th Volksgrenadier Division, which had just arrived from the Eastern Front, attacked to sever the Bastogne corridor from the

Above: German infantry in a half-track carrier roll past an American half-track that had become stuck in a roadside ditch. Motor transport was something of a German rarity by this stage of World War II.

123

Above: Complete US Army cold weather/winter kit c.1944.
Howard Hendricks Collection

northeast. In response, III Corps' experienced 35th Division, the battered 4th Armored Division (down to 42 tanks), artillery, and aircraft of the US XIXth Tactical Air Command stopped this threat. The day ended with the Luftwaffe's largest and final major attack on Bastogne. The next day as German attacks continued, III Corps moved around the east of Bastogne toward St. Vith.

Montgomery unleashed Collins' 100,000-man VII Corps toward Houffalize on January 3 with units of the British XXX Corps on their right. In the worst weather yet seen in the battle, four of Collins' divisions plowed into remnants of the 2nd SS Panzer and 12th and 560th Volksgrenadier Divisions with some 12,000 men. Wind-driven snow and icy roads made tracked vehicle movement dangerous and slow. Infantrymen quickly tired struggling through deep snow, and a foggy overcast negated Allied air superiority, enabling tenacious German defenses to stall the advance.

By January 5, the threat to Bastogne ended as Germans shifted units from the shattered town to stop Patton and Montgomery. Two days later VII Corps cut the La Roche–Vielsalm road, leaving the Germans only one east-west route, and Model demanded to withdraw units west of Houffalize before they were cut off. Finally admitting his operation had failed, on January 8, Hitler ordered von Manteuffel to withdraw to a defensive line west of the Bastogne–Liège highway between Dochamps and Longchamps. Dietrich was to defend northeast of St. Vith and east of Wiltz. The following day, the Führer ordered his four SS panzer divisions, two werfer brigades, and the two "Hitler" brigades to the rear of Army Group G for rehabilitation. Finally, Patton was able to break free from Bastogne and advance toward Houffalize, though it took him another week to cover the seven miles (11km) to the rendezvous.

On January 12, in Poland, the Soviets launched their

Above: Two soldiers of the US 28th Infantry Division, smashed in the first days of the German onslaught, rest in Bastogne after linking with elements of the US 101st Airborne Division that had just arrived in this town.

winter offensive across the Vistula and Hitler ordered Dietrich's Sixth SS Panzer Army to the Eastern Front. Four days later, after advancing only 15 miles (24km) in nearly two weeks, lead elements of First Army met Third Army at Houffalize. The skies again cleared on January 22, and Allied pilots and artillery pummelled bumper-to-bumper German vehicles waiting to flee across icy bridges. By January 28, the Allies had pushed the Germans back to their December 15 start-line, and the US Army declared the Ardennes campaign officially over.

If Hitler hoped to split the Anglo–American alliance, he failed. Montgomery infuriated Eisenhower at the end of December with a letter charging that the broad-front strategy had failed and that Eisenhower should make Montgomery his land forces commander over Bradley. Eisenhower, knowing he had Prime Minister Churchill's and US Army Chief of Staff Marshall's support, prepared to ask the Combined Chiefs of Staff to choose between him or Montgomery. Montgomery apologized and retracted the letter.

Another misunderstanding soon emerged. To correct misleading British press accounts of the battle that offended Americans by making it seem that Montgomery had saved them from defeat and would "lead all the Allies to victory," Montgomery called a press conference on January 7. It backfired. Montgomery revealed his devotion to Eisenhower, "the captain of the team," praised the American soldier, and applauded American stands on the northern shoulder, St. Vith, and Bastogne.

Below: German prisoners of war, watched by their American guards, dig graves for just a few of the men killed in the defence of Bastogne by the US 101st Airborne Division against the 15th Panzergrenadier Division.

But Monty was self-congratulatory and implied that the Americans would have collapsed had he not been "thinking ahead" and had Eisenhower not given him command of the northern front. By failing to explain Eisenhower's decision or that the arrangement was temporary, Montgomery insinuated he alone could have saved the Americans. Montgomery overlooked the fact that the Americans were in control of the battlefield before the command shift. Montgomery said he "employed the whole available power of the British Group of Armies," obscuring the fact that he had cautiously used only the 29th Armoured Brigade, two battalions of the 6th Airborne Division, and the 53rd (Welsh) Division. Bradley and Patton protested to Eisenhower, refusing ever to serve under Montgomery. Montgomery admitted that his gloating statement appeared "to be triumphant – not over the Germans but over the Americans."

Churchill intervened, telling the House of Commons that, "the Americans have engaged 30 or 40 men for every one we have engaged and they have lost 60 to 80 men for every one of us." Churchill called it "the greatest American battle of the war . . . an ever famous American victory." Montgomery was chastened. It was clear that he was fallible, dispensable, and subordinate to Eisenhower. As a result of these episodes, Eisenhower's authority became far stronger. Montgomery was no longer in a position to challenge it, and Anglo–American operational command unity solidified.

Nearly 850,000 US soldiers of the 12th Army Group participated in the battle and suffered 81,000 casualties, including 15,000 captured and 19,000 killed. Some 55,000 British soldiers participated, incurring 200 killed and 1,200 other casualties. Estimates of German casualties vary widely, between 80,000 to 120,000 of nearly 500,000 soldiers involved. Equipment losses were heavy on both sides, around 800 tanks each and about 1,000 German planes. Yet the Americans quickly replaced their losses while the Germans could not. Hitler had expended the last of his manpower and equipment reserves. Although *Herbstnebel* delayed the Allies' final offensive in the west by six weeks, it accelerated Germany's collapse. Hitler committed one of the worst military blunders by significantly underestimating his foe, and he paid dearly. His massing of units in the west had left his armies vulnerable to the Soviets in the east. By February 1945, his forces in the west were severely weakened, and without air support they were no longer in the same league as the Allies. Overwhelming Allied armies were pinching a hollow and grossly overmatched Wehrmacht led by a physically, mentally, and emotionally drained dictator. Hitler had wrecked both himself and his army and doomed his Reich.

Above: As revealed by the wreckage of this PzKpfw IV medium tank, the German offensive could not finally survive against the overwhelming might of the Allies' armored formations, artillery and tactical air power.

V Eight

Crossing the Rhine

John Pimlott

"There are thousands of eyes keeping watch on the Rhine; thousands of German eyes . . . It has the feel of the last barrier, and I know that when the Allied armies cross this brown river, it will be the end of Nazi Germany."
R.W. Thompson, War Correspondent, November 24, 1944

By the end of January 1945 the Allies had recovered all the ground lost during the Battle of the Bulge. It had been a hard fight, with cruel American losses, but the Germans had been decisively weakened. As Gen. Eisenhower prepared to make his next move, the end of the campaign in Northwest Europe was clearly in sight.

But there was a lot of fighting still to do. German soldiers, withdrawing into their homeland, were unlikely to give up easily, and it was fully expected that the next major barrier – the Rhine – would be defended to the death. The river, stretching 825 miles (1,320km) from Switzerland to the North Sea, was a natural moat, forcing any invader from the west to pause before attempting to cross it. By early 1945, the Germans had constructed an additional barrier further west – the West Wall, or Siegfried Line – to protect their border, while the appalling winter weather created floods that were sure to hamper Allied progress. Any campaign to approach and then cross the Rhine was going to be time-consuming and costly.

Eisenhower's plan was a cautious one. The failure of Field Marshal Montgomery's attempt to "jump" the Lower Rhine in September 1944 (Operation *Market Garden*) made the supreme commander wary of any similar "single thrust" that might leave Allied troops exposed to German counterattack. Instead, he favored a "broad front" advance from positions on the German border, designed to ensure that all Allied armies reached the Rhine without leaving enemy pockets behind. This also had the advantage of satisfying critics who argued that Montgomery was trying to steal all the glory. By

Left: American troops across the Rhine at the Ludendorff bridge at Remagen. The capture of the bridge intact provided an unexpected coup for Allied commanders; though it did not change their overall plan for crossing this last major natural barrier defending the heart of Germany.

129

early 1945 US troops in Europe outnumbered those from Britain and the Commonwealth. Eisenhower had to make sure that Americans were seen to be taking a major role in the defeat of Germany.

The result was a four-phase campaign. In the north, where Montgomery commanded the 21st Army Group, which included the US Ninth Army under Lt. Gen. William H. Simpson, two interconnected operations were to clear the way to the Rhine opposite Wesel. The first of these, Operation *Veritable*, would involve a re-inforced British XXX Corps advancing from east of Nij-megen through the forests of the Reichswald. The second, Operation *Grenade*, would see the US Ninth Army pushing northeast through Mönchengladbach to link up with the British. Once the area had been con-solidated, Montgomery would prepare for an assault crossing of the Rhine in his sector to outflank the in-dustrial heartland of the Ruhr from the north and break out onto the good tank country of the North German plain. This would lead him directly to Berlin.

Lt. Gen. Bradley, commanding the US 12th Army Group to Montgomery's south, was to clear the approaches to the Rhine from Cologne to Koblenz in Operation *Lumberjack*. One of his armies – the US Third under Lt. Gen. Patton – was to contribute to this before swinging southeast towards Mainz and Mannheim, link-ing up with elements of Lt. Gen. Devers' 6th Army Group, advancing from the Saar in Operation *Under-tone*. Bridgeheads over the Rhine would be seized in the south, but only to divert German reserves away from Montgomery's assault and to provide a southern pincer against the Ruhr. Both Bradley and Patton were dis-satisfied with the apparently secondary role given to US armies, exerting pressure on Eisenhower that would eventually lead to a dramatic change of emphasis in the Allied advance once the Rhine had been crossed.

But this was in the future. In early 1945 the priority was to reach the Rhine quickly and prepare for assault crossings. It was not an easy task. The West Wall was a formidable obstacle, comprising blockhouses and anti-tank defenses all along the German frontier. German losses in the Ardennes may have been severe, but enough troops remained to man the defenses and im-pose heavy casualties. Of equal significance was the weather, for as snow gave way to rain in early February, the battle area became waterlogged, hampering the movement of Allied mechanized forces. Furthermore, in Ninth Army's sector in the north, the Germans con-trolled a series of dams on the Rur River which, if breached, would flood the entire region to a depth of at least three feet (0.9m). In these circumstances, full coordination of the four Allied assaults was next to impossible.

Below: Men of the US 63rd Infantry Division's 255th Infantry Regiment cross the 'dragon's teeth' outer antitank defences of the Siegfried Line on the US Seventh Army's front near Wurzbach on March 20, 1945.

The campaign began in the north, where Operations *Veritable* and *Grenade* were meant to take place simultaneously, splitting German opposition and opening the way to the Rhine. Montgomery's preparations were, as always, meticulous, but his forces faced formidable problems. Responsibility for *Veritable* was given to Lt. Gen. Henry Crerar's Canadian First Army, which included the British XXX Corps under Lt. Gen. Brian Horrocks. Horrocks had five divisions under his command – the 2nd and 3rd Canadian as well as the 15th (Scottish), 51st (Highland) and 53rd (Welsh) – and his immediate reserves included the Guards and 11th Armoured, plus the 43rd (Wessex) and 52nd (Lowland) Divisions: a total of nearly 80,000 men and 1,000 tanks. They were opposed by a mere 12,000 soldiers and 36 self-propelled assault guns of Lt. Gen. Alfred Schlemm's First Parachute Army, but numbers were misleading. German defenses, prepared since the time of *Market Garden*, were deep, the troops knew the ground intimately and the terrain favored the defender. By February 1945 ground to both north and south of XXX Corps was flooded, the advance axis was along narrow roads through the thick forests of the Reichswald, and the enemy occupied the high ground.

Veritable began at 05:00 on February 8. Nearly 1,000 guns bombarded German positions for two and a half hours, then paused. Enemy batteries sprang into life, allowing their positions to be pinpointed, after which

Above: This was the view from France into Germany in the area of the wrecked town of Steinfeld. The orderliness of the 'dragon's teeth' defences contrasts strongly with the destruction behind them.

the Allied guns opened up again for a further three hours. Under the cover of smoke, the infantry moved forward, but progress was slow. Heavy rain, that was to continue throughout the period of the battle, turned the area into "an ocean of mud" and flooded the only roads, making command communications impossible. Almost immediately, the infantry entered thick forest and the battle degenerated into a series of hard-fought platoon actions. Tanks found it difficult to negotiate the terrain; because of the weather, close air support was impossible. Twenty-five years later, Horrocks described it as "the worst battle I ever experienced."

British XXX Corps was expected to achieve its objective in three or four days, but this was an impossible schedule. The town of Cleve did not fall until February 11 despite heavy air bombardment, by which time the Allied battle plan was in tatters. Horrocks, in an attempt to gain momentum, committed the 43rd Division. As they moved forward they encountered horrific traffic jams and could only be fed into the battle piecemeal. To cap it all, the Germans opened the Rur dams, preventing all movement in Ninth Army area and freeing reserves to oppose the Anglo–Canadian assault. Goch was finally entered on February 19, but was not completely cleared for another three days. The remaining German defenders pulled back across the Rhine, destroying all bridges in the area. Horrocks could congratulate his troops on achieving their objectives, but the battle had been far harder than anyone had expected. It was a sign of German determination to defend the Fatherland.

Because of the Rur floods, Operation *Grenade*, which should have begun 24 hours after *Veritable*, had to be postponed. It did not begin until February 23, when the water levels subsided. In the event, the Americans encountered only weak opposition — most of the

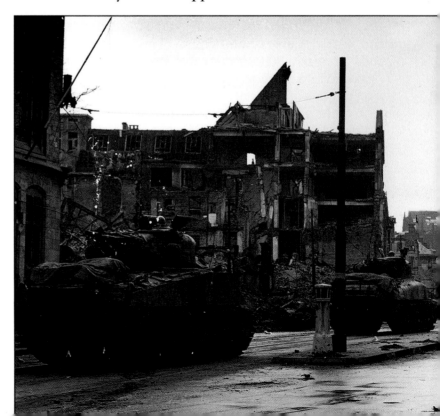

German forces in their path had been moved north – and a link up with the Anglo–Canadians was made at Geldorn on March 3. This cleared the approaches to the Rhine from Nijmegen to Düsseldorf, enabling Montgomery to begin detailed preparations for his assault crossing, scheduled for March 23/24.

No bridges had been seized in this area, although elements of Ninth Army had come close. On March 2, US Intelligence reported that two bridges – at Oberkassel and Uerdingen – were still intact. A composite force from the US 83rd Infantry Division, disguised as Germans, moved towards Oberkassel; although they advanced to within sight of the bridge, their ruse was discovered and the bridge blown up before their eyes. At the same time, men of the US 2nd Armored and 95th Infantry Divisions motored at speed to capture the Adolf Hitler Bridge at Uerdingen. Some infantry soldiers crossed the structure before being forced back; they too witnessed the destruction of their objective. An assault crossing in the north was now unavoidable.

Further south, Bradley's two armies – Lt. Gen. Hodges' First and Patton's Third – opened their assault on February 28. Operation *Lumberjack* began well, chiefly because German forces in the assault area had been weakened by the movement of reserves to oppose Montgomery's advance. On the left, Hodges' troops crossed the Rur once the flood waters had subsided and pushed across the Cologne plain with comparative ease, flushing enemy defenders out of small villages by using tanks and infantry in self-contained "teams." Cologne itself was taken on March 5/6.

Meanwhile, other elements of the US First Army had thrust towards Bonn, with the 9th Armored Division veering southeast to link up with Patton's men on the Ahr River at Sinzig. Their task was regarded as secondary

Left: Against a backdrop created by the twin spires of the city's celebrated cathedral, tanks of the US 3rd Armored Division roll through the rubble-littered streets of Cologne which fell to the US First Army on March 5, 1945.

Above: The two sides of the famous hand-painted sign put up over the Ludendorff bridge by the 9th Armored Division. This metal plaque is nearly ten feet (3m) long and as can be seen once advertised the Cologne-Düsseldorf ferry.
Patton Museum of Cavalry and Armor

Below: Seizure of the damaged Ludendorff bridge over the Rhine River at Remagen gave the Allies a superb chance to surge across this natural barrier, and the bridge survived for 11 days before collapsing.

to the main attack on Cologne. Late on March 6, 9th Armored reached the town of Meckenheim, about 10 miles (16km) west of the Rhine, and prepared to move forward against scattered opposition. Brig. Gen. William M. Hoge's Combat Command B was ordered to close to the Rhine at Remagen, shielding other elements of the division which would advance down the Ahr valley to make contact with Patton. Hoge divided his units into task forces, one of which, commanded by Col. Leonard Engemann (comprising part of 14th Tank Battalion and the whole of 27th Armored Infantry Battalion, plus engineer support) set out early on March 7 to take Remagen. At 13:00, Co. A of the 27th Armored Infantry, commanded by 2nd Lt. Karl Timmermann, emerged from woods above the town. Timmermann was amazed by what he saw – the Ludendorff railway bridge across the Rhine was still intact. After a hasty reconnaissance, Engemann urged his men into Remagen, but it was not until German attempts to demolish the bridge had failed that he decided to force a crossing. Just before 16:00, Timmermann led his company across the bridge to seize a foothold on the east bank.

News of this unexpected coup spread quickly through the Allied chain of command. By nightfall on March 7, Hodges had informed Bradley – whose response was, "Hot Dog, Courtney! This'll bust him wide open!" – and Eisenhower had ordered as many units as possible to cross to the east bank. But not everyone was enthusiastic. Maj. Gen. Harold R. Bull, Eisenhower's operations chief, pointed out that "it just doesn't fit into the overall plan," and to an extent he was right. Although, in Bradley's words, "A bridge is a bridge, and mighty damn good anywhere across the Rhine," and the intention was still to concentrate on Montgomery's assault in the north, particularly as the Remagen bridgehead led into the hills of the Westerwald, with little opportunity for decisive advances. Psychologically, the sudden breaching of the

Rhine barrier had incalculable effects on enemy morale, while the existence of the bridgehead forced the Germans to divert units away from the north, but on its own the capture of the Ludendorff bridge (which collapsed into the river on March 17) did not lead to an immediate shift of Allied emphasis.

Meanwhile, Patton's Third Army had carried out its part of Operation *Lumberjack*, linking up with Hodges' troops at Sinzig on March 9 and clearing the west bank of the Rhine as far as Koblenz, captured on the 18th. Without pausing, Patton diverted units southeast towards Mainz and Mannheim, threatening to cut off German forces in the Saar that were already under attack from the US Seventh Army, commanded by Lt. Gen. Alexander M. Patch, as part of Operation *Undertone*. Jealous of Hodges' success at Remagen and annoyed by Eisenhower's insistence that the main assault crossing should still be in the north, Patton did not halt at the Rhine. On March 22 the US 11th Infantry Regiment, supported by engineers, simply paddled across the river at Nierstein and Oppenheim against minimal enemy opposition. In a communiqué deliberately worded to cause embarrassment to Montgomery, whose elaborate preparations

Above: Before its collapse on March 17, 1945, the Ludendorff bridge was used by the US First Army's III Corps to create a strategically vital bridgehead on the eastern side of the Rhine River.

135

Above: The shoulder insignia of the British XXX Corps, part of Field Marshal Montgomery's 21st Army Group. The corps had played a striking role in British operations since the D-Day landings.
Salamander Books

Right: Officer's service dress uniform, bearing the insignia of the Royal Engineers XXX Corps.
Memorial Museum, Bayeux

were nearing completion, Bradley announced: "Without benefit of aerial bombardments, ground smoke, artillery preparation and airborne assistance, the Third Army at 22:00 hours Thursday evening, 22nd March, crossed the Rhine river." Patton was ecstatic; as he said, with reference to Montgomery, "I can outfight that little fart anytime."

Comments such as this were indicative of American disquiet about the emphasis on Montgomery's operations in the north, especially as they seemed to be geared to an Anglo–Canadian capture of Berlin. Eisenhower made no move at this stage to alter his "master plan," but pressure was building on him to give the Americans a

more decisive role. Allied political leaders had already decided, at the Yalta Conference in February 1945, that Berlin would be in the Soviet zone of occupied Germany once the war was over. Eisenhower was understandably wary of sacrificing his troops in what promised to be a costly battle for a city that was outside his sphere of operations. In addition, the existence of American bridgeheads at Remagen and further south opened up the possibility of advances deep into central and southern Germany, where defenses were weak. It would not take much to persuade the supreme commander to shift the main weight of his attack away from Berlin.

Montgomery was unaware of these arguments and no attempt was made to disrupt the elaborate preparations he was making for his assault crossing of the Rhine. Eisenhower remained convinced that the Ruhr was a vital objective that could not be taken without such an assault, while the continued concentration of German forces in the north to oppose Montgomery would clearly help any American breakout further south. Operation *Plunder*, the codename chosen for the assault by 21st Army Group, still had much to achieve; it was subsequent objectives, however, that were being queried.

By early March, when Anglo–Canadian and US troops linked up at Geldorn, planning for *Plunder* was already well advanced. Montgomery had been aware since before D-Day in June 1944 that the Rhine would be a major obstacle. He viewed the assault in his sector in much the same way as the Normandy invasion: in other words, an operation that required the full exploitation of Allied assets. Intelligence about German defenses would have to be detailed, enabling artillery and air strikes to be effective. This in turn would require close cooperation between air and ground forces as well as between the various units involved in the actual assault. Infantry would lead the way, carving out bridgeheads on the east bank, but they would have to be supported by artillery; engineers would be needed to build pontoons and, eventually, more permanent bridges across the Rhine so that armor and supplies could be committed for the breakout onto the North German plain. Close air support would be essential at all times.

All these factors were reflected in the plan, issued by Montgomery's headquarters as early as March 9. The assault was to be carried out on the night of March 23/24, preceded by a massive air and artillery bombardment that was designed to stun the enemy and open up gaps in German defenses along the east bank of the river. The main attack would be carried out by the British Second Army under Lt. Gen. Sir Miles Dempsey, which would seize the towns of Rees and Wesel on the Allied left. A secondary attack, designed to split German defenders, would take place simultaneously on the right,

Above: The France and Germany Star; awarded to British and Commonwealth personnel for service in northwest Europe, June 6, 1944 to May 8, 1945. *Salamander Books*

Below: Shoulder insignia of HQ 21st Army Group. *Salamander Books*

between Wesel and Duisburg. This would be the responsibility of Simpson's US Ninth Army. As soon as the infantry had seized bridgeheads, having crossed the river in amphibious vehicles and landing craft, engineers would move forward to construct ferries and Bailey bridges. The tanks would then be committed.

Montgomery added a further refinement. In daylight on March 24, Maj. Gen. Matthew B. Ridgway's US XVIII Airborne Corps, comprising the US 17th and British 6th Airborne Divisions, would be dropped on the east bank to reinforce the bridgeheads. This was a reversal of the usual deployment of airborne troops – as at Arnhem the previous September, the norm was to drop them in advance of ground forces, which would then link up – but Montgomery was convinced that they would be equally useful (and far less vulnerable to counterattack) if used as follow-up units. Operation *Varsity*, as the airborne drop was codenamed, would avoid the problems of traffic jams that were likely to affect the ground forces as they advanced across the river and increase the weight of available resources to deal with inevitable German responses on the first day. The overall intention was to carve out a bridgehead 40 miles (64km) long and 10 miles (16km) deep within the first 24 hours, out of which the bulk of 21st Army Group would advance to encircle the Ruhr before deploying in strength onto the North German plain. As a final element of the *Plunder*

plan, Canadian forces would cross the Rhine at Emmerich, on the extreme left, once the main assault had succeeded. They would then advance north into Holland. It was typical of Montgomery – an elaborate plan, based on the provision of overwhelming forces to ensure victory. It may have lacked the sort of flair associated with Patton, but the situation in Montgomery's sector, where the Germans were expecting the main assault to take place, left little opportunity for anything more than a set-piece operation.

The area chosen for *Plunder*'s main assault posed a number of practical problems. Chief among these was the Rhine itself, for its normal width of about 1,000 feet (300m) had been increased by the winter rains to 1,500 feet (450m) in places, and the approaches to the west bank were sodden and extremely slippery. Engineers were brought in to build roads, construct hard-standings for the stockpile of supplies and prepare bridging sites. By March 19, more than 25,000 tons (25,400 tonnes) of bridging equipment had been delivered and a number of suitable sites selected, but it was vitally important to hide the details from German defenders on the opposite bank. For 10 days before the assault, therefore, special smoke generators were used to create an impenetrable fog along 20 miles (32km) of the river. Captain Andrew Wilson, commanding a troop of Crocodile flamethrower tanks, described the scene as he moved forward: "Long

Left: The Churchill Crocodile was a flamethrower version of the British Infantry Tank Mk IV Churchill, and was very useful for assaults on strongpoints. The flame had a typical range of 80yds (72m).

139

before you came to the Rhine you saw the smokescreen. It stretched along the front without a break; a tall white cloud, two or three hundred feet [60–90m] high, curling at its top like a wave-crest caught in slow motion." It was surreal, but with nearly a million troops packed into the form-up areas, essential to prevent enemy preemptive artillery bombardments.

Such arrangements clearly precluded any chance of gaining surprise. German defenders – the remnants of Schlemm's First Parachute Army – had been expecting an attack since their withdrawal across the Rhine, and had not wasted the opportunity to dig in. But their morale was low, made worse on March 22 when Schlemm was wounded during an artillery strike against his headquarters. By then, the German command chain was in tatters, for Field Marshal von Rundstedt, the highly experienced Commander-in-Chief West, had been relieved by Hitler on March 8, being replaced by Field Marshal Albrecht Kesselring, who had been in Italy and knew nothing about the situation on the Rhine. Moreover, any attempt at a local level to consolidate defenses was disrupted by the Allied air and artillery attacks. Strategic bombers had been hitting transportation targets in and around the Ruhr since February, aiming to prevent the movement of German reinforcements and supplies. As the date for *Plunder* drew near, fighter-bombers were committed to destroy enemy positions on the east bank of the Rhine, supplementing an artillery barrage that involved over 5,500 guns of various calibers, some of which fired more than 600 rounds. It was this sort of obvious superiority that made many of the assault troops – the 15th (Scottish) and 51st (Highland) Divisions, plus 1st Commando Brigade, in the British sector; the 30th and 79th Infantry Divisions in the

Right: A Sherman DD amphibious tank of the 4th Armored Brigade passes men of the King's Own Scottish Borderers after crossing the Rhine near Bergen on March 25, 1945 in the sector of the British 15th Infantry Division.

American – confident that they were about to embark on the last great offensive of the war in the west.

This confidence was shared by Prime Minister Winston Churchill, who insisted on traveling to Montgomery's headquarters at Venlo to witness the forthcoming battle. Accompanied by the Chief of the Imperial General Staff, Field Marshal Sir Alan Brooke, he set out on March 23. While he was airborne over the Channel, Montgomery issued the final attack order, ending it with the stirring words, "Over the Rhine, then, let us go. And good hunting to you all on the other side."

The artillery bombardment, carried out by a total of 3,500 field guns and 2,000 antitank guns and rocket projectors, began at 18:00 on March 23, building up to an overwhelming crescendo. Assault troops, having spent the day resting in uncharacteristic sunshine, filed down to the river bank and boarded a variety of amphibious craft, while special Duplex Drive (DD) tanks, belonging to Maj. Gen. Percy Hobart's 79th Armoured Division, prepared to "swim" the Rhine. Those who were there remembered the scene with crystal clarity. Maj. Martin Lindsay, commanding the 1st Battalion Gordon Highlanders in 51st (Highland) Division on the left flank of the assault area, described it as "a lovely night with a three-quarter moon" and remembered "the long ghostly files of men marching up to [the Buffalo amphibious vehicles] . . . a few busy figures darting here and there in the moonlight directing people to this or that Buffalo". Andrew Wilson, with his troop of Crocodiles, was equally lyrical: "East and west as far as [I] could see, the night was lit with gunfire; it flickered through the trees and flashed on the underside of the clouds. The ground shook ceaselessly, and now and again there was a violent, continuing explosion, like a pack of cards being snapped."

Above: Men of a Scottish unit land on the eastern bank of the Rhine River after crossing near Rees on March 23, 1945. With this great obstacle behind them, the Allies were poised for a drive deep into Germany.

In the event, the actual crossing was almost an anticlimax, reflecting the benefits of elaborate preparations and overwhelming firepower. At 21:00, vehicles carrying the first assault wave, comprising the 7th Battalion Black Watch and 7th Battalion Argyll and Sutherland Highlanders of the 51st (Highland) Division, entered the murky waters of the Rhine. Exactly two and a half minutes later, they reached the far bank to the west of Rees; despite some casualties from antipersonnel mines, the infantry quickly pushed forward to create a bridgehead, ably supported by amphibious tanks. At 21:04 Gen. Horrocks, waiting anxiously for news, received the historic message: "The Black Watch has landed safely on the far bank." The left flank was secure.

An hour later, it was the turn of 1st Commando Brigade, tasked to carve out a bridgehead on the extreme right of the British assault area, close to Wesel. Their crossing also went smoothly, although a number of assault boats and a Buffalo amphibian were hit by German artillery, firing blind through the smoke and darkness. The commandos set up a defensive perimeter on the east bank, waiting for a promised air strike on Wesel before they advanced into the town. They were not to be disappointed. At 22:30, 218 Avro Lancaster and de Havilland Mosquito bombers of the RAF appeared over the battle area, dropping more than 1,000 tons (1,016 tonnes) of high-explosives to add to the devastation already caused by the artillery bombardments: it was reckoned that over 97 percent of the buildings in the main part of the town had been reduced to rubble by the end of this raid. As the dust settled, the commandos (supported by the 1st Battalion Cheshire Regiment) burst into Wesel from the west. Their advance was not unopposed – German troops who survived hid in the ruins and forced the commandos to fight for every yard of ground – but another bridgehead had been successfully established.

With both flanks secure, the third of the British assault formations – 15th (Scottish) Division – was able to cross the river virtually unopposed. At 02:00 on March 24, the 8th Battalion Royal Scots and 6th Battalion Royal Scots Fusiliers were ferried across to take the village of Bislich, to the west of Wesel, while over to their left the 10th Battalion Highland Light Infantry and 2nd Battalion Argyll and Sutherland Highlanders crossed with the aim of taking Haffen and, eventually, linking up with 51st (Highland) Division around Rees. By dawn, both assaults had been reinforced and initial objectives taken. Included among the follow-up battalions was a Canadian formation, the Highland Light Infantry of Canada, attached to 51st (Highland) Division. It was truly a "Scottish" affair.

Similar success was achieved by the Americans

Below: The C-46 Commando had two rather than the C-47's one door for the speedy despatch of 38 rather than 18 paratroops, but these advantages were offset by the type's tendency to catch fire after enemy hits.

further south, where a hurricane artillery bombardment caught the Germans by surprise. Starting at 01:00 on March 24, over 2,000 guns fired a staggering total of 65,261 shells across the Rhine in an hour, while up to 1,500 heavy bombers flew overhead to destroy pre-selected targets. At 02:00, coinciding with the assault by 15th (Scottish) Division, men of the US 30th Infantry Division were ferried across at Büderich, Wallach and Rheinburg, creating bridgeheads at little cost. An hour later, the US 79th Infantry Division landed to their right, around Walsum and Orsay. They encountered problems with the strong river current – so much so that one of the amphibious craft was turned round in mid-stream, its occupants conducting an assault landing back at their embarkation point – but casualties were minimal. As Lt. Whitney O. Refvem, commanding a company of the 117th Infantry Regiment, remarked: "There was no real fight to it. The artillery had done the job for us."

In all sectors, engineers now came forward to ferry supplies across and to begin the laborious task of building pontoon bridges, often under enemy fire. By dawn on March 24, five bridgeheads had been firmly established and, although heavy fighting was taking place in both Rees and Wesel, the German response had been poorly coordinated and ineffective. As the day wore on, Kesselring committed the 116th Panzer and 15th Panzergrenadier Divisions from his meager reserve, but their chances of decisive action were curtailed as the second part of Montgomery's plan – Operation *Varsity* – took place. It ensured that the Allies had overwhelming forces available on the east bank.

Men of the British 6th Airborne Division, packed aboard transport planes and gliders, left airfields in England at 07:00 on March 24. Two hours later the US 17th Airborne Division took off from bases in France. When the two streams joined forces over Brussels, they constituted the largest airborne armada of the war: a

Above: The C-46 was used by the US IX Troop Carrier Command led by Maj. Gen. Paul L. Williams, and was employed to deliver much of the US 17th Airborne Division in the landing east of the Rhine between Wesel and Hamminkeln.

total of 1,572 aircraft towing 1,326 gliders, designed to commit over 21,000 troops to battle in one lift. The stream took more than three hours to pass over a given point on the ground, symbolizing the power and strength of Allied capabilities. Over 2,000 fighter aircraft gave protection, although by this stage the chances of any interference by the Luftwaffe were slim.

The landings began at 10:00, watched by Churchill and his entourage on the west bank. It was a tricky operation, involving the simultaneous landing of both airborne divisions into an area no more than five miles (8km) wide by six miles (10km) long, situated to the north and west of Wesel. The aim was to prevent any German reinforcements from entering the bridgeheads and this involved the seizure of the Diersfordter Forest, together with bridges over the River Issel around Hamminkeln. The British were given responsibility for the northern part of the attack area, the Americans for the southern, although, inevitably, confusion occurred. Some of the transport pilots, disorientated by ground haze, dropped their paratroopers in the wrong place, while a number of gliders, released too early or too late, crashed to the ground in unpredictable locations. Despite the events of the previous night, German machinegunners and antiaircraft crews were active, imposing significant casualties on both aircraft and men. Although the drop took only two hours to complete, more than 100 aircraft and gliders were destroyed and 332 severely damaged. Particularly worrying were the losses suffered by the Curtiss C-46 Commando transports, used for the first time on this operation. Those carrying the US 513th Parachute Infantry Regiment, for example were caught in antiaircraft fire before they

Below: Men of the US 17th Airborne Division round up German prisoners: by the time the airborne soldiers were relieved by the swiftly advancing ground forces, they had captured some 1,500 of the enemy.

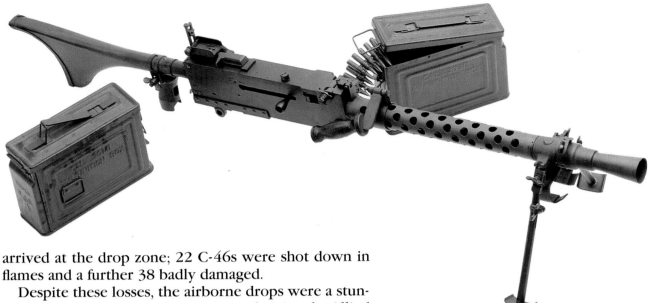

arrived at the drop zone; 22 C-46s were shot down in flames and a further 38 badly damaged.

Despite these losses, the airborne drops were a stunning success, confusing the enemy and giving the Allied ground forces a welcome boost. By 14:00 all objectives had been secured, including the town of Hamminkeln and its adjacent bridges over the Issel, the latter seized by the 2nd Battalion Oxfordshire and Buckinghamshire Light Infantry in a repetition of their gliderborne assault on the Bénouville Bridge on June 6, 1944. Casualties overall were not light – the British lost 1,078 men, killed or wounded, while the American figure was 881 – but despite the losses the bridgeheads were now unassailable.

The fighting was not over yet. In Rees, the 51st (Highland) Division had to clear the remains of the town in bitter clashes with diehard German paratroopers. In the process, the divisional commander, Maj. Gen. Thomas Rennie, was killed, but this did not stop the momentum. Even so, it took until March 26 for the town to be secured. On the opposite flank of the British assault area, men of the 15th (Scottish) Division faced similar problems in Wesel, while all along the front nasty firefights occurred as small villages, woods and hills were taken. It was not until March 28, by which time Montgomery had 20 divisions and over 1,000 tanks over the Rhine (including Canadian units that crossed at Emmerich), that consolidation was complete. German defenses were crumbling in the face of such overwhelming force, opening the way to a breakout that would outflank the Ruhr and project Anglo–Canadian armies towards Berlin.

Unfortunately, this was not to happen: Eisenhower was about to shift the emphasis of the Allied advance much further south, leaving an extremely angry Montgomery with little more than a secondary role in the final defeat of Germany. It seemed poor recompense for an assault crossing that was almost perfect in its planning and execution.

Above: A US .30 caliber, Model 1919A6 Browning light machine gun. Late in the war these company support weapons began to be produced with a shoulder stock and bipod instead of the usual tripod.
War Memorial Museum of Virginia

Below: After landing a paratrooper of the US 17th Airborne Division crawls forward carrying a late model 1919A6 LMG.

V Nine
The Soviets Enter Germany: The Winter Offensive

David Glantz

In early 1945, while the western Allies were planning their crossing of the Rhine, away in the east, the Red Army was continuing its inexorable advance westward on a continent-wide front which now stretched from the Baltic to the Balkans.

By the end of August 1944, the Soviet summer strategic offensive had run its course. In the central sector of the Eastern Front, the three Soviet Belorussian Fronts fought along the East Prussian borders, approached the Narew River north of Warsaw, and clung to tenuous bridgeheads across the Vistula River south of the Polish capital. During July and August, German reserves had gravitated to the central sector to contest every mile of ground and, if possible, hold Soviet forces east of the German heartland and the Narew and Vistula River barriers. Bitter fighting raged throughout September and into October as worn-down Soviet forces at the end of frayed logistical lines sought to improve their position for another winter offensive against equally worn and heavily attrited German forces, who now fought more out of desperation than conviction.

Soviet units fought their way into the Augustow forests west of the Neiman River, to the very gates of Warsaw, and into bridgeheads over the Vistula River at Magnushev, Pulavy, and Sandomierz. In the Narew and Vistula bridgeheads, the Soviets dug in and successfully fended off counterattack after counterattack by German panzer forces trying to drive them back across the rivers. By mid-October, however, quiet had set in on the Warsaw–Berlin axis as both sides regrouped and prepared for the inevitable resumption of the Soviet offensive.

Meanwhile, Soviet attention again shifted to the flanks, where fighting raged throughout late fall and into winter. In the Baltic region, the three Baltic Fronts launched offensive after offensive and slowly drove German Army Group North back from its 'Panther' fortified

Left: A Soviet SU-76 self-propelled gun lurks on the edge of a Hungarian village as units of the 3rd Ukrainian Front prepare for the Battle of Lake Balaton, Germany's last offensive of World War II.

147

line toward Tallinn and Riga. The well-constructed German defenses and the shrinking size of the front combined to thwart any hope for a rapid Soviet advance. The city of Riga became a magnet, attracting the offensive efforts of the Soviets until mid-October, when a sudden secret Soviet maneuver shifted the focus of battle and propelled Soviet forces to the Baltic coast, cutting off Army Group North in the Courland pocket.

In the south, the Soviets capitalized on their August destruction of the bulk of Army Group South Ukraine by seizing Bucharest and forcing Romania to switch her allegiance. Soon after, Soviet forces crossed the Danube into Bulgaria and, in October, forced the Bulgarians to join the Allied cause. In mid-October, 2nd Ukrainian Front swung west across the Carpathians into eastern Hungary, engaging the newly reorganized Sixth and Eighth Armies of Army Group South Ukraine, which had now been reinforced by three Hungarian armies. Meanwhile, 3rd Ukrainian Front poised for a thrust into southern Yugoslavia against Army Group F to seize Belgrade and destroy Germany's position in the Balkan peninsula.

Finally, during September and October, 1st Ukrainian Front's left wing and 4th Ukrainian Front's right wing began heavy combat to pierce the Carpathian Mountain barrier into Slovakia and eastern Hungary. Konev's 38th Army struck on September 8, in an attempt to force the Dukla Pass, but failed after heavy fighting. Throughout the month and into October, the fighting expanded to encompass 1st Guards Army and 4th Ukrainian Front's 18th Army. Despite the enlarged Soviet effort, skillful defense by the German First Panzer Army under Gen. Gotthard Heinrici thwarted any rapid Soviet advance. Soviet success in the Carpathians would ultimately become a byproduct of successful Soviet operations

Below: Citizens of Sofia cheer units of the advancing 3rd Ukrainian Front as they pass through the Bulgarian capital in October 1944 during their westerward sweep along each side of the Danube River.

further south in Hungary. For his efforts, Heinrici would later be elevated to command German defenses along the Oder River.

The Soviet advances in the Baltic and into southwestern Europe represented strategic diversions, albeit diversions with definite concrete objectives. During the transitional period between the summer offensive of 1944 and the winter offensive of 1945, the Soviet thrust into the Danube basin threatened not only Germany's military position but also its already weakened political and economic state. Should Budapest fall, Germany's last ally, Hungary, would certainly abandon her, while the Balaton oil fields and food supplies of the Hungarian plain were essential for continuation of the German war effort.

Hitler knew this and had long stressed the value of the southern peripheral. The Soviets knew he would defend it at all costs. More important, a continued Soviet offensive into the Danube basin would inexorably draw German reserves from the central portion of the front and weaken the Germans there, thus improving Soviet chances for a decisive drive during the winter along the main strategic approach to the Oder River and Berlin. Therefore, Soviet operations on the flanks in the fall of 1944 were necessary preconditions for what would occur in the center in January 1945.

By the end of September 1944, Marshal L. A. Govorov's Leningrad Front had cleared virtually all of Estonia of

Above: An unidentified Guards cavalry unit exploits its mobility to probe into the Carpathian mountains during August 1944 as elements of the 4th Ukrainian Front prepare for the Soviet drive into Hungary.

Above: As the Red Army began its long drive west, it found itself fighting not just Germans, but a whole host of non-German volunteer units raised from collaborators and those eager to free themselves from Soviet rule. From the top are the shoulder insignia of the Ukrainian; Albanian Waffen-SS; Estonian Waffen-SS.
Salamander Books

German forces except the Baltic coastal islands. General I. I. Maslennikov's and Marshal A. I. Eremenko's 3rd and 2nd Baltic Fronts had reached the close approaches to Riga, and Marshal I. Kh. Bagramian's 1st Baltic Front had seized Elgava and Dobele and threatened Riga from the south. However, resistance by Gen. Ferdinand Schoerner's Army Group North had stiffened, bolstered by prepared defenses covering the approaches to Riga.

In these circumstances, the *Stavka* decided to change the direction of attack of its *fronts*, in particular that of 1st Baltic. On September 24, a *Stavka* directive ordered the Leningrad Front and Baltic Fleet to complete the liberation of Estonia and the 3rd and 2nd Baltic Fronts to seize Riga and clear the Baltic coast of Germans. Meanwhile, 1st Baltic and part of the 3rd Belorussian Front were to conduct a powerful blow on the Memel axis, cut off the entire enemy Baltic group from East Prussia, and create the prerequisites for destroying all German forces in the Baltic region.

The *Stavka* ordered the secret redeployment of four armies in the Riga region to reinforce Bagramian's 1st Baltic Front. Bagramian was to use these forces, spearheaded by refitted 5th Guards Tank Army, to conduct the Memel operation, a surprise thrust from the Shiauliai region to the Baltic coast. In secret, between September 24 and October 4, Bagramian successfully regrouped five armies (50 rifle divisions, 15 tank brigades, and 93 artillery regiments) into new attack positions. The Germans detected Soviet attack preparations too late to prepare a response.

On October 5, Bagramian's forces struck and, by evening, 5th Guards Tank Army was exploiting into the depths of the German defenses. By October 9, 5th Guards Tank Army had overrun Third Panzer Army headquarters and reached the Baltic coast north and south of Memel, irrevocably severing contact between Army Groups North and Center and isolating German XXVIII Corps in the city. Within days Soviet forces commenced operations on the Gumbinnen approach into East Prussia, ending all German hopes of restoring the situation in the Memel area and re-establishing contact with Army Group North, which remained until war's end locked uselessly in Courland.

After months of heavy fighting, 1st Baltic Front had broken a virtual stalemate in the north and reached the Baltic Sea. On October 6, one day after the Memel operation began, Malinovsky's 2nd Ukrainian Front struck westward into Hungary, thus forcing the German High Command to add new concerns for the viability of its southern flank to its concern about the situation in the north.

By the end of September, Tolbukhin's 3rd Ukrainian Front had completed its sweep of Bulgaria and neared the Yugoslavian border, while Malinovsky's 2nd Ukrainian Front had occupied the passes through the Carpathians on a 496-mile (800km) front and was preparing to advance into Hungary to engage German and Hungarian forces of Army Group South Ukraine. Malinovsky's Front consisted of five combined-arms armies, one tank

Below: Poorly led, poorly trained and poorly equipped at the beginning of the war, the Soviet infantryman of 1944 was an altogether more formidable creature of vastly improved fighting abilities.

army (6th Guards), a cavalry-mechanized group, several separate mobile corps and two Romanian armies newly incorporated into the Soviet fold. The *Stavka* ordered Malinovsky to destroy enemy forces in Hungary and drive Hungary from the German fold in cooperation with 4th Ukrainian Front, which had deployed from the Crimea to the northern Carpathian region.

The *Stavka* reinforced Malinovsky's Front with an additional army (soon joined by another), two mechanized corps, and Lt. Gen. I. A. Pliev's cavalry-mechanized group. Since the 2nd Ukrainian Front was deployed on an exceedingly broad front, its force densities remained low throughout the operations, and logistical sustainment was tenuous at best. Temporary force concentrations and routine resupply produced periodic advances in given sectors but could not result in decisive deep operations such as occurred in other sectors. Consequently Malinovsky's Front was forced to conduct a series of successive army or multi-army operations, each preceded by a short operational pause and limited regrouping of forces, in particular of the Front's mobile elements.

Malinovsky's initial plan called for an advance in the center northwestward toward Debrecen, while flank armies pushed toward Cluj and Szeged. Malinovsky sought to trap all German forces in eastern Hungary in a pincer between his 2nd and Gen. I. E. Petrov's 4th Ukrainian Front, which, in early September, had begun a thrust into the Carpathian Mountains. Thereafter, he intended to shift his direction of attack westward toward the Hungarian capital Budapest. The Debrecen operation began on October 6 and, within three days, Group Pliev had advanced 62 miles (100km) northwest to the Tisza River. When 6th Guards Tank Army failed to seize Debrecen, Malinovsky quickly shifted Pliev's Group

Below right: One of the most widely used Soviet pistols of the period was the Nagant revolver Model 1892/5. This weapon fired a 7.62mm cartridge and chambered seven rounds. The pistol was unusual in that when cocked, the entire chamber moved forward to create a gas-tight seal with the barrel. Inset is the revolver's ordnance mark and date stamp.
Imperial War Museum, London

eastward to assist the tank army. Together, on October 20, the combined mobile forces seized Debrecen. Subsequently, Pliev's and Gorshkov's Cavalry-Mechanized Groups sped north and seized Nyiregyhaza on October 22, only to be struck by a coordinated German panzer counterstroke which severed the Groups' communications and, by October 27, forced them to abandon much of their equipment and withdraw south.

With both German and Soviet forces tied down in heavy combat north of Debrecen, the *Stavka* and Malinovsky capitalized on German weakness further south by mounting a drive on Budapest from 2nd Ukrainian Front's left flank. On October 29, his forces, spearheaded by two mechanized corps, penetrated Hungarian defenses and advanced through Kiskoros and Kecskemet to the southern approaches to Budapest, where, on November 3, German resistance brought the Soviet advance to an abrupt halt. After regrouping, on November 10, Malinovsky struck again east of Budapest but, by November 20, the redeployed German IV Panzer Corps again halted the Soviet drive short of the city. Further south, on November 27, Tolbukhin's 3rd Ukrainian Front deployed secretly to the banks of the Danube River near Sombor and attacked across the river with two armies, which, by December 3, had advanced to the shores of Lake Balaton, southwest of Budapest.

Malinovsky struck again on December 5, this time simultaneously north and south of Budapest in a two-pronged attack to envelop and seize the city. In the north, 6th Guards Tank Army and Pliev's cavalry-mechanized group advanced to envelop the city from the north, and a second force advanced from the south to seize Szekesfehervar and Esztergom, west of Budapest. Despite a successful initial Soviet advance, the Germans shifted operational reserves, and Budapest did not fall, nor was it encircled. The Soviet advance south of the city bogged down against the German Margareithe Defense Line between Lake Balaton and the southern outskirts of Budapest, and both 6th Guards Tank Army and Pliev's cavalry-mechanized group penetrated into the hills north of the Danube but failed to encircle the city.

Subsequently, on December 20, 2nd and 3rd Ukrainian Fronts finally conducted a coordinated offensive which successfully penetrated the Margareithe defenses and encircled IX SS Mountain Corps and Hungarian forces in the city. Throughout the remainder of the month and into January 1945, the Soviets successfully parried several heavy counterattacks by IV SS Panzer Corps to relieve the beleaguered garrison.

The operations along the German flanks, in the Baltic and in southeastern Europe, clearly achieved their intent. While the Soviets made important gains, they also

Above: The Germans also created volunteer units from Georgia (in the southern USSR); Russia (the Russian Army of Liberation badge features the old Tsarist colors of blue and white) and Turkistan in Soviet Central Asia. *Salamander Books and the George Fistrovich Collection*

Above: A destroyed bridge over the Danube gives some indication of the severe fighting for Budapest, which was encircled by the 3rd Ukrainian Front on December 24, 1944 but fell only on February 14, 1945.

achieved their greater purpose – to deflect German attention and resources from the critical central sector of the front. Although German intelligence continually stressed the ultimate importance of the direct approach to Berlin, troops flowed to sectors where combat was the most intense, especially if German political and economic interests were also threatened. The Soviets appreciated German political and economic sensitivities over the Baltic and Danubian basin regions, and they played on those sensitivities. Bagramian's, Malinovsky's, and Tolbukhin's forces successfully threatened the German position in both areas; and, in fact, if reinforcements had not been sent, the situation would have become even more critical. This, combined with Soviet inactivity in November and December along the Narew and Vistula Rivers, inevitably drew German forces to the flanks. Hitler's preoccupation with his counteroffensive in the Ardennes only exacerbated the situation in Poland as events in January would confirm.

In late October 1944, the *Stavka* and Soviet General Staff developed the general concept for a winter strategic offensive designed to end the war. It mandated a two-stage campaign commencing in November to destroy German Army Group Center and occupy East Prussia, to defeat Germany Army Groups A and South, in Poland, Czechoslovakia, Hungary and Austria, and to advance to a line running from the mouth of the Vistula, through Poznan and Breslau to Vienna. The Warsaw–Berlin axis, 1st Belorussian Front's sector, was designated as the direction of the main effort. The *Stavka* ordered 1st and 2nd Baltic Fronts and the Baltic Fleet to

destroy German Army Group North in Courland and prevent transfer of enemy forces to other fronts.

During November and December, Soviet offensives in the Baltic region and Hungary, which formed the first stage of the winter campaign, confirmed the *Stavka's* judgement that these operations would draw German forces from the critical Warsaw–Berlin axis. The second stage of the campaign was to consist of two large scale operations, both focused on the western strategic axis. The first, conducted by 3rd and 2nd Belorussian Fronts, would strike heavily entrenched German Army Group Center in East Prussia, with 3rd Belorussian Front advancing directly on the Baltic port of Königsberg, through the main German defenses and 2nd Belorussian Front enveloping East Prussia from the south and west, to isolate German forces in the region and to protect the northern flank of the main strategic thrust across Poland.

At the same time, 1st Belorussian and 1st Ukrainian Fronts would jointly launch the main strategic offensive across Poland against German Army Group A to the Poznan–Breslau region. Subsequently, the offensive would be continued, if feasible. Ultimately, the planned Vistula–Poznan operation became the Vistula-Oder operation when original operational objectives were quickly exceeded. In these operations, the *Stavka* dispensed with the use of special representatives to plan and coordinate each operation. Instead it worked directly with each Front commander: Zhukov for 1st Belorussian; Rokossovsky for 2nd Belorussian; Gen. I. D. Cherniakhovsky for 3rd Belorussian; Konev for 1st Ukrainian Front; and Marshal A. M. Vasilevsky for 1st and 2nd Baltic Front operations on the northern flank. In late December, the *Stavka* approached initial *front* plans and ordered an attack date of January 12, eight days earlier than originally planned, to assist the Allies, then struggling in the Ardennes.

Zhukov planned three major attacks. His main attack would come from the Magnushev bridgehead, launched by three combined-arms armies to penetrate German defenses, and two tank armies (1st Guards and 2nd Guards), and one cavalry corps to exploit toward Poznan. Two other armies, backed up by three mobile corps, would conduct a secondary attack from the Pulavy bridgehead toward Lodz, and one army, cooperating with 1st Polish Army, would envelop and seize Warsaw.

Above: SKS semi-automatic rifle and bayonet. This weapon underwent field trials with the Red Army throughout 1944-45. It fired a 7.62mm cartridge held in a 10-round clip.
Imperial War Museum, London

Below: The Soviets made effective use of their 'Katyusha' rocket-launcher batteries as they drove the German forces back to their homeland. Such rockets lacked accuracy but were fearsome in barrage fire.

Konev planned one powerful assault from the larger Sandomierz bridgehead. Six armies, supported by three tank corps, would penetrate German defenses, and 3rd Guards and 4th Tank Armies would then exploit toward Breslau. Two reserve armies would join the attack from second echelon and advance to seize Krakow and the Polish industrial region around Katowice. To confuse the Germans, the two *fronts* were to attack in time-phased sequence. Konev's forces would initiate the attack on January 12, from the Sandomierz bridgehead, and two days later Zhukov would commence his assaults from Pulavy and Magnushev.

Before the offensive, the *Stavka* reinforced Zhukov's and Konev's Fronts with seven combined-arms and two tank armies (60 rifle divisions, four tank corps, one mechanized corps, and over 120 artillery regiments), forces needed to sustain the advance through the depths of Poland. This 50 percent increase in the strength of the two *fronts* was skillfully, and largely successfully, concealed by stringent deception plans. Deception measures hid the scale of Soviet concentration and, combined with economy of forces measures elsewhere, permitted the Soviets to achieve force superiorities in critical sectors of over ten to one in manpower and six to one in armor.

Konev's assault on January 12 swept away German defenders in a matter of hours and destroyed the coherence of two reinforced German panzer divisions (16th and 17th) backing up the tactical defenses. Within two days, Gen. P. S. Rybalko's 3rd Guards and Gen. D. D. Leliushenko's 4th Tank Armies, with a combined strength of over 1,700 tanks and SP guns, had streamed into the German operational rear. Zhukov's initial assaults on January 13 penetrated German defenses and obliterated two German infantry divisions. On the second and third days of the operation, he committed Gen. M. E. Katukov's 1st Guards and Gen. S. I. Bogdanov's 2nd Guards Tank Armies, whose 1,635 tanks and SP guns began an exploitation west of Warsaw and towards Lodz. So complete was the destruction of forward German forces and so powerful was the momentum of the four exploitation tank armies that, within days, they had swept around and encircled German operational reserves (Panzer Corps Grossdeutschland) deployed in haste from East Prussia and forced that corps itself to fight in encirclement for its very survival.

Within a week Soviet forces, spearheaded by the four tank armies, swept westward in an avalanche of armor past Lodz and Krakow towards Poznan and Breslau, virtually obliterating organized German defenses across a 155 mile (250km) front. Warsaw fell to Soviet and Polish forces on January 17.

While 1st Guards, 2nd Guards, and 4th Tank Armies

Below: The Germans made extensive use of thick-walled Polish houses as defensive strongpoints, but these proved little obstacle to Soviet infantry units amply provided with light yet powerful artillery.

plunged westward towards the Oder River, 3rd Guards Tank Army and second echelon Soviet armies were ordered to deal with newly arrived German reserves, which had formed a major pocket of resistance around the Katowice industrial region in southern Poland. On the evening of January 20, Rybalko received orders from Konev to turn his army abruptly southward, ninety degrees away from its projected line of advance westward toward Breslau. Within hours, Rybalko reoriented his forward detachments along the new direction of advance and followed, the next day, with the remainder of his army in an attack which ultimately forced the Germans to abandon their defensive bastion around Katowice. By February 1, lead elements of Soviet forces had reached the Oder River from Küstrin, 37 miles (60km) east of Berlin, to south of Oppeln and had secured small bridgeheads across the river 62 miles (100km) beyond their planned objective, Poznan. Swept away by optimism, the *Stavka* drafted plans for continuing the advance to Berlin.

The Soviets planned their second major strategic thrust in January 1945 against the heavy Germany Army Group Center defenses in East Prussia. The Germans had recognized the likelihood of such a Soviet attack since late October and had prepared accordingly, with an ardor that reflected German concern over maintaining their position in the "heartland" of Prussia.

The *Stavka* concept for the East Prussian operation, developed in late November, required Cherniakhovsky's 3rd and Rokossovsky's 2nd Belorussian Fronts to launch coordinated assaults to cut off German forces in

Above: A column of German prisoners taken in the Polish fortress city of Poznan moves forlornly eastward into a long and extremely arduous period of captivity in the hinterland regions of the USSR.

Below: A metal and enamel Red Army cap badge.
Imperial War Museum, London

157

Above: A Nagant Model 38 carbine. This weapon fired the 7.62mm cartridge. It was commonly issued to rear echelon troops.
Imperial War Museum, London

East Prussia from those in Poland and to pin them against the Baltic coast. Then, in subsequent operations, 3rd Belorussian and 1st Baltic Fronts would fragment and destroy the encircled German force. After reaching the Vistula River south of Danzig, 2nd Belorussian Front, in coordination with 1st Belorussian Front, would continue its operations on the main axis across the Vistula River and through eastern Pomerania to Stettin on the Oder River. The operation was timed to coincide with the Vistula operation.

Cherniakhovsky planned his main attack with four combined armies and two tank corps directly into the teeth of main German defenses, through Insterberg directly toward Königsberg along the boundary of the defending German Third Panzer and Fourth Armies. A single army would defend the *front*'s extended left flank, and two armies would cover the right flank. Rokossovsky planned his main attack with three armies from a small bridgehead across the Narew River through Germany Fourth Army defenses toward Mlava and Marienburg. Gen. V. T. Vol'sky's 5th Guards Tank Army would exploit westward with the penetrating armies, and the *front*'s flank armies would brush past and isolate German forces in East Prussia.

Regrouping of forces was less extensive than in the case of the Vistula operation, but the most important involved the 2nd Belorussian Front's exploitation force, 5th Guards Tank Army, which had to be moved secretly southward from 1st Baltic Front's sector into new attack positions along the Narew River. The successful regrouping accorded the Soviets significant force superiority.

The East Prussian operation began on January 13 when Cherniakhovsky's forces struck German defenses on the Königsberg axis. The 3rd Belorussian Front's direct thrust toward Königsberg quickly turned into a prolonged penetration operation, which limited the utility of the two tank corps serving as army mobile groups. Ultimately, after costly heavy fighting, Cherniakhovsky committed his second echelon 11th Guards Army against the German left flank, unhinging the German defenses and forcing an agonizingly slow German

withdrawal toward the Königsberg outer defenses.

Further south, Rokossovsky's 2nd Belorussian Front succeeded in penetrating the German defenses rapidly and unleashed its operational maneuver forces into the German rear. Vol'sky's 5th Guards Tank Army and three mobile corps drove in an immense armored wedge to the outskirts of Marienburg fortress, the banks of the Vistula, and the Baltic coast. German resistance, however, drew main Soviet rifle forces into fierce battles, firstly against units conducting a fighting withdrawal into East Prussia, and secondly in fending off German attempts to break through the Soviet cordon of defenses separating the now encircled German Army Group Center forces from the main German front lines along the west bank of the Vistula. So intense was the fighting that 2nd Belorussian Front's thrust gravitated away from that of 1st Belorussian, leaving the latter's right flank along the Vistula somewhat unprotected.

At this juncture, in late January, based on the rapid progress of Zhukov's forces, *Stavka* still hoped to continue the advance on Berlin. Conditions during the last few days of January and the first few days of February caused a reversal of that decision. Large German forces were defending Breslau and were encircled in Torun and Poznan, while German resistance had stiffened along the Oder River, particularly from the air. German reserves seemed to be massing along the Soviet flanks in Pomerania and Silesia, and 2nd Belorussian Front, tied down in heavy fighting for East Prussia, was unable to join 1st Belorussian Front's advance, and all *fronts* required resupply and refitting. As a result, the *Stavka* cancelled its further offensive plans until the flanks could be secured

Below: The troops of the 2nd Belorussian Front cleared the Bay of Danzig by the end of March 1945. The Germans with their backs to the Baltic Sea suffered terrible manpower losses and the destruction of many hundreds of armored fighting vehicles.

Above: In keeping with their doctrine of using heavy firepower to support any assault, the Soviets equipped their forces with large numbers of automatic weapons such as this SG43 heavy machine gun.

and its forces could properly be reprovisioned for the final thrust on Berlin.

There was a problem on the Soviet's flank, although it was not as severe as the *Stavka* supposed. After his front in Poland had been smashed, on January 23, Hitler placed his Interior Minister, Reichsführer Heinrich Himmler in command of the new Army Group Vistula with orders to hold Pomerania in the gap between the struggling Soviet 1st and 2nd Belorussian Fronts and Army Groups Center and A and to prevent the Soviets from severing East Prussia from Germany proper. Himmler's makeshift force consisted of three improvised corps headquarters, reinforced by Ninth Army deployed along the Oder River, and assorted Volkssturm units. Hitler also renamed many of his army groups and began dispatching reinforcements to Himmler. Army Group North, which he refused to evacuate from Courland, became Army Group Courland, while Center became North, and A became Center.

Meanwhile, on February 8, Konev's 1st Ukrainian Front struck along the Oder River north and south of Breslau and committed 3rd Guards and 4th Tank Armies in a drive, which, by the end of the month, had encircled 35,000 German troops in Breslau, a similar number in Glogau, and had propelled *front* forces to the Neisse River line adjacent to Zhukov's forces.

Fearing an immediate assault on Berlin, in

mid-February Hitler ordered Himmler to launch a counteroffensive from Pomerania against 1st Belorussian Front's flank and the 2nd Belorussian Front, which had already begun an attack into Pomerania on February 10. The German attack, launched on February 16, in piecemeal fashion by Eleventh SS Panzer Army, failed, but it did prompt the *Stavka* to turn more of Zhukov's forces northward for a concerted attack on bothersome German forces in Pomerania. The renewed Soviet attack on February 24 ultimately reached the shores of the Baltic, cutting off German forces in eastern Pomerania and Danzig.

In October and November 1944, Soviet forces had slashed away at the German strategic flanks and reached the Baltic and Budapest. German forces, dispatched to meet the crisis, failed to stem the Soviet tide. Then, in less than two months, German defenses in Poland and East Prussia had been torn asunder, and Soviet forces advanced up to 434 miles (700km) to the west, in the process decimating Germany Army Groups Center and A. As a result, by early March 1945, Soviet forces had reached or were approaching the Oder–Neisse River line on a broad front from Stettin on the Baltic to Görlitz near the Czech border and were now poised to begin final operations to Berlin.

Although German losses in these operations were high (600,000), replacements and transfers from other theaters caused German troop strength in the east to decline only from 2,030,000 (and 190,000 Allies) to just under 2,000,000 at the end of February. However, 556,000 of these troops were isolated in Courland and East Prussia and virtually irrelevant. To make matters worse, the Soviet's 6,461,000 troops could now be concentrated on the most critical axes. For over one third of these forces, the next target would be Berlin.

Below: The SG43 air-cooled heavy machine gun and carriage. This weapon was introduced into the Red Army to replace the water-cooled Maxim (the date stamp on the breech of this particular example is 1944). The gun was belt-fed and had a fire rate of 650 rounds per minute. Its range was anything up to 2,300m (2,500yds). *Imperial War Museum, London*

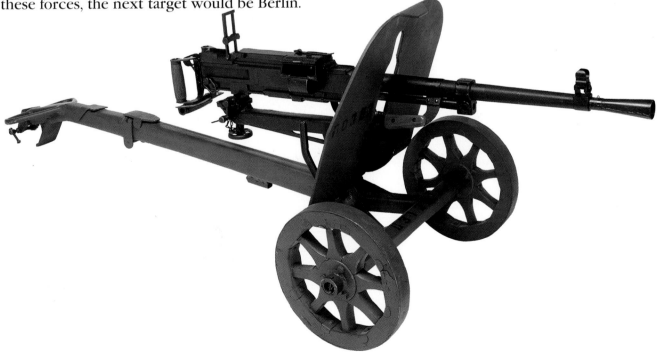

V Ten

Burma Reconquered, 1944-45

Raymond Callahan

While the Soviets were advancing on the borders of the German Reich, in Southeast Asia, men of Britain's "Forgotten Army" were about to launch their long-awaited assault on the Japanese Army in Burma.

The attention of men and women in the British Isles and North America was focused intently on Western Europe in June 1944. Rome fell on the 4th; two days later American, British and Canadian soldiers dropped from the sky and splashed ashore in Normandy to begin the long-awaited liberation of western Europe. Half a world away, under the leaden skies of monsoon season northern Burma, Britain's "Forgotten Army", Lt. Gen. William Slim's Fourteenth Army, simultaneously set out on another campaign of reconquest, revenge and liberation.

Burma had always been a theater of frustration — its priority low, the attention the Allied high command devoted to it intermittent. The war there had opened in 1942 with the longest retreat in British military history, a disastrous episode relieved only by the first gleams of Slim's subsequent luster as a commander. The following year, a premature counterattack brought a defeat even more complete, though, as Churchill sarcastically minuted, on a mercifully small scale. Anglo–American arguments over the place of Burma operations in their overall strategy, and the scope and purpose of any campaign there, resulted in the creation, early in 1942, of a semi-autonomous American command "CBI". (China–Burma–India) with its own area of operations, the Northern Combat Area Command. CBI troops were largely Chinese, equipped and trained by Americans.

CBI nestled uncomfortably within the supposedly integrated Allied South East Asia Command (SEAC) created in the fall of 1943. CBI's commander, Lt. Gen. Joseph W. Stilwell (who was also SEAC's deputy commander and, at least notionally, chief of staff to the

Left: Sikh soldiers of the Anglo-Indian Fourteenth Army rush a Japanese foxhole in Burma to kill any of the enemy seeking to escape from this trap, hit with white phosphorus grenades just a few moments earlier.

163

Chinese generalissimo, Chiang Kai-Shek) hated England in the abstract, and most Englishmen personally. He was there to achieve America's aim in Burma — a restored overland link with China — the famous Burma Road — to support a major Chinese war effort.

Anglo–American tensions, and the frustration of being repeatedly beaten by smaller Japanese forces, also combined to make Burma the scene of the war's greatest experiment in light infantry tactics, the Chindit epic. The brainchild of the eccentric but charismatic Orde Wingate (whose first Chindit raid into Burma in 1943 provided a desperately needed gleam of success in a theater hitherto dogged by defeat), the Chindits thereafter blossomed under the joint sponsorship of Churchill and the Americans into the corps-size "Special Force" of 1944. Its large scale operations inside Japanese-held Burma — Operation *Thursday* (at the inception of which Wingate died in a plane crash) — provided a veritable Iliad of courage, endurance and tactical skill, though the results and significance of the episode are still debated today.

Into this welter of argument and cross purposes came, in the early months of 1944, several great simplifications that opened the way for what would happen in Burma after June. In the fall of 1943, Slim had become commander of the newly created Fourteenth Army, an army that, as Britain's manpower crisis worsened in 1944–45, was bound to be made up largely of Indian Army units. Slim himself was an Indian Army officer, and that legendary service, badly scarred by the defeats its raw units had

Below: Lt. Gen. Joseph 'Vinegar Joe' Stilwell was the US commander in China, and is seen here with the leader of the Chinese Republic, Generalissimo Chiang Kai-Shek, and his influential wife.

suffered at the hands of the Japanese in 1941–43, was simultaneously being nursed back to health by two other distinguished Indian Army officers. Gen. Sir Claude Auchinleck became Commander-in-Chief, India, in mid-1943, while at the same time, Maj. Gen. Reginald Savory became the Indian Army's Director of Infantry. These two men gave Slim a refurbished weapon. The Japanese promptly gave him a chance to use it.

Alarmed both by Wingate's first Chindit raid and mounting evidence of British preparations for an offensive into Burma, the Japanese resolved on a preemptive strike to seize the British base area at Imphal in the eastern Indian state of Assam, bordering Burma. Four

Above: Two safe-passage documents or 'blood chits.' These were carried by Allied aviators in operations over Asia. If forced down, messages in local languages told the inhabitants which side the flyer was on and usually offered a reward for his safe return. *John T. Frawner Collection*

Below: Men of the 77th Infantry Brigade prepare to blow a railway bridge behind Japanese lines in the first "Chindit" raid of February/April 1943, which was designed to disrupt Japanese lines of communication.

months of very complicated fighting followed (February–May, 1944). Japanese defeats were on two widely separated battlefields: the Arakan, where the attacking Japanese force lost 5,000 of its 8,000 men; and at Imphal, where the Japanese Fifteenth Army suffered casualties amounting to 53,000 of its original 84,000 men. It was the acid test of both the rebuilt Indian Army and Slim's generalship. The Arakan and Imphal battles were both defensive battles in which Slim turned the relentless and inflexibly aggressive tactical and operational ethos of the Imperial Japanese Army, hitherto its strong point, into a liability. Utilizing his superior firepower, sustained by air supply when Japanese encircling tactics cut communications, he produced killing grounds and allowed the Japanese to immolate themselves on them. It was the turning point in Burma.

Successful exploitation is the brightest gem in a general's crown. How then would Slim now exploit his army's great victory? He had a ready answer: by following up the retreating Japanese, even through the torrential rainfall and liquid mud of the monsoon. When the dry weather came again in the fall he planned to have his army poised on the edge of the central plains of Burma where his combination of armor, artillery and tactical airpower could be exploited to the fullest, giving his enemy no respite. "Some of what we owed we had paid back," he wrote later in his classic memoir, *Defeat Into Victory*, "Now we were going to pay back the rest with interest."

As the Anglo–American armies landed in France, conducted their complex battle in Normandy, broke out

Right: Lt. Gen. Sir William Slim turned a motley collection of British and Indian formations into the highly effective Fourteenth Army that finally encompassed the total defeat of the Japanese in Burma.

and then raced to the frontiers of the Reich, Slim's XXXIII Corps under Lt. Gen. Montagu Stopford pushed steadily forward in conditions hitherto believed to preclude large scale military operations. The corps' average weekly strength, from July to November, was 88,500, of whom half were maintained forward to Imphal, following up the shattered Japanese. Indicative of the conditions in which the fighting took place, total XXXIII Corps casualties for the monsoon campaign were 50,300, but only 372 of these were actually killed in action. Some 47,000 became ill enough to be evacuated to India. It is a measure of how much Slim, Stopford and Fourteenth Army owed to improved medical care and air transport that even with the anti-malarial drug mepacrine available, there were still 20,000 cases of the disease. Without new drugs, and air evacuation of the sick, the monsoon campaign would have failed dismally. Progress, however was maintained and, by the time the Allies stalled on the borders of Germany, Slim had his troops across the Chindwin River and into Burma proper. The monsoon was now giving way the dry weather and Fourteenth Army was poised to launch Operation *Capital*, Slim's brilliant design to smash the Japanese in Central Burma, opening the way to the overland recovery of the country from north to south – something else that had hitherto been regarded as unfeasible.

Another simplification now occurred. Slim's superior, Adm. Lord Louis Mountbatten, the SEAC Commander, had planned a series of amphibious operations for 1944–45 which would have become the theater's strategic focus. They depended, however, on the war in

Above: Japanese service handguns. On the left is a modified 8mm Nambu semi-automatic, Type A with holster and spare clip. The Nambu was the standard Japanese handgun of the war. On the right is a modified 7.65mm Colt 1903 semi-automatic. The holster and ammunition are of Japanese manufacture.
Eugene C. Gibson Collection

Below: The shoulder insignia of the USAAF 10th Air Force.
Salamander Books

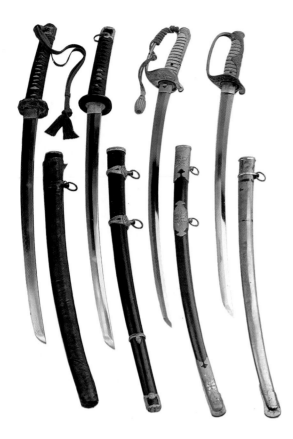

Europe ending in the early fall of 1944, thus allowing the transfer of ships, landing craft and men to the east. The prolongation of the European war made this impossible, thus removing any threat to the primacy of Slim's campaign. (The American war in north Burma had reached its climax when Stilwell's forces, powerfully assisted by the Chindit formations the American commander shamefully misused, took the key town of Myitkyina in August. A road link with China was now assured and American interest in Burma waned rapidly thereafter. Stilwell himself left the theater in October, lamented by few.)

Fourteenth Army's dry weather campaign now came sharply into focus as the principal SEAC endeavor for 1944–45. Slim had vowed on a grim monsoon morning in May 1942, as he watched the tattered remnants of the corps he had led in a three-month, thousand-mile (1,500km) retreat, march past him to win it all back. Sir William, as he now was after being knighted for his Imphal victory, had learned from defeat and forged an army able to command victory. Now he was ready to erase the stigma of 1942. His monsoon campaign had preempted any Japanese attempt to consolidate and hold him at bay short of the dry belt of central Burma where British superiority in tanks, guns and tactical airpower could be deployed with even more devastating effect than in the fighting around Imphal. Slim hoped to use that superiority to smash the Japanese in relatively open country –

Above and far right: A selection of Japanese officer's swords. All are from the army except for the center blades, above, which originate from the Imperial Japanese Navy. Most were part of the personal collection of Gen. Douglas MacArthur.
MacArthur Memorial Collection

Right: Air supply was a vital feature of the Burma campaign, and here British gunners man a 40mm Bofors gun near Kalewa to protect a C-47 drop on an area prepared by the 11th East African Division in December 1944.

with the great Irrawaddy River at their back. The Japanese theater commander, Lt. Gen. Hoyotaro Kimura, acknowledging the success of Slim's monsoon drive, prepared to counter it by retiring behind the river.

The Japanese decision to fall back behind the Irrawaddy forced Slim to recast him plans. Stopford's XXXIII Corps would continue to close up to the river both north and south of the city of Mandalay. This, Slim appreciated, would focus Japanese attention, while the decisive stroke came elsewhere. Fourteenth Army's other corps, the IV, now under Lt. Gen. Frank Messervy – (Slim, going over to the offensive, exchanged Sir Geoffrey Scoones, the cautious infantryman who had commanded the corps in the Imphal fighting, for an aggressive cavalryman) – would move, via the fever-ridden Myittha Valley, to a point on the Irrawaddy well below Mandalay. Crossing there, Messervy would launch a tank-infantry striking force to seize the communications center at Meiktila. With that in his hands, Slim would be able to throttle all the Japanese units facing both Stopford and the Chinese–American force in north Burma. This latter force, comprising the British 36th Division, the Chinese divisions Stilwell had led to Myitkyina, an American Regimental Combat Team known as "Mars Force", and the Kachin irregulars raised and directed by the Office of Strategic Services (OSS) – the American version of SOE – would push south against the remnants of the Japanese formations that had been decimated in the Myitkina campaign. Their objective was not, however, the reconquest of Burma but simply defensive depth in front of the new road link to China. Not for the first time disparate Allied objectives were on display.

Capital's opening phase went very well. The great victories of 1944 had transformed Fourteenth Army into a

Below: Men of the US Mars Force use a commanding height to good effect during a firefight with the Japanese between Wauting and Lashio on the Burma Road that was the main supply route from India to China.

Above: The light machine gun formed an essential role in Japanese infantry tactics. These two examples are (top) the Type 99 (1939), 7.7mm caliber, and (bottom), the Type 96 (1931), 6.5mm caliber.
US Army Ordnance Museum, Aberdeen, Md.

self-confident, veteran force. The increasingly difficult logistics of campaigning in central Burma meant Slim had to limit the number of formations he employed, so it was the cream of Fourteenth Army that fought in this last stage of the Burma campaign. The near impossibility by 1945 of keeping British formations up to strength (even Montgomery's 21st Army Group in Europe was running out of men) meant that Slim's force, always predominately Indian Army in composition, was now overwhelmingly so – by January 1945 only 13 percent of the land forces in SEAC were British while 60 percent were Indian Army, with the balance being mostly African.

It was one of the Indian Army's most aggressive divisional commanders, Maj. Gen. Peter Rees, who, between January 14–16 moved his 19th Indian Division across the Irrawaddy above Mandalay, covered by the heaviest artillery concentration yet employed in Burma. This fixed Japanese attention, as Slim had expected it would. Meanwhile, Messervy's corps – its march concealed by an elaborate deception plan, Operation *Cloak* (and the virtual disappearance of the Japanese air force from the skies of Burma) – closed up to the Irrawaddy and prepared to cross. The Chinese–American–Kachin force (now commanded by Lt. Gen. Daniel Sultan, one of the three American lieutenant generals among whom Stilwell's kingdom had been divided) pressed down from the north.

Both Stopford's divisions were across the Irrawaddy, drawing a typically furious Japanese response, by the time Messervy sprang Slim's great surprise. Crossing the mile-wide (1.6km) river barrier, weakly and ineffectively held by units of the "Indian National Army" (recruited from among the mass of Indian prisoners taken

by the Japanese in 1941–42), IV Corps drove for Meiktila, where its spearhead was promptly reinforced by an
air-mobile brigade that had been standing by at Imphal.
The effect of Messervy's coup was to unhinge the
Japanese command much as the German thrust across
the Meuse at Sedan had unbalanced the French in 1940.
The Japanese commanders, like their French counterparts, never again had full control of the battle they were
fighting. The Japanese soldier remained an extremely
formidable opponent, but his willingness to die could no
longer be used in an operationally significant fashion.
Around Meiktila swirled a series of battles that effectively destroyed Kimura's Burma Area Army. Slim had
created a situation in which he could again combine the
strategic offensive with the tactical defensive, one in
which the lethal firepower of Fourteenth Army could be
deployed with crushing effect – the situation he had exploited, first in the Arakan and then during the Imphal
battle. The brilliance of Slim's handling of these battles
was overshadowed by the great struggle on the borders
of Germany in the winter of 1944–45 but, noticed or not,
Slim had won another great victory which he was now
ready to exploit.

The Mandalay–Meiktila battles set the stage for Slim's
final operation, *Extended Capital*, an overland drive to
take Rangoon from the north before the monsoon broke

Left: Always hampered by lack of motor
transport and fuel, the Japanese in
Burma eagerly exploited the transport
capabilities of the elephant to keep
their front-line units supplied with
essentials.

in May. By this time, it was abundantly clear SEAC would be unable to launch any major amphibious assault until after the 1945 monsoon, ie not until the fall. Although an overland reconquest of Burma was not what Churchill, the British Chiefs of Staff, or Mountbatten had originally wanted, it was clear that the only offensive option now open to them was *Extended Capital*, with a limited amphibious assault, christened *Dracula*, held in reserve for possible use against Rangoon as Slim approached from the north. Scarcely had this been settled, however, when the Americans did what the Japanese were no longer able to do to Fourteenth Army, and nearly derailed the plan.

The capture of Mandalay on March 21 signalled the effective end of any significant American controlled operations in CBI. China, of course, had always been the focus of all American endeavor in CBI and the USAAF transport squadrons – a very high proportion of the theater's air transport assets, and about to become even more vital to Slim – remained under exclusively American control. This became significant as ominous developments began to unfold in China. Stilwell had predicted that once the USAAF bombers based there began seriously to annoy them, the Japanese would simply mount an offensive to overrun their airfields, an offensive which the ramshackle Chinese Army would not be able to stop. Coincidentally with Stilwell's departure,

Below: A contrast in old and new as a mortar team of the 1st Battalion, West Yorkshire Regiment, pound Japanese positions in Meiktila, a vital target which fell to the Fourteenth Army on March 3, 1945.

Left: Men of the British 36th Infantry Division's 29th Brigade load ammunition onto boats in preparation for their crossing of the river Irrawaddy near Katha and then the drive south to Mandalay.

the Japanese vindicated his prophecy, launching their last offensive campaign of the war. As they drove toward the American airbases, the obvious source of modernized, battle-tested divisions to oppose them was the group of Chinese divisions under CBI command in north Burma. The only way to move those divisions to China rapidly enough was by air.

This would cast a lengthening shadow over *Extended Capital*, as the progress of the Japanese offensive in China quickly made the presence there of the CBI Chinese divisions, and Mars Force, more important in American eyes than anything they might now do in Burma. The first truck convoy over the reopened Burma Road had reached Chungking in January. Slim's victories had removed any possibility that the Japanese could again cut the road. Although the OSS's Kachins – now, with victory imminent, more numerous than ever – continued to operate aggressively against Japanese road communications, no Chinese or American objectives remained unattained in Burma. On behalf of Generalissimo Chiang Kai-Shek, Lt. Gen. Alfred Wedemeyer, Chiang's American chief of staff (and another of Stilwell's troika of successors) asked for the return of all Chinese forces serving there. The air transport squadrons necessary to shift them, however, had to come from the pool whose most important customer was Slim.

Fourteenth Army's line of communication was by this time a logistic wonder, stretching from India and the docks at Calcutta, in an enormous horseshoe via Assam and Imphal to the divisions poised in central Burma to drive back to the sea at Rangoon. It employed virtually every known form of transport – road (some of it "surfaced" with tar-covered burlap), river, rail (in two gauges), porters, mules, elephants, and above all the DC-3, the "Dakota," the real wonder weapon in Burma.

Below: A Republican Chinese propaganda leaflet and the shoulder patch insignia of the China–Burma–India Theater.
Salamander Books

Above: The road between India and China traversed some of southeast Asia's worst terrain, as indicated by this photograph of a US truck convoy negotiating the famous 21-curve section near Annan in China.

Already creaking ominously, this line of communications would no longer function when the monsoon broke in May. Slim had to take Rangoon in what remained of the dry season. By early April 1945, he had pared his force to the bare minimum and stood ready to drive the 300 miles (480km) to Rangoon in the few weeks remaining before the monsoon. The air transport squadrons were critical, because Slim now intended to drop his overland communications and rely exclusively on them for the climactic "SOB" (Sea or Bust) phase of the campaign. A less tough and self-confident commander would certainly have paused when the vital link in his communications was threatened with severance. Slim, however, pushed on, relying on Mountbatten to somehow produce the Dakotas. Over his head flew a heavy barrage of signals culminating in a furious message from Churchill to Gen. George Marshall, in Washington, pointing out that the Burma campaign had turned out to serve primarily American objectives and demanding fair treatment now that Slim's army was poised on the brink of decisive victory. The Americans grudgingly agreed that their aircraft could stay until Rangoon fell – or May 1, whichever came first.

Early in April, "Sea or Bust" began, with Messervy's corps in the lead. The chief staff officer of Rees' 19th Indian Division, watching Messervy's corps jump off, recorded for posterity the opening of the old Indian Army's last great offensive as Slim, Messervy and three divisional commanders . . . :

watched the leading division crash past the start point. The dust thickened under the trees lining the road until the column was motoring into a thunderous yellow tunnel, first the tanks, infantry all over them, then trucks filled with men, then more tanks going fast, nose to tail, guns, more trucks, more guns – British, Sikhs, Gurkhas, Madrassis, Pathans – this was the old Indian Army, going down to attack, for the last time in history . . .

Combat engineers, moving with Messervy's leading units, opened a new airhead about every 60 miles (96km), into which supplies were flown by transports flying far more sorties than their theoretical maximum. Japanese resistance, although poorly coordinated, was as intense as ever. Messervy's spearhead – the 17th Indian Division, which had been through the 1942 retreat and all the subsequent fighting – was at Pegu, some 30 miles (48km) from Rangoon, when the monsoon (early that year) began.

Slim's drive to Rangoon compares favorably with the great blitzes of the European war – Messervy had averaged nearly 15 miles (24km) a day, in spite of resistance, logistic problems and the clammy pre-monsoon heat varied only by occasional downpours. Guderian in 1940 and Patton four years later did no better – and they did not face opponents prepared to die where they stood. *Dracula*, the insurance policy against the "Bust" in SOB, was launched on May 1. Rangoon, however, was un-defended, abandoned by the Japanese as Slim drew near. Exhibiting great operational versatility, Slim's Forgotten Army had won a remarkable victory that, ironically, coinciding as it did with VE Day, was barely noticed in Britain or the United States.

The reopened Burma Road carried about 38,000 tons (38,600 tonnes) of supplies to China between January and VJ Day. The American trans-Himalaya (or "Hump") airlift's last full month of operation carried 39,000 (39,600 tonnes). By early 1945, the acceleration of their Pacific drives had made China essentially irrelevant to American military calculations regarding the final stages of the war with Japan, while Burma had sunk totally out of sight. In August 1945, the atomic bomb ended the war before SEAC had a chance finally to launch a major amphibious assault on Malaya, and whose aim was the reconquest of Singapore for which Churchill so fer-vently hoped. No one, in the end, achieved what they hoped for out in Burma – except possibly Slim.

What are the lessons learned from the final stages of the war in Burma? These seem to fall into two categories: operational and the nature of coalition war.

Above: The shoulder patch of the 14th Air Force USAAF, featuring its famous 'flying tiger' emblem.
Salamander Books

Below: Rangoon eventually fell to the Fourteenth Army without a battle and men of this Anglo–Indian army, here epitomized by Gurkha riflemen, were able to take control of the Burmese capital on May 3, 1945.

Throughout the fighting in Burma, the Japanese displayed a remarkable aggressiveness and tenacity, together with the capacity to endure food so bad, medical care so poor, and length of time in combat so great that the combination would have rapidly eroded the fighting power of any western army (and in this regard the Indian Army must qualify as substantially western). Ferocious discipline – and an equally ferocious training regimen – can explain some of this. Training and discipline can only tell part of the story, however. They built upon foundations laid by Japanese culture and society. To explain the Imperial Japanese Army (about which one Chindit brigadier later remarked that nearly every man in it could have been awarded the Victoria Cross or Congressional Medal of Honor) would however draw us far beyond the confines of these pages.

The largest body of troops to fight the Japanese in Burma were Indian, drawn, like Stilwell's Chinese divisions, from pre-industrial agricultural peasantries. The experience of both forces underscored the importance of careful training and good leadership in determining the outcome of combat. Stilwell's American-trained Chinese, like the products of the Auchinleck–Savory overhaul of Indian Army training; performed in 1944–45 in ways scarcely creditable to those who had witnessed the 1942 collapse. One persistent problem for British and Indian Army formations, however, was the western "high tech" style of warfare that clogged the scanty communications with masses of transport, thus slowing their

Below: The Chindits had some motor vehicles, but their most important transport asset was the mule, even if it was sometimes difficult to load these obstinate beasts into the aircraft that were to deliver them.

movement and rendering them highly vulnerable to the standard Japanese infiltration and encirclement tactics.

One of the most interesting aspects of the war in Burma, in fact, is the record of tactical and operational innovation compiled there. Here the Imperial Japanese Army's record was as weak as its urge to combat was strong. Its command structure was rigid and Japanese military culture inhibited flexible responses to changing conditions. On the offensive, Japanese tactics were stereotyped: aggressive advance to contact, infiltration, encirclement, the severing of communications. Once retrained, opponents were no longer hustled by this approach into precipitate retreat – something that was the case after Slim's assumption of command – and the Japanese had no further cards to play. (Nor did they have a solution to the problem they faced at Imphal when, lacking a sound logistic system themselves, they could no longer depend on "Churchill supplies" – captured stores.) Superior artillery, armor and airpower, deployed in favorable terrain, could also stop them, as it did on the edges of the Imphal plain in 1944 and later around Meiktila. Their own guns and tanks were obsolescent by Anglo–American standards, and their airpower, after 1943, was fading. On the defensive they produced, with their well-designed, carefully sited and thoroughly camouflaged bunkers, a formidable obstacle, but one that veteran tank-infantry teams could overcome. But of course the most important Japanese asset when standing on the defensive was the Japanese soldier himself.

On the Allied side, the most interesting tactical experiment was the large-scale creation of light infantry units; the most striking operational innovation was their deployment for prolonged periods deep in the enemy's rear sustained by air. Certainly the Chindits demonstrated, in their early operations, the flexibility and striking power of such formations, imaginatively employed. After Wingate's death, and Stilwell's decision to use the Chindits to help him take Myitkyina, the inherent problems of such formations came rapidly to the fore. Their lack of both the firepower, "heavy" formations they could deploy, and manpower sustainability, caused them to erode rapidly in numbers and combat effectiveness. The Chindit story contains remarkable examples of courage, endurance and leadership, but it is hard to see the Burma campaign as anything but a cautionary tale where light infantry are concerned.

Perhaps the most important innovation of the 1944–45 campaigns was the massive use of air transport to solve otherwise daunting problems of both logistics and operational mobility. Air supply was not invented by or for the Chindits, although the scale of Wingate's operations rapidly matured its techniques. Slim, an

Above: Generally known as Chindits, the men of the 3rd Indian Division were wholly reliant on air supply of the type seen here as a C-47 drops equipment over 'White City,' near Mawlu, in spring 1944.

Above: The Burma Star. This medal was awarded to British and Commonwealth personnel who served in Burma from December 11, 1941 to September 2, 1945. It also gave its name to the Burma veterans association established after the war.
Salamander Books

imaginative but essentially orthodox soldier would later say that "special forces" were a mistake – well trained infantry, properly led, could, he maintained, do whatever was needed. This, obviously a reaction to Wingate's denigration of regular, and especially Indian Army-units, may need some qualification.

It is clear that the Chindit operations of 1944 revealed possibilities which had their impact on the great campaign in which Slim's well trained and competently led infantry retook Burma. The 1944 Chindit campaign was the largest air mobile operation yet launched. When Slim flew a brigade into Meiktila, or dropped his overland supply line in SOB, he was making use of techniques which the Chindits had helped to develop. Although experiments like putting an Indian division on a "light" scale of transport – mules and jeeps – helped, air supply and mobility proved to be the keys to campaigning in Burma. To Slim, Wingate, Stilwell and the Burma Road, as symbols of the war in Burma, must be added the ubiquitous, indispensable Dakota.

The greatest of the lessons of the Burma campaign, however, must surely be the complexity of coalition war. In the much rehearsed controversies that accompanied the Allied war against Germany, the central argument came to be the relative weight that would be assigned to the Italian campaign versus the cross-channel reentry into Europe. This argument about emphasis pales before the fundamental divergences in Burma. CBI existed solely to support the Chinese war effort, first by airlift, then by overland supply. American thinking about the role China was to play when properly supported shifted, however, over time and finally faded away altogether, leaving Stilwell and his successors developing the means to an end which was no longer clear. SEAC aimed to contribute more directly to the defeat of Japan, using an amphibious strategy that had the additional attraction (never absent from Winston Churchill's calculations) of redeeming the Empire's lost territories and tattered prestige in southeast Asia. Lack of amphibious resources (and American pressure) constrained SEAC however, to fight a land war in Burma to reopen the road to China. Once that objective had been attained, the Americans showed an indifference to further developments that almost aborted Slim's final offensive. In Europe, Britain and the United States agreed on fundamentals while quarreling over means. In Burma, there was little agreement on anything.

The experience of great powers in the modern era has been that major wars are coalition wars. Burma demonstrates, as in a laboratory test, why such wars often present to posterity a puzzling inconsequence in direction – as Napoleon observed so long ago when he said that his favorite opponent was a coalition.

The campaign in Burma demonstrates one other thing – and that is the crucial role, even in an era of mass armies and industrialized war, of imaginative and inspiring leadership. A young British soldier, far from home, fighting around Meiktila a savage war against a relentless foe, a war moreover in which he knew the "home front" took little interest, was dazzled to encounter the army commander in person, virtually unaccompanied, carbine slung on his shoulder. Making his rounds of units, feeling the pulse of his army, Slim told the soldier and his companions that, the sooner they took Rangoon, the sooner they would be on the "big ships" home. There was none of Montgomery's careful stagecraft or Patton's histrionics in this, but it was exactly the right touch for that soldier and his companions, so exactly right that he was able to recall the dialogue clearly nearly half a century later.

The British Empire in the east was on borrowed time by May 1945. Slightly more than two years after the Fourteenth Army's great victory, the Indian Empire and its army, which had been the foundation of Slim's campaign, were no more, while Burma itself became independent the year after that. Sir William Slim and the troops he commanded had provided that Empire with a sunset moment of martial glory.

Above: Lightly equipped and subject to the utmost difficulty of terrain and operational conditions, the "Chindits" achieved wonders of endurance in a campaign that is still highly controversial.

V

Eleven

From the Rhine to the Elbe

Lloyd Clark

While Japanese power was crumbling in Southeast Asia, the Nazi Reich was facing imminent destruction. For the Allies the questions now remained: where would they link up with the Russians and who was to take Berlin, the center of Hitler's power?

By the end of March 1945 the Allies, having crossed the Rhine, were just one final push from victory. The advance from the Rhine bridgeheads was to be conducted by three Army Groups; Field Marshal Montgomery's 21st Army Group consisting of the British Second, Canadian First and US Ninth Armies; Bradley's 12th Army Group consisting of the US First, Third and Fifteenth Armies, together with the 6th Army Group, commanded by Lt. Gen. Jacob Devers and consisting of the US Seventh Army and the First French Army — forces totaling 73 divisions in all.

These forces could rely upon strong air support, large stocks of equipment, plentiful supplies and high morale. The Allies had good reasons therefore, to feel confident about their future prospects, especially when the weaknesses of the enemy were also taken into account.

The German forces, by late March 1945, were in a precarious state, indeed Gen. Eisenhower, wrote in his memoirs, "Militarily, the thing for [Hitler] to do at that moment would have been to surrender." Hitler's army was a spent force with poor lines of communication, scant resources, virtually no air support and widespread demoralization. The Germans were, quite clearly, the antithesis of their Allied counterparts. Günther Blumentritt was horrified at the weaknesses of First Parachute Army, supposedly the strongest German army in the western theater, when he took over its command in late March 1945. As he recalled after the war:

I found that there were great gaps in my front, that I had no reserves, that my artillery was weak, that I had

Left: German refugees walk through the wreckage of Bremen. This industrial city on the Elbe River served as one of Germany's biggest ports and was a center for U-boat production. Bombed throughout the war in consequence, it had first been attacked by RAF Bomber Command in 1940 and had suffered a thousand bomber raid in 1942.

no air support whatever and hardly any tanks. My communications and signal facilities were entirely in-adequate [and] . . . reinforcements that still came to me were hastily trained and badly equipped.

The situation was no better in any of Field Marshal Kesselring's armies. Kesselring, Commander-in-Chief of the German forces in the west, was having a difficult time controlling any of his three Army Groups. In the north were Army Group H, commanded by Gen. Johannes Blaskowitz, consisting of the First Parachute Army and Twenty-Fifth Army. In the centre were Army Group B, commanded by Field Marshal Walter Model, consisting of Fifth Panzer Army, Seventh Army and Fifteenth Army. In the south were Army Group G, commanded by Gen. Paul Hausser, consisting of First Army and Nineteenth Army.

Kesselring had neither the quality nor the quantity of troops that he would have wished. So bad was the troop shortage that the German manpower barrel, already scraped virtually clean, was plundered for one last time. It was now the turn of the Volkssturm – the Home Guard – to help stop the Allied advance. Even taking into account the use of the sick and elderly, the Germans could still only manage to raise 26 full strength divisions in the west. Moreover, many of the troops lacked any desire to continue fighting in a war that they perceived as already lost. The German High Command was compelled to initiate new awards in the hope that it would help soldiers find from within themselves some as yet untapped source of fighting spirit. There were medals for fighting out of an encirclement and back to friendly lines and there was even the offer of a signed photograph

Below: Men of the 22nd Infantry Regiment round up demoralized SS troopers in the Dachau area of southern Germany at the end of April 1945 as the US Seventh Army advanced toward western Austria.

Left: A Waffen-SS 'Soldbuch.' This booklet was issued to every recruit and served as a paybook and identification document. It also recorded the soldier's service numbers, blood group, and gas mask size. Unfortunately the name of this particular example is indecipherable.

of von Rundstedt for acts of bravery – although few, unsurprisingly, applied for such an award. In such circumstances, the High Command was forced to use the direct threat of the firing squad in order to regain discipline. Failure to blow a bridge or withdrawing without orders were just two of a plethora of offences made punishable by death.

Thus a once loyal and successful army which demanded that every man swear an oath of "unconditional obedience to the Führer" was, by late March 1945, having to be gripped by an iron fist of fear which squeezed relentlessly. The German army was on the point of destruction and ready to exacerbate this situation were four million Allied soldiers.

The scene was set for the climax of the war in western Europe. Kesselring's front was about to be ripped apart.

March 28 was a turning point in World War II. Up to this point Eisenhower had often stated that his strategic objective was Berlin, an objective that had certainly caught the imagination of the public on both sides of the Atlantic. However, on the 28th, just as 21st Army Group were beginning their advance across the north German plain towards the German capital, Montgomery received a telegram outlining a change in strategy. Eisenhower now declared that the main thrust was to be moved away from 21st Army Group and Berlin and towards 12th Army Group and the Elbe and Mulde Rivers. The aim was to cut the German army in half and ultimately, to facilitate a smooth union with Stalin's Red Army.

To aid the advance, Bradley was to regain Ninth Army from Montgomery's command and was to also use the newly created Fifteenth Army, commanded by Lt. Gen. Leonard Gerow, to conduct the defense of the west bank of the Rhine. 21st Army Group were to protect Bradley's left flank and then clear Holland, seize the north German ports, cut off Denmark and reach the Baltic before the

Below: On the left are German Army rank insignia of (from the top): lance-corporal-major (stabsgefreiter); senior lance-corporal (obergefreiter); lance corporal (gefreiter). The insignia on the right are trade and proficiency badges, (from the top): Luftwaffe and Army transport sergeant (schirrmeister); artillery gun layer, Army (richtkanonier).
Salamander Books

Soviets. 6th Army Group were to support Bradley's right flank and then drive into southern Germany and on into Austria.

Why had Eisenhower, the man who had written in September 1944, ". . . clearing Berlin is the main prize . . . we should concentrate all our energies and resources on a rapid thrust to Berlin" now changed his mind?

Firstly the American, Soviet and British political leaders had agreed in July 1944 that after the war Germany was to be carved up into National Zones of Occupation. These arrangements, confirmed at Yalta in February 1945, ensured that Berlin would become an area controlled by all three powers even though it was deep inside the proposed Soviet zone. Thus the capture of Berlin could no longer be considered a priority for the British and Americans unless it was deemed either vital strategically, or necessary in trying to keep the Soviets out of central Germany.

The second reason for the change in strategy stemmed from Eisenhower's own belief that Berlin was no longer strategically important. The supreme commander argued that the war could be shortened more effectively if other, more critical, military objectives were seized instead of Berlin. To this end he wrote in his telegram to Montgomery on March 28:

> You will see that in none of [my plan] do I mention Berlin. So far as I am concerned, that place has become nothing but a geographical location; I have never been interested in these.

Indeed, Eisenhower now wanted to seize the Ruhr as a matter of priority. The Ruhr was Germany's industrial heartland and contained Model's Fifth Panzer and Fifteenth Armies. Even if SHAEF did believe reports that the region's industrial output had suffered a mortal blow through Allied bombing raids, Eisenhower wanted to make sure and thus despatched the US Ninth and First Armies to encircle it. The Supreme Allied Commander was clearly not in the business of taking any chances at this stage in the war.

The third reason for the strategic realignment was the perceived necessity of advancing south into the mountains of Bavaria and Austria. It was believed that in this area, some 240 miles (384km) long and 80 miles (128km) deep, the Allies would find the "German National Redoubt," the final ideological demonstration of National Socialist resistance. SHAEF intelligence talked of SS troops, jet aircraft and crucially, "some of the most important ministries and personalities of the Nazi regime" moving into the area. This National Redoubt, because it was sited in such treacherous terrain, threatened to be an awkward and costly fortress to clear

Below: The nature of the war's last campaigns was shaped as much by political decisions on the part of the "big three" (from left to right Churchill, Roosevelt and Stalin) as by purely military considerations. The three leaders are seen here at the Yalta Conference in February 1945.

if the Germans were given time to consolidate in the area. Eisenhower was adamant that the Nazi's were to be given no such time.

The fourth reason for the change in strategy was based upon distance and weight of numbers. By the end of March, the Soviets had over two million men just 30 miles (48km) from Berlin whilst the Allies were 200 miles (320km) away, back on the Rhine. The supreme commander was also influenced by Bradley's estimate that it would cost approximately 100,000 casualties to take Berlin, a price that was generally regarded as too high for a "mere symbol."

Whilst these four reasons for changing stgrategic priorities were confessed by Eisenhower, there was also, very probably, an unconfessed influence upon his decision to change tack. The supreme commander was under a great deal of pressure not to allow the British to capture the prestigious prize of Berlin whilst the Americans played a merely supportive role. The United States were clearly the driving force behind the western war effort and Bradley in particular thought that the Americans should gain the lion's share of the glory when victory eventually came – or at least that the glory should be denied the British. Bradley argued that both his own reputation and that of the United States Army had been tarnished when Montgomery had been given command of a large part of 12th Army Group at a critical phase in the German Ardennes counteroffensive of the previous December. It seems less than likely that Eisenhower was left uninfluenced by Bradley's comments.

Thus, despite British protest, the Allied strategy was altered. 12th Army Group were now to lead an offensive aimed at the Elbe and Mulde Rivers and a successful union with the Soviet forces advancing from the east. Boldness had been replaced by caution.

On March 28, Lt. Gen. Dempsey's British Second Army, advancing on a three-corps front, broke out of its Rhine bridgehead at Wesel. By April 5, with their right directed on Uelzen and their left on Bremen, the British were fast approaching the Weser River. Three days later two corps had crossed the Weser and one of them, VIII Corps, had also gained a bridgehead over the Leine River just north of Hanover. It was at this point, however, that VIII Corps ran into Panzer Training Battalion 'Grossdeutschland' and were held up. Although the Germans were generally weak in the west they did often make good use of defensive positions and fought bravely to slow the Allied onslaught. Indeed, Montgomery used the delay on the Leine to justify his claim for more troops to aid his advance. The 21st Army Group commander thought that extra manpower was vital if the Second Army had any hope of blocking a Soviet advance to the North Sea. Help was eventually to come in two forms

Above: Allied and German propaganda leaflets, designed to destroy enemy morale. Top left: A leaflet sent to German troops in Normandy in August 1944, playing on the German army's role in the Hitler assassination plot. Top right and center: German leaflets claiming that Allied sacrifices were being exploited by Stalin. Bottom: A German leaflet to the Allied troops in Normandy during the stalemated fighting of June/July, 1944.
D-Day Museum, Portsmouth

Above: A US M1 bayonet. This was introduced for use on the M1 Garand rifle in 1943. The single-edged blade is 10in (25cm) long; the weapon overall being 14.5in (36cm) long.
Salamander Books

from Eisenhower. It was decided that Bradley could look after his own left flank (thus freeing more British troops to concentrate on the Second Army advance) and also, that Dempsey was to be given the use of US XVIII Airborne Corps to help seize a line from the Elbe to the Baltic Sea.

By April 18 all three British corps were advancing well: on the left, XXX Corps were on the outskirts of Bremen; XII Corps, in the center, were moving towards Hamburg; and VIII Corps, on the right, having snatched Lüneburg, were just short of the Elbe. The British had advanced some 200 miles (320km) in just three weeks.

The Canadian First Army, commanded by Lt. Gen. Crerar, advanced on a two-corps front with the aim of clearing eastern Holland, the area south of the Zuider Zee and the Wilhelmshaven Peninsula.

The Canadians advanced out of their Emmerich bridgehead on April 2, and within two days had reached the Twente Canal. From here, II Corps were to break north and northeast whilst I Corps were to attack west across the Ijssel River. By the second week in April the Canadians were making fast progress; indeed, on April 8, II Corps crossed the Eems River at Meppen and by the 10th had not only taken Deventer and Zwolle but were also moving towards Oldenburg in Germany.

On April 12, a division from I Corps attacked across the Ijssel River towards Arnhem. The town that had been the focus of so much attention and fighting in September 1944 took just three days to overcome in April 1945. Canadian success continued when the Zuider Zee was eventually reached on April 18, after Apeldoorn had been overrun two days earlier. By the third week of April, therefore, I Corps were looking across the Eem and Grebbe Rivers towards a starving Dutch population which desperately needed help.

The US Ninth and First Armies, commanded by Lt. Gen. William Simpson and Gen. Courtney Hodges respectively, began their encirclement of the Ruhr on March 28. Field Marshal Model did try to break out by counterattacking in the north near Hamm and in the south near Siegen, but both attempts failed and, on April 1, the two American armies met at Lippstadt.

The mopping up of the Ruhr was a relatively slow process because of both the terrain and the nature of the built-up industrial environment As the Americans advanced they could clearly see the ragged state of both the army and the civilian population in the pocket. The bombing had devastated three quarters of the housing in the region and communications were hopeless. For the besieged Germans, what little food and ammunition there was could not get to where it was most needed and by April 12, as the Americans reached Essen, it was impossible to send anything anywhere at all.

Gen. Kochling, a commander of LXXXI Corps, one of the encircled formations, later said of these dark days:

> The continuation of resistance in the Ruhr pocket was a crime. It was Model's duty to surrender . . . only the danger of reprisals against my family prevented me from taking this step myself.

What little fighting spirit there had been in the German troops soon evaporated as the Americans advanced, indeed it was not uncommon for the Wehrmacht soldiers to celebrate upon hearing that another town had fallen.

By April 14, the Germans were surrendering at such a rate that dealing with them became a problem for the Americans. On this day, the pocket had been split when a corps from Ninth Army and two from First Army met near Hagen on the Ruhr River. On April 16, some 80,000 Germans surrendered in just 24 hours. Two days later, a massive 325,000 German soldiers (including 30 generals) were taken prisoner and all organized armed resistance came to an end. On April 29, Field Marshal Model, the man who had criticized Field Marshal Paulus for surrendering at Stalingrad in January 1943, walked out into some woods near Düsseldorf and shot himself.

The Ninth Army continued to push east towards the Elbe River in the opening days of April. On April 4 elements of the Ninth Army were on the Weser River, on the 8th they had bridged the Leine, on the 10th Hanover was seized and, remarkably, on the 11th the Elbe River was reached just south of Magdeburg.

This incredible advance prompted Eisenhower into a statement about exactly where the 12th Army Group stop-line would be. It was decided that the line would run from Wittenberge in the north to Bayreuth in the south, connecting Dessau, Leipzig and Chemnitz on the Elbe and Mulde Rivers. It was therefore the case that by April 11, Ninth Army's forward element had moved as far east as Eisenhower would allow – despite the fact that Berlin was only two days away at the current rate of advance. Eisenhower was not drawn into a mad dash to Berlin despite the pressure put on him by some commanders. The supreme commander, emphasized the need to clear his flanks, to achieve a problem-free union with the Soviets and, as he wrote to the Combined Chiefs of Staff on April 15, "It must be remembered that only our spearheads are up to the river; our centre of gravity is way back of there."

The First Army also made great progress towards their eastern objectives from a very early stage. By April 9, with Kassel and Göttingen already seized, Gen. Hodges' troops were heading for the Harz mountains, where they cooperated with the Ninth Army in the envelopment of some 15,000 German troops. These were members

Below: Oblivious to the passing men from the 180th Infantry Regiment of the US Seventh Army's 45th Division, a German woman looks despairingly at the ruination of her home in Bensheim. March 27, 1945.

Above: The cap badge, collar badge, button and shoulder title (post-1920) of the Royal Scots Greys. The regiment swapped its famous grey mounts for tanks before the war and was one of the leading units in the Allied drive to the Baltic. The eagle emblem makes reference to one of the regiment's most famous battle honors, that of Waterloo in 1815. The regiment was amalgamated in the 1960s.
Salamander Books

of Wenck's newly formed Eleventh Army, which had only just been formed and which was supposed, in theory, to have gone to Model's assistance in the Ruhr. In practice however, the Germans had been overwhelmed by the speed of the American advance and as a result, on April 18, were encircled. By this point the First Army had reached their stop-line on the Mulde River at Dessau and had to call a halt to their advance.

The Third Army, commanded by Gen. George Patton, had also broken out of their bridgehead at the end of March and immediately fanned out. Some units cleared Frankfurt, others moved in on Kassel and Gotha (both eventually overrun on April 4) whilst others still advanced towards the Thüringian Forest.

By the second week in April, large areas of the forest had been cleared and by the 14th Chemnitz, Hoth and Bayreuth had been reached. Indeed, the advance was going so well that Patton asked Eisenhower for permission to advance into Czechoslovakia. The supreme commander replied that he could not order any such move until the flanks of 12th Army Group had been cleared, but in principle he was in favor of an advance up to the line Carlsbad–Pilsen–Budejovice.

Although for the time being any thrust into Czechoslovakia had to be put on hold, Patton was asked to move down into the Bohemian Forest to link up with the Soviets in the Danube Valley. This advance was to be co-ordinated with 6th Army Group who had already begun the clearance of southern Germany.

By April 4 the US Seventh Army, commanded by Lt. Gen. Patch, were on the outskirts of Würzburg whilst the First French, commanded by Gen. Jean de Lattre de Tassigny, were busy in Karlsruhe. Both armies came up against stiffer opposition here than could be found elsewhere on the front. On April 7, for example, 10th Armored Division were forced to withdraw after an attack on Crailsheim failed due to the strength of the German defense. It seems that at this stage Hausser's troops of Army Group G were not as demoralized as those who bore the brunt of the Allied offensive further to the north.

The Germans were not, of course, strong enough to halt the American advance altogether. By April 8, Seventh Army had captured Schweinfurt and were soon on their way, via the Hohe Rhön Mountains, to Nuremberg which was eventually reached nine days later. By this stage the French had started to engage the German Nineteenth Army in the Stuttgart–Black Forest area and were already focusing on the Austrian border.

With the Allies having taken over one million prisoners since the beginning of April, the German army in the west was clearly on the point of disintegration. Even though President Roosevelt had died on April 12, the

Allies remained calm and assured whilst the Germans sank further into a state of panic and confusion.

By April 18, Hitler had little of Germany, save Bavaria, under his command. By the fourth week of April, Zhukov's lead tanks had penetrated the eastern suburbs of Berlin whilst in northern Italy, Field Marshal Alexander's offensive was progressing well. Yet whilst Hitler was still alive German commanders, possibly due to their oath of allegiance but more probably due to the fear of retribution, would not surrender.

In the last week of April, with the British Second Army on the Elbe, on the outskirts of Hamburg and in the vicinity of Bremen, Montgomery and Dempsey discussed the next phase of their operations. The British were to clear Bremen and the Cuxhaven Peninsula, across the Elbe, advance up to the Danish border and, as a matter of priority, reach the Baltic before the Soviets managed to slip through to the North Sea.

At Bremen, XXX Corps commander, Lt. Gen. Horrocks, decided to give the Germans a chance to surrender before he attacked. Nobody in the city, however, had the courage to take the necessary decision and as a result fighting lasted for five days. Once again the German people were made to suffer for Hitler's tyranny. On April 25, medium and heavy bombers hit Bremen levelling many areas. A ground attack followed. As the British soldiers entered the devastated city, it was quite clear that the Germans were both disoriented and dispirited. The British took possession of Bremen on the 27th April and immediately turned north to face their next objective, the Cuxhaven Peninsula.

Meanwhile, with Berlin finally encircled by Soviet troops on April 25, the British had now to reach the Baltic as quickly as possible. Dempsey crossed the Elbe at Lauenburg on April 28 and from there advanced north to Lübeck and west to Hamburg – both capitulated on May 2. US XVIII Airborne Corps meanwhile, joined by British 6th Airborne Division, crossed the Elbe at Darchau and sped north for the Baltic. Wismar was reached on May 2, just hours before the Soviets.

Stalin was never in any doubt as to Eisenhower's intentions, because on April 30, the Allied Supreme Commander had sent him a telegram outlining his plans. The 21st Army Group would hold a line from Wismar to Dömitz on the Elbe and also occupy the area up to the Kiel Canal. The 12th Army Group would hold their position on the Elbe and Mulde Rivers although Third Army, resources allowing, would advance into Czechoslovakia. The 6th Army Group would continue to advance deeper into southern Germany and penetrate into Austria. Eisenhower now eagerly awaited Stalin's response to these plans and continued to withhold Patton's thrust into Czechoslovakia until one was received.

Below: The Sherman Firefly was the US M4 medium tank carrying the potent British 17-pounder gun. These Fireflies are of the Royal Scots Greys in Wismar, eastern limit of the British advance, on May 2, 1945.

The Canadians meanwhile, although not having the problem of encroaching upon territory earmarked by the Soviets, did have difficulties of their own. Whilst II Corps, firmly established across the Küsten Canal, continued to advance slowly up into the Wilhelmshaven Peninsula, I Corps awaited orders to advance over the Eem and Grebbe Rivers to relieve the starving Dutch population – but the orders never came. Montgomery feared that the German commander in the region, Gen. Blaskowitz and Reichskommissar Seyss-Inquart would carry out their threat to open dykes protecting The Netherlands from the damaging salt waters of the North Sea and the Zuider Zee if the Canadians continued to advance. Thus, on April 30, Eisenhower sent his chief-of-staff, Lt. Gen. Walter Bedell-Smith to talk to the two men. The Germans agreed to a truce period during which time the Allies could drop food behind their lines, but when Bedell-Smith mentioned surrender it was clear that neither man wanted the responsibility.

In the 12th Army Group area, with Ninth Army firmly established along their stop-line, the First Army continued to mop up the remaining pockets of German resistance on their front. Halle and Leipzig were captured on April 19, after a great deal of street fighting, and Dessau was taken on the 22nd. Two days later, Hodges' men reached their own stop line on the Mulde and, on the following day, the forward elements of 69th Division linked up with Marshal Konev's 58th Guards Division

Below: An M4 Sherman medium tank of the US Third Army's 11th Armored Division trundles past streams of German prisoners in Gallneukirchen on the Czech/Austrian border during the last days of the war May 4, 1945.

on the Elbe. The first link had been successfully made and soon Soviet and American troops were shaking hands all along the front.

Patton meanwhile, still awaited orders from Eisenhower to move into Czechoslovakia, but while he was waiting his Third Army continued their thrust south. On April 25, Patton's men crossed the Danube River and on the following day, overran Regensburg before heading for Austria and Linz. Linz was finally captured on May 5, just one day after Eisenhower received word that the Soviet High Command had agreed to his boundaries. As a result the Third Army was ordered to seize the line Carlsbad–Pilsen–Budejovice whilst the Soviets, much to Patton's dismay, were left the rest of Czechoslovakia including Prague.

On Third Army's right, the US Seventh Army and French First Army were still making good progress. On April 20, the Americans finally captured Nuremberg after a five-day battle and the French took Stuttgart. By April 22, both Armies had crossed the Danube and in so doing finally shattered Gen. Hausser's Army Group G. Ulm was taken by the Americans on the 23rd, whilst the

Above: An embroidered flag presented to Gen. George Patton by the officers of the Third Army on his relinquishment of that command on October 7, 1945, a little over two months before his death. The flag bears the emblems of every Third Army Division.
Patton Museum of Cavalry and Armor

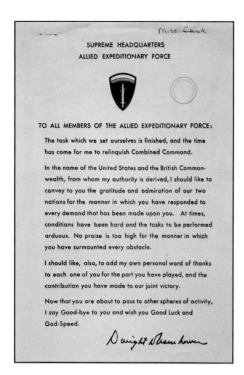

SUPREME HEADQUARTERS
ALLIED EXPEDITIONARY FORCE

TO ALL MEMBERS OF THE ALLIED EXPEDITIONARY FORCE:

The task which we set ourselves is finished, and the time has come for me to relinquish Combined Command.

In the name of the United States and the British Commonwealth, from whom my authority is derived, I should like to convey to you the gratitude and admiration of our two nations for the manner in which you have responded to every demand that has been made upon you. At times, conditions have been hard and the tasks to be performed arduous. No praise is too high for the manner in which you have surmounted every obstacle.

I should like, also, to add my own personal word of thanks to each one of you for the part you have played, and the contribution you have made to our joint victory.

Now that you are about to pass to other spheres of activity, I say Good-bye to you and wish you Good Luck and God-Speed.

Dwight D Eisenhower

Above: Gen. Eisenhower's farewell message to the Allied Expeditionary Force, issued July 14, 1945 on the formal ending of SHAEF's combined command.
Eisenhower Library and Museum

Right: Full circle at the end of a long and totally disastrous road for Germany a German soldier, morally broken but still alive, is posed in front of the Reichstag in Berlin for Soviet propaganda photography.

French were to reach Lake Constance on the Swiss border a few days later. By the end of the month, Seventh Army had moved into Dachau and Munich and the First French had entered Austria. By May 3, the American forces were in Austria, at Innsbruck where they quickly advanced to the Brenner Pass and linked up with the US Fifth Army which had fought its way up through Italy. Other units meanwhile seized Salzburg on May 4 and some even penetrated as far as the bombed ruins of Hitler's mountain retreat, the Berchtesgaden. German resistance had all but vanished.

By the last week in April, it was clear to everyone that the war was nearly over. Indeed, it was at this time that Heinrich Himmler tried to seek surrender without Hitler's approval. On April 23 Himmler, Hitler's SS Reichsführer, contacted the head of the Swedish Red Cross at Lübeck and told him that he felt at liberty to ask the Swedish Government to let the Allies know that the

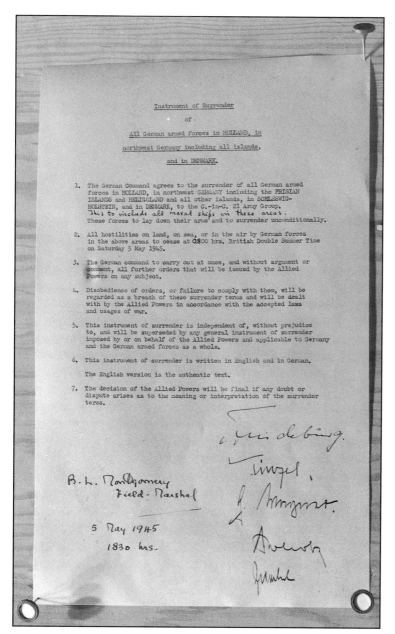

Left: The first of the German surrender documents was that signed on Lüneburg heath outside Hamburg on May 3, 1945 and signaling the capitulation of the German forces in northern Germany.

Below: Field Marshal Wilhelm Keitel, the Chief of the High Command of the German Armed Forces, signs the final German surrender document in Berlin on May 7, 1945 at the headquarters of the 1st Belorussian Front.

German Government were prepared to surrender on the Western Front.

Himmler's attempts to initiate a surrender failed immediately. The British Prime Minister, Winston Churchill, quickly informed both the Americans and the Soviets of Himmler's overtures in accordance with a secret 1943 protocol. This protocol pledged that the American, Soviet and British Governments would consult each other if the German Government ever came forward with a surrender proposal. The British Cabinet made it quite clear in their reply to Himmler that whilst the surrender of a front, or an army, or indeed any lower formation, by a German commander was acceptable in the field (as this was a tactical and military matter) the German Government could only surrender unconditionally on all fronts.

Above: The closing stages of the war saw some extraordinary events: shot as they left their SdKfz 250/1 half-track in Berlin, these men were Swedish volunteers of the 11th SS Panzergrenadier Division 'Nordland.'

Whilst Himmler was making his offer to the British, the Germans were finally beaten in Italy. On April 29, as the result of the Allied offensive, General von Vietinghoff signed unconditional surrender at Alexander's headquarters (see Chapter 6). The thirty days of April had not been happy ones for Field Marshal Kesselring; indeed the month had seen the western powers take over 1.65 million prisoners including Field Marshals von Kleist, von Leeb, Weichs, List and von Rundstedt. This brought the total number of prisoners taken since June 1944 to almost three million. The German army simply could not withstand this sort of pressure for much longer.

Even Hitler, hidden away in his underground bunker at the heart of a smouldering Berlin, recognized the gravity of the situation. On April 29, the Führer appointed Grand Adm. Dönitz as his successor in the event of his death. Dönitz did not have to wait long before he took up his unenviable new position. On April 30, ten days after his 56th birthday, Hitler and his new wife, Eva Braun, committed suicide as the Soviets reached the Reichstag.

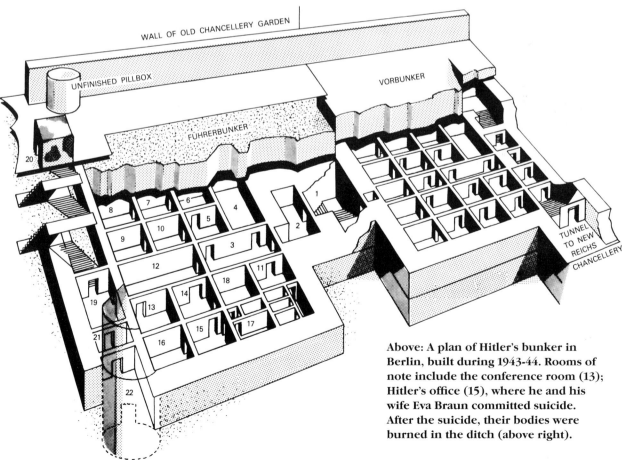

WALL OF OLD CHANCELLERY GARDEN

UNFINISHED PILLBOX

VORBUNKER

FÜHRERBUNKER

TUNNEL TO NEW REICHS CHANCELLERY

Above: A plan of Hitler's bunker in Berlin, built during 1943-44. Rooms of note include the conference room (13); Hitler's office (15), where he and his wife Eva Braun committed suicide. After the suicide, their bodies were burned in the ditch (above right).

195

Above: Uniforms and post-war awards of Gen. Eisenhower. These include from the left (top), a piece of the SHAEF dinner service; gold dagger presented by Marshal Zhukov; diamond and ruby-encrusted Soviet Order of Victory; Gen. Eisenhower's overcoat and service jacket and cap; a jewel-encrusted gold saber and scabbard presented by the Royal Family and People of Holland; the general's lucky coins; and inset and not to scale, a gold Cartier cigarette case presented by Gen. Charles de Gaulle. *Eisenhower Library and Museum*

As news of Hitler's death and Dönitz's appointment reached the front, the remaining pockets of resistance began to negotiate for peace independently. Floods of German soldiers moved across the increasingly small strip of land dividing the Eastern and Western Fronts so that they could surrender to the Anglo–American forces.

On May 4, at Montgomery's headquarters at Lüneburg Heath, Dönitz's envoys agreed to the unconditional surrender of German forces in Holland, Denmark and North Germany with effect from 08:30 hours on May 5.

The 21st Army Group immediately received a tour by the effervescent Field Marshal Montgomery who addressed his victorious troops. Montgomery said that

they had been successful for four main reasons: enemy mistakes, Allied dominance, Anglo–American cooperation and the fighting abilities of the British, Canadian and American soldiers.

On May 5, Dönitz's representatives arrived at Eisenhower's headquarters at Reims in France to negotiate unconditional surrender. Once again the Germans tried to stall the process but the supreme commander demanded the surrender immediately. At 02:40 on May 7, Adm. von Friedeburg and Gen. Jodl signed the surrender document with British, Soviet and French representatives present. Operations ceased at 23:01 hours central European time on May 8.

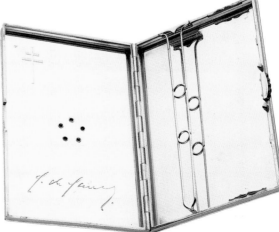

V Twelve
The Battle for Berlin:
April-May 1945

David Glantz

For Stalin and the Soviets, their "Great Patriotic War" could end in only one place – Berlin. As the Red Army juggernaut closed in on the German capital, the world watched and waited for the end.

In retrospect, the battle for Berlin in April 1945 served as a dénouement to the bitter fighting which had occurred over almost four years of war. The Soviets' offensive action had endured for so long, and successive German disasters had been so numerous that one could dismiss the Berlin operation as just the final humiliation of a once proud and mighty German army. True, the results of the operation were foreordained. Allied victory was but weeks away, for someone was going to seize Berlin, and soon. The only question was, which army would engage the remnants of the German military establishment in the final *Götterdämmerung*, the Soviets' or those of their western allies. It was only fitting that this task fell to the Soviets, as Roosevelt and Churchill had earlier ordained. The soundless cries of over ten million Soviet military dead compelled the *Stavka* to undertake the last great operation of her "Great Patriotic War."

The Soviets did not undertake the task lightly. As astute students of history, they recalled the fate of earlier Russian armies, at the gates of Berlin in 1760 and at the gates of Warsaw in 1920, when Russian hopes had been dashed by over-optimism and unfortunate circumstances. The Soviets determined that history would not repeat itself. The Soviet command estimated the Germans would field a force of one million – the desperate remnants of the German army, and, deep down, they were unsure of how many Germans in the west would join their comrades along the Oder to face the more dreaded and feared Soviet army. Experience had demonstrated that a force of one million men could render credible resistance along a river barrier (the Oder),

Left: Signals of victory: triumphant Soviet soldiers raise their flags over the Brandenburg Gate in the middle of Berlin as the capital of Germany falls to the Red Army on May 2, 1945.

Above: Vienna, the capital of Austria that had been annexed to Germany in 1938, fell on April 14, 1945. Yet again the German defense was determined if ultimately doomed, and here Soviet troops fight for the Emperor Bridge.

even against a force more than twice its size.

Thus the Soviets prepared an offensive fitting the task – an offensive that would leave little in doubt – an offensive whose conduct would do the Soviets credit in the eyes of her allies who were approaching from the west.

In early March 1945, while Soviet forces were clearing German forces from the flanks of their advanced positions along the Oder River, the German High Command organized and conducted its last major offensive of the war, an attempt to defeat Soviet forces around Budapest and recapture the economically important Balaton oil fields. Hitler redeployed his elite Sixth SS Panzer Army from the Ardennes to Hungary and ordered it, together with Sixth Army and Second Panzer Army, to smash Soviet defenses in Hungary and retake Budapest. The German operational concept called for Sixth SS Panzer and Sixth Armies to attack southeast on March 6 from positions north of Lake Balaton and link up along the Danube River with the Second Panzer Army advancing eastward, south of Lake Balaton. The combined force would then push Soviet forces to the banks of the Danube River and reoccupy Budapest.

Coincidentally, while the Germans planned their offensive, the Soviet 2nd and 3rd Ukrainian Fronts planned an offensive of their own to begin on March 15 to clear Hungary of German forces, invade Austria, and divert German attention from the Berlin axis. The Soviet plan called for three combined-arms armies, including

Below: Based on a design produced in Leningrad during the siege, the Soviet PPS43 submachine gun was a robust, but crudely made weapon of pressed steel. It fired the standard pistol cartridge of 7.62mm, held in a 35 round magazine. Its rate of fire was a phenomenal 700 rounds per minute. *Imperial War Museum, London*

9th Guards Army, a special army designated to be employed only in offensive actions, and 6th Guards Tank Army to attack from positions west of Budapest to destroy defending German forces and advance on Vienna.

More than two weeks prior to the German offensive, the Soviets learned of the Germans' intent and formed a dense and deep defense west of Budapest. The *Stavka* specifically prohibited defensive use of 9th Guards and 6th Guards Tank Armies and directed that their offensive preparations continue even during the impending defensive operation. The two Soviet *fronts*, less 9th Guards Army and 6th Guards Tank Army, were to be prepared to defend by March 5, after a force regrouping.

The German offensive commenced on March 6, when III Panzer, II SS Panzer, and I Cavalry Corps assaulted Soviet positions north of Lake Balaton. An agonizingly slow and costly German advance ensued. By March 15, German forces had penetrated only 6–15 miles (10–25km) into the Soviet defenses. Judiciously using its reserves, 3rd Ukrainian Front absorbed the shock of the German offensive; its defenses bent, but did not break.

Once the German assault had been halted, and without a pause, on March 16, the two Soviet *fronts* launched their own offensive. The subsequent Soviet Vienna offensive operation developed slowly, but ultimately drove German forces from Hungary to the gates of Vienna, which fell on April 15, after only desultory fighting, only one day before Soviet artillery opened its devastating barrage along the Oder River announcing the final Soviet drive on Berlin.

Below: Soviet infantrymen stand guard near Vienna's town hall at the beginning of an occupation that was to be considerably shorter than that of any other European capital seized by the Soviet armies in 1944 and 1945.

Above: The Soviet order of Lenin. This award was instituted in 1930 by the Central Executive Committee of the USSR. It could be presented to Soviet citizens, organizations, institutions and foreigners for service to the state both civil and military. The inscription reads: "Lenin."
Imperial War Museum, London

The Berlin operation, the concluding Soviet wartime strategic offensive operation in the west, was conducted by Soviet forces from April 16 to May 8, 1945. *Stavka* aims were to destroy German forces defending the Berlin axis, secure Berlin, and link up with advancing Allied forces on the Elbe River. By mid-April 1945, American and British forces had reached the Elbe only 62–75 miles (100–120km) from the German capital, and there were very real Soviet concerns that Allied armies would themselves advance on Berlin. These concerns accelerated the Berlin operation. In addition, the Soviets feared that German forces would be shifted east to join the defenders of the Oder–Neisse line.

German forces defending the approaches to Berlin included German Army Group Vistula (Third Panzer and Ninth Armies), commanded by Gen. Heinrici, elements of Army Group Center, commanded by Field Marshal Schoerner (Fourth Panzer Army), and the ill-defined Berlin Garrison. Army Group Vistula consisted of six corps (25 divisions) and a large number of separate and specialized units and formations. Army Group Center committed elements of two corps to the operation, and the Berlin Garrison consisted of one corps (LVI Panzer of 5–6 divisions) and over 50 volkssturm battalions. The combined force totalled about 800,000 men.

German defenses along the Berlin axis were deep, but only partially occupied by troops. They consisted of the fully occupied Oder–Neisse defense line to a depth of 12–24 miles (20–40km), which in turn consisted of three defensive belts, and the Berlin defensive region, which consisted of three defensive rings (external,

Left: The Soviets knew that the battle for Berlin would be as bloody as any they had encountered. Here Marshal Georgi Zhukov and other commanders of the 1st Belorussian Front attend an April 1945 planning meeting.

internal, and city). To control units effectively, the city was subdivided into nine sectors. The central sector, which included governmental and administrative organs (Reichstag and Imperial Chancellery), was best prepared for defense. All defensive positions were interconnected by means of integrated communications. The metro (subway) system was employed to maneuver forces secretly. In an engineering sense, the defenses opposite the Küstrin bridgehead held the strongest German concentrations located as they were on the highway to the German capital. Hitler intended to fight to the end in Berlin, and hoped in vain for a breach in the Anglo–American–Soviet alliance. Instead the Soviets and the Allies agreed to fight for nothing short of an unconditional surrender.

Soviet forces assembled to conduct the operation consisted of Marshal K. K. Rokossovsky's 2nd Belorussian Front (five combined armies, one air army, and five mobile corps), Marshal G. K. Zhukov's 1st Belorussian Front (seven Soviet and one Polish combined-arms armies, two tank armies, two air armies, and four mobile corps), and Marshal I. S. Konev's 1st Ukrainian Front (five Soviet and one Polish combined-arms armies, two tank armies, one air army, and four mobile corps), totalling 2,500,000 troops. Baltic Fleet and Dnieper Flotilla units and three air defense corps (PVO Strany) supported.

Planning for the Berlin operation commenced on April 1, the day after 1st Ukrainian Front completed operations in Upper Silesia and three days before 1st and 2nd Belorussian Fronts completed their operations to clear German forces from eastern Pomerania. That day

Below: The heaviest piece of artillery operated by the Soviet armies was a 203mm howitzer produced in six variants on a tracked rather than wheeled carriage. The weapon fired a 220.5 lb shell to 17,500 yds (15,750m).

Zhukov and Konev met in Moscow with Stalin, the *Stavka*, and the General Staff to formulate plans for the Berlin operation. Rokossovsky joined them on April 6. The *Stavka* approved the *front* commanders' plans and set the attack date for April 16, leaving just two weeks for detailed preparations.

The *Stavka* plan called for the destruction of German forces defending the Berlin axis by "the delivery of several powerful blows on a wide front to encircle and dismember the Berlin group and destroy each segment individually". Subsequently, within 12–15 days, Soviet forces were to capture Berlin and advance to the Elbe to link up with Allied armies. Zhukov's 1st Belorussian Front was to launch its main attack from the Küstrin bridgehead, with four armies supported by one tank corps. On the first day, these armies were to penetrate strong German tactical defenses on the Seelow Heights and secure commitment of 1st Guards and 2nd Guards Tank Armies into battle. The two tank armies would then lead the advance directly into Berlin, which was supposed to fall on the sixth day of battle. Zhukov planned two secondary attacks; one north of Küstrin with two armies and one south of Küstrin with two armies and a cavalry corps. Zhukov's assault was to begin in darkness and be illuminated by 143 searchlights to light the terrain and disorient the enemy.

On Zhukov's left flank, Konev's 1st Ukrainian Front was to launch its main attack with three armies supported by two tank corps across the Neisse River towards Cottbus. Lead forces were to reach the Spree River by the end of the second day and secure commitment to combat of 3rd and 4th Guards Tank Armies, which would then exploit toward Brandenburg, Dessau, and the southern limits of Berlin. Two reserve armies would reinforce Konev's main attack as it penetrated deep into Germany. Konev also planned a secondary attack with parts of two armies and two mobile corps towards Dresden to cover his left flank.

To the north, on Zhukov's right flank, Rokossovsky's 2nd Belorussian Front was to attack in the Stettin–Schwedt sector with three armies, supported by five mobile corps, to destroy German forces around Stettin, prevent Third Panzer Army from reinforcing German forces in Berlin, and advance to occupy northern Brandenburg and link up with British forces along the Elbe. Simultaneous with the Berlin offensive, 4th, 2nd, and 3rd Ukrainian Fronts, operating further south were to conduct demonstrative actions.

To create the shock groups necessary for the offensive, required extensive regrouping by all three *fronts*, which had to move from positions they occupied at the end of previous operations into new positions along the Oder River. A total of 29 armies had to regroup, 15 of them a distance of up to 238 miles (385km) and three between 328 and 186 miles (530 and 300km). All these movements had to be accomplished in 15 days (compared with 22–48 days available to move forces prior to the Belorussian, East Prussian, and Vistula–Oder operations).

Extensive support operations took place before the offensive. On six occasions reconnaissance aviation prepared aerial photo surveys of Berlin, all approaches to the city, and the defensive belts. On the basis of these surveys, captured documents, and POW interrogations, useful schemes, plans, and maps were distributed to all commanders and staffs. Engineer forces in 1st Belorussian Front sector constructed 25 bridges and 40 ferry crossings over the Oder River. To assist in crossing the Neisse River, 1st Ukrainian Front prepared 2,440 wooden sapper boats, 750 assault bridges, and more than 1,000 elements for wooden bridges. During the preparatory period, reserve equipment and materials were created in a relatively short period. All forces sharpened their skills in river crossings, and conducted exercises in city, forest, and night fighting. In particular, cooperation was worked out between forces for street fighting in large cities.

Just before the commencement of the operation, the Soviets conducted combat reconnaissance in the 1st Belorussian and 1st Ukrainian Front sectors. On April 14, after a 15–20-minute fire raid, reinforced rifle battalions from 1st Belorussian Front first echelon divisions began operations on the main attack axis. In some sectors, first echelon regiments joined the battle. In two days of combat, some succeeded in wedging up to three miles (5km) deep into enemy defenses. Subsequently, the operation developed in three distinct stages.

Below: Arguably the finest ground-attack warplane of World War II, the Il-1 'Shturmovik' was produced in vast numbers for the tactical support of the Soviet ground forces with cannon, bombs and rockets.

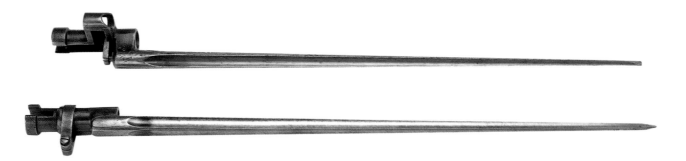

Above: Soviet Nagant rifle Model 91 spike bayonets.
Imperial War Museum

The first stage saw 1st Belorussian and 1st Ukrainian Front main forces attacking early on April 16. The night before, 4th and 16th Air Army planes struck German defenses in 1st Belorussian Front's sector, and, after the offensive began, four aviation corps of 18th Air Army struck strong points in the enemy's second defensive belt. The infantry and tanks advanced up to a mile (1.6km) but met strong enemy resistance and were themselves disoriented by the glaring searchlights. In order to accelerate the advance, on the first day Zhukov committed both 1st and 2nd Guards Tank Armies into battle. However, they too became involved in heavy combat, were intermixed with advancing infantry, and could not break through the strong defenses. Thereafter, *front* forces had to penetrate in succession, and in painstaking and costly fashion, a series of consecutive defensive belts. In the main attack sector facing Seelow

Right: Another able leader was Col. Gen. V. I. Chuikov, who ended the war as commander of the 8th Guards Army and is seen between Lt. Gens. Telegin and Kazakov of the 1st Belorrussian Front's command.

Heights, 8th Guards Army and 1st Guards Tank Army succeeded in penetrating the defenses only on April 17. By the end of April 19, they finally penetrated the third Oder defensive line and began a slow advance on Berlin proper. An impatient Stalin alternatively threatened and cajoled Zhukov on. Meanwhile, on Zhukov's right flank, 47th and 3rd Shock Armies developed the offensive more successfully and began to envelop Berlin from the north and northwest. On the left wing, Soviet successes cut off German Ninth Army from Berlin and paved the way for its envelopment from the north.

First Ukrainian Front forces, supported by 25th and 4th Guards Tank Corps and the forward detachments of 3rd and 4th Guards Tank Armies, forded the Neisse River, penetrated the enemy main defensive belt on the first day, and wedged up to a mile (1.6 km) into the second belt. By the end of April 18, Konev's forces had completed penetration of the Neisse defensive line and crossed the Spree River, creating conditions for the encirclement of Berlin from the south. On the Dresden axis, formations of 52nd Army repelled increasingly intense German counterattacks from the Görlitz region.

Impatient with the Zhukov's slow advance, Stalin personally altered original *front* missions by erasing a portion of the extended boundary line between Zhukov's 1st Belorussian and Konev's 1st Ukrainian Fronts on the *Stavka* operational map, thus implying that the latter could participate in the seizure of Berlin by attacking from the south, if the situation permitted. Meanwhile, on April 18 and 19, 2nd Belorussian Front joined the action by fording the eastern channel of the Oder River and occupying jumping-off positions on river islands for fording of the western channel.

On April 20, while the 1st Belorussian Front continued its offensive, the long-range artillery of 3rd Shock Army's 79th Rifle Corps first opened fire on Berlin, beginning the operation's second stage. The following day intermixed units of 3rd Shock, 2nd Guards Tanks, 47th, 8th Guards, and 1st Guards Tank Army penetrated into the suburbs of Berlin and began heavy and difficult urban combat.

Konev's Front maneuvered to complete the envelopment of German Ninth Army from the south and, at the same time, reach the southern outskirts of Berlin. On April 19–20 his 3rd and 4th Guards Tank armies advanced 58 miles (95km), and the following day 3rd Guards Tank Army elements penetrated into the southern suburbs of Berlin, and 4th Guards Tank Army reached the southern approaches to Potsdam. Combined-arms armies of the *front* shock group rapidly advanced westward, engaging in the process German Twelfth Army, the infamous new army of General Wenck, which had been turned eastward from the

Below: Berlin took a ghastly pounding in the fighting of April and May 1945 as the Soviet forces ground down the defense with armored vehicles and artillery of all calibers firing at pointblank range.

Above: Troops of the Western Allies and the USSR met along the line of the Elbe River from April 25, 1945. Here US and Soviet officers finalize the details of the line demarcating their zones of responsibility.

Above: The shoulder patch insignia of the US 69th Infantry Division. The 69th had entered Germany on March 8, and had crossed the Rhine by March 28. By April 16 it had fought its way across half of Germany and was in the suburbs of Leipzig, a city it took after hand-to-hand fighting on April 19. Forward elements of the division made contact with the Soviet 5th Guards Army at Torgau on the Elbe River six days later. *Salamander Books*

Right: Soviet troops rattle the sky above Berlin with a fusillade of small arms fire to signal their joy and relief at the end of this grim battle, which was one of the finest victories won by the Red Army.

Western Front to link up with German Ninth Army and save Berlin. From April 20–26, 2nd Polish and 52nd Army on 1st Ukrainian Front's extended left flank repelled Army Group Center counterattacks from the Görlitz region designed to break through and relieve German Ninth Army.

On April 24, Zhukov's 8th Guards and 1st Guards Tank Armies linked up with units from 1st Ukrainian Front's 3rd Guards Tank and 28th Armies southeast of Berlin, thus completing the encirclement of German Ninth Army southeast of Berlin. The next day forces of their *fronts* also united west of Berlin completing the encirclement of the entire Berlin Grouping, the same day that 5th Guards Army forces met at Torgau with advancing units of the American First Army. At the same time, 2nd Belorussian Front forces forded the western channel of the Oder River, penetrated German defenses on its western bank, and pinned down Third Panzer Army, depriving it of the opportunity to deliver a counterblow from the north on Soviet forces encircling Berlin.

In the third and last operational stage, the destruction of encircled German Ninth Army was completed between April 26 and May 1. Liquidation of German forces encircled in the city proper continued until May 2. By April 30, Soviet forces had cut the defending force into four isolated parts, and they set about smashing each in piecemeal fashion. In heavy fighting, which lasted several days, they succeeded in clearing the enemy from over 300 city blocks. Every street and house was taken by storm, using task-organized assault detachments and groups made up of infantry, artillery and tanks firing directly over open sights, and sappers armed with explosives. Heavy fighting occurred in the Metro and in underground communications installations.

On April 29, against strong resistance, 79th Rifle Corps of 1st Belorussian Front's 3rd Shock Army began the struggle for the Reichstag. The following day scouts from the 150th Rifle Division hoisted the Red Banner over the Reichstag, this symbolic act coming on the

Above: A Soviet TT33 7.62mm automatic pistol. This example, of 1942, reveals shortcuts taken in wartime production, such as the crude machining and wooden grips. *Imperial War Museum*

same day as Adolf Hitler's suicide in his bunker under the Reichs Chancellery. The battle for the Reichstag, however, continued until the morning of May 1, as Russian rooted bedraggled but stubborn groups out of basement cellars. On May 1, 3rd Shock Army forces attacking from the north linked up just south of the Reichstag with 8th Guards Army units advancing from the south. By the evening of May 2, German resistance fully ceased, and remnants of the Berlin Garrison, under the command of Gen. Weidling, finally surrendered.

While the German Berlin Garrison was capitulating, 1st Ukrainian Front forces began regrouping to prepare for an advance into Czechoslovakia along the Prague axis, while 1st Belorussian Front forces advanced

Right: The utter defeat of Germany is symbolized by this photograph taken on May 7, 1945, revealing the devastation of Berlin: the gutted Reichstag and the ruins around it.

Left: Troops of the British Second Army and Soviet 2nd Belorussian Front meet during May 7, 1945 on the Elbe River, which had been designated as the dividing line between the Allied and Soviet forces.

Below: Pockets of German resistance continued along the coast of the Baltic Sea as the Soviets swept west, but were soon reduced. These are German prisoners in Königsberg, which fell on April 9, 1945.

westward and, on May 7, reached the Elbe on a broad front. The 2nd Belorussian Front forces reached the shores of the Baltic Sea and the line of the Elbe where they linked up with Second British Army. At Karlshorst, on May 8, 1945, representatives of the German High Command signed the final act of unconditional surrender to the Allied powers. Meanwhile, Soviet forces eliminated resisting pockets of German forces in Courland and the Samland Peninsula, west of Königsberg.

During the course of the Berlin operation, Soviet forces crushed the remnants of the once vaunted Wehrmacht and captured 480,000 men. The cost, however, had been great, as 352,475 Soviet soldiers fell in the effort.

The Berlin operation was prepared in a relatively short period and its main aims – the encirclement and destruction of the main enemy shock grouping and the capture of Berlin – were achieved in 16–17 days. The Soviets considered the operation a classic example of an offensive by a group of *fronts* conducted with decisive aims in an almost ceremonial fashion. The simultaneous offensive by three *fronts* in a 186 mile (300km) sector with the delivery of six blows tied down enemy reserves, helped disorganize his command and control and, in some instances, led to the achievement of operational-tactical surprise.

The Berlin operation, in particular the poor performance of Zhukov's *front*, was instructive in other ways as well. As high level commissions formed after the war to study the operation determined, its nature and course

was somewhat different from the heavy combat Soviets had experienced on more open terrain further east. Combat in more heavily urban and wooded terrain exacted a far more costly toll on the attackers than Soviet planners had anticipated.

The final operation in the war on the Eastern Front involved the elimination of the Soviet's old nemesis, Army Group Center, a force which for over two years had been poised threateningly on the distant approaches to Moscow. In May 1945, over 600,000 men of this Army Group, now commanded by Gen. Schoerner, awaited inevitable destruction, ironically, not in Germany, but in Czechoslovakia, which back in 1938 had been one of Hitler's initial victims.

The Soviets turned their attention to this last remnant of German military power while the Reichstag was still under assault. Between May 1 and 6, the forces of Konev's 1st Ukrainian Front, Malinovsky's 2nd Ukrainian Front, and Gen. Eremenko's 4th Ukrainian Front regrouped to launch an overwhelming assault on Schoerner's force in conjunction, if not in competition, with George S. Patton's US Third Army, which was poised to enter Czechoslovakia from Bavaria. The combined force of over two million soldiers planned to use heavy tank forces, including two tank armies, to spearhead a rapid thrust directly on the Czech capital, Prague.

Taking advantage of local German withdrawals, Konev struck from the north of May 6, with three combined-arms armies and 3rd and 4th Guards Tank Armies, making his main attack from the Risa area. The next day he launched two secondary attacks with slightly smaller forces (including a Polish Army) further to the east. Malinovsky's Front struck northward from Brno toward Olomouc with four combined-arms armies, 6th Guards Tank Army, and 1st Guards Cavalry-Mechanized Group, with a supporting attack by two armies. In between Konev's and Malinovsky's forces, Eremenko's Front pressured German defenses across the entire front. The advance was timed to coincide with an uprising inside

Facing page: Soviet troops pose for their passport to immortality in front of the burned-out, pockmarked and rubble-strewn Reichstag in the center of Berlin, the wholly devastated German capital.

Below: A 'Cnopm' (Sport) camera produced in 1935 by Gomz in Leningrad. An example of one of the earliest single lens reflex cameras. The high quality of the camera suggests that it was in fact manufactured in Germany and assembled in Leningrad. Imperial War Museum

213

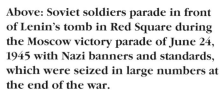

Above: Soviet soldiers parade in front of Lenin's tomb in Red Square during the Moscow victory parade of June 24, 1945 with Nazi banners and standards, which were seized in large numbers at the end of the war.

the city by the Prague resistance movement.

Within two days Konev's forces occupied Dresden, Bautzen, and Görlitz against dwindling German resistance, and 4th Ukrainian Front seized Olomouc and a day later linked up with advancing 2nd Ukrainian Front troops for a combined drive on Prague. To accelerate the advance, on the night of May 8–9, Konev ordered Rybalko's and Leliushenko's 3rd and 4th Guards Tank Armies to begin a dash for Prague. By first light the two armies had traversed 49 miles (80km) and linked up in the city with forward mobile elements of 2nd and 4th Ukrainian Fronts, which included Czech forces of the 1st Separate Czechoslovak Tank Brigade. During the following two days, Soviet forces liquidated and accepted the surrender of over 600,000 remaining German troops. On May 11, advance elements of 4th Guards Tank Army linked up with US Third Army forces east of Pilsen, completing the last operation of what the Soviets afterwards called "The Great Patriotic War."

The military consequences of operations in spring 1945 were clear. The remaining forces of the once proud and seemingly indestructible armies of Nazi Germany were crushed by the combined efforts of Allied forces assaulting from east and west. Nazi Germany, which had based its power and built its empire on the foundations of unprecedented warfare and violence, was felled in an equally violent and decisive fashion. The colossal scope

Left: The Nazi banners cast down during the Soviet victory parade were later placed in the Central Museum of the Soviet Armed Forces in Moscow. Symbolically, the 'Adolf Hitler' standard lies at the feet of the bronze eagle taken from the Reichs Chancellery in Berlin.

and scale of the Berlin operation, with the appalling Soviet casualties and equally massive destruction of the German capital, was a fitting end to a war which was unlike other wars. As more than one German veteran observed, war in the west was proper sport, while war in the east was unmitigated horror. This final horror had eliminated the remaining two million men of the Wehrmacht and had reduced Germany to ashes.

The political consequences of these last operations reflected a process which had been going on for over a year, a process which the victorious Allies had largely overlooked in their search for victory. That process now became crystal clear during the peace which followed. For, in the baggage of the victorious Red Army came political power in the guise of newly formed national armies for the liberated states and governments to go with those armies. Two Polish, three Romanian, and two Bulgarian armies fought alongside the Soviets, together with a Czech corps and other smaller national formations. Once returned to their liberated lands, they cooperated with local partisan formations, many also sponsored and equipped by the Soviet Union. These armed forces and the governments-in-exile which accompanied them, under protection of the Soviet Army, quickly transformed military into political power. Within a few short years, the horrors of war had been replaced by the menace of the Cold War.

Above: Men of the victorious Red Army heap the martial emblems of a defeated and indeed crushed Nazi Germany on the cobbles of Red Square in front of Stalin and the Soviet leadership, during the Moscow victory parade.

V Thirteen

Island by Island

Andrew Steed

**VE Day may have come to Europe,
but for the Americans in the Pacific
the war was far from over.
Each step closer to their Home Islands
produced greater fanaticism in the
Japanese defenders and more and more
bloodshed. Some began to wonder
how it would ever end.**

By attacking the United States at Pearl Harbor on December 7, 1941, Japan widened the "Second European Civil War" into a world war and facilitated American entry into the conflict – much to the relief of Britain. The attack on an unprepared base resulted in catastrophic losses to the defenders and negligible losses to the attackers; by noon on that Sunday, eight battleships, three cruisers, three destroyers and eight auxiliary craft had been immobilized, with 224 aircraft damaged and 3,400 people killed or wounded.

It appeared a model preemptive strike inflicting a crippling blow; the US Pacific Fleet had been virtually wiped out, enabling the Japanese to advance into the southwest Pacific, free from American interference. In the weeks that followed, the Japanese swept aside Dutch and British resistance and established an empire of sizeable proportions.

However, with the advantage of hindsight, the Japanese victory seems less than complete. One can argue that the Japanese actually did the Americans a service, for the attack missed the US aircraft carriers completely, and, in so doing, forced the American navy to re-think its strategy, as the carriers had to replace the battleship as the essential feature of the fleet organization. In addition, by failing to destroy the oil reserves next to Pearl Harbor, the Japanese left the base in working order, ready to support a new fleet.

Japan had secured an impressive tactical victory, but now found herself pitted against a power with enormous industrial and military potential. The battles that were fought in the Pacific in 1942 (Coral Sea on May 6–8 and

Left: US marines raise the Stars and Stripes on the summit of Mount Suribachi on Iwo Jima. Although the flag was first raised only four days after the invasion of this island stronghold began, it would take another month of intense fighting before Japanese resistance finally ceased.

Midway June 4–6) were between evenly matched prewar navies, but by 1943 the US Navy was already growing at an ominous rate; in that year alone the Americans commissioned, in tonnage terms, almost the equivalent of the Japanese Navy at its wartime peak. It soon became apparent that Japan lacked the resources to wage a war of this scale and found it difficult to maintain a balanced fleet and merchant marine. Japan also found herself outpaced technically in terms of aircraft and radar development, VT shells, control systems and TBS radios, all of which ensured a massive qualitative improvement of the US Pacific Fleet during and after 1943. When one considers that the Americans also had the capacity to read all the Japanese intelligence signals, it is hardly surprising that by 1944 the Americans had won a series of victories on land which had done much to restore Allied belief in their own abilities, and go some way to refute the idea of Japanese supermen. By a succession of naval encounters – 1944 saw the Battle of the Philippine Sea in June and the Battle of Leyte Gulf in October – it was obvious even to the Japanese Imperial General Headquarters (IGHQ) that a negotiated peace to discuss what parts of the Imperial Empire Japan would retain was no longer an

Below: This photograph of the preinvasion bombardment reveals Iwo Jima's dismal nature with the commanding Mount Suribachi at its southern tip. The island was honeycombed with the Japanese defenders' tunnels.

option. Rather, by June 1944 Japanese policy was directed to securing a negotiated peace that would avoid unconditional surrender.

The Allied *Sextant* Conference in Cairo in 1943 had established a timetable for Adm. Chester Nimitz's central Pacific approach, which took priority over Gen. Douglas MacArthur's drive from the southwest, through the Philippines. Plans for the invasion of Formosa (Operation *Causeway*) had reached an advanced stage of preparation, but the decision was taken that with the war in Europe continuing, there were insufficient army troops available to take an island of that size. Adms. Spruance and Nimitz claimed, however, that there were enough army and marine troops for Iwo Jima and Okinawa. This coincided with a belief that the Americans could go it alone and did not need Chinese Nationalist support to defeat Japan. As it was, the May 1944 Japanese offensive which saw the capture of US air bases in China had further weakened the Formosa strategy. Accordingly, the resources earmarked for Formosa were redeployed for Iwo Jima and Okinawa.

As the Americans advanced across the central Pacific, Iwo Jima was assuming an importance out of all proportion for an island 4½ miles (7km) long, and 2¼ miles (3.5km) wide. Positioned at the southern end of the Bonin chain, Iwo Jima was 700 miles (1,120km) from the coast of Japan.

For the Japanese, the island was an important staging post on the route to the central and southern Pacific and was used as a base to bomb the Marianas, which had been taken by the Americans in July 1944. The Japanese

Above: Men of the 2nd Battalion, 27th Marine Regiment land on the black volcanic sand of Iwo Jima's southwest coast on February 19, 1945 at the start of a campaign that was to last five blood-soaked weeks.

Above top: The US Army Distinguished Service Medal: instituted in 1918 for service not involving gallantry. Above: The US Asiatic-Pacific Campaign medal for service in these theaters from December 7, 1941 to March 2, 1946.

were aware of the potential of the island as the Americans gradually worked their way back across the Pacific, and began to contemplate taking the war to the Japanese homeland. The airfields on Iwo Jima would provide a base for fighters – the B-29 Superfortress bombers on missions to Japan were suffering high losses as they had no fighter protection, as none of the American fighters had the range to make the 2,800 miles (4,480km) trip between the Marianas and Japan. As Gen. Curtis Le May was to tell the Chief of the American Task Force bearing down on the island in January 1945: "Without Iwo Jima I couldn't bomb Japan effectively." In addition, the island was traditional Japanese territory – its loss would be a psychological blow to the Japanese people.

In early 1944, command of the island was given to Lt. Gen. Kuribayashi, who immediately began to strengthen the defenses. Over the past two years, Japanese defensive doctrine changed from encountering the Americans on the beaches to concentrating on the construction of defenses in depth. Kuribayashi realized that the Americans would be able to bring more guns, planes and ships to the battle for Iwo Jima. In the absence of materiel, he was forced to rely on clever tactics, and high troop morale. He focused his defense around the old volcano Mount Suribachi, and the Motoyama plateau, building over 750 gun emplacements and scores of blockhouses with five-foot (1.5m) concrete walls. Beneath Mount Suribachi, a complete hospital and four-storey gallery were built, while the sides of the volcano bristled with pill boxes. By January 1945, the garrison numbered over 21,000 troops – they even had their own song, urging the defenders to:

Work and struggle, strive and thrust
'Til the hated Anglo Saxons
Lie before us in the dust.

The American assault on Iwo Jima (Operation *Detachment*) began in January 1945. Spruance instructed the Seventh US Army Air Force to attack the island's defenses with B-24's, then a naval bombardment was to follow to soften up the Japanese. The campaign actually involved the longest pre-invasion bombardment of the war – 72 days. In that time, it is estimated the Seventh US Air Force flew 2,700 missions and dropped 5,800 tons (5,892 tonnes) of bombs.

American intelligence was helped by the Japanese opening up their heavy artillery – hitherto concealed – against the American Support Force, which arrived off Iwo Jima on February 16. The main force, commanded by Rear Adm. Kelly Turner was in position by the morning of the 19th, and comprised some 450 vessels. The prelanding bombardment began at dawn, with the first carrier force strafing the beaches, known defensive positions and camouflaged artillery.

Unfortunately, for the first marines who landed on the southeastern beaches, the damage inflicted on the Japanese defenses was limited. After the war was over there was to be some argument over this prelanding bombardment. In particular, marines were to say that there should have been a larger naval bombardment prior to their assault. One has to appreciate, however, that factors such as the worsening weather situation, the supply of naval shells and the timetable for the next operation – Operation *Iceberg* – the attack on Okinawa, meant a longer naval bombardment was not really a possible option.

Before long, members of the US V Amphibious Corps, commanded by Maj. Gen. Henry Schmidt, found themselves pinned down on the beaches. By landing on the soft volcanic ash, the men found themselves unable to dig in. In the words of one marine it was like "trying to dig a foxhole in a bag of wheat." The marines were not helped by the deteriorating weather, which, with the strong ocean currents, made landing reinforcements and other equipment more difficult. Nevertheless, by the evening of the 19th, 30,000 marines had been landed but casualties were high; it is estimated that at the end of the first day 3,000 marines had been killed.

Robert Sherwood, the American war correspondent, was to comment, "The first night on Iwo Jima can only be described as a nightmare in hell . . ." Despite this inauspicious start to Operation *Detachment*, by the end of

Above: The shoulder patch insignia of the 4th Marine Division.
Salamander Books

Below: This reenactment is one of World War II's most abiding images: men of the 2nd Battalion, 28th Marine Regiment plant the Stars and Stripes on the summit of Mount Suribachi, February 23, 1945.

Above: Some 1,300 ships were involved in the Okinawa landing of April 1, 1945. The *kamikaze* threat was taken very seriously, the last-ditch defence being entrusted to weapons such as this quadruple 40mm mount.

the following day, the west coast of Iwo Jima had been reached and by the morning of the 23rd, a patrol was able to raise the Stars and Stripes on the summit of Mount Suribachi. A subsequent raising of the flag that same day was the image captured on film by photographer Joe Rosenthal, which was to become one of the most famous photographs of the war.

The American assault on the island was led by Maj. Gen. Cates' 4th Marine Division, who advanced along the eastern half of the island, and the 5th Marine Division led by Maj. Gen. Rockey who had landed, turned southwest to take Mount Suribachi and then moved north to advance along the west coast. On February 25, the 3rd Marine Division, commanded by Maj. Gen. Erskine, joined the assault. Increasingly the advance of the marines became held up as they encountered the elaborate Japanese defensive positions. The terrain was not suitable for tanks and the artillery proved difficult to manuever. As the American progress became agonizingly slow, casualties increased at an alarming rate. Eventually, after intense fighting, elements of the 3rd Division reached the northeast shore of the island, and on the northwestern tip of the island, near Kitano Point, the Japanese forces were finally isolated. For the marines there followed a prolonged mopping-up operation as they uncovered the underground bunkers and caves which had protected the Japanese so well. The campaign is generally considered to have ended on March 26, when the remaining Japanese performed a courageous, but futile, *banzai* charge.

Japanese casualty rates on the island serve to illustrate the fanatical nature of their fighting; only 1,083 were taken prisoner. The marine casualties totalled 6,812 killed and 19,189 wounded. The Fifth Fleet of Adm. Spruance did not escape during the battle; on February 20/21 Japanese aircraft hit the fast carrier force of Rear Adm. Marc Mitscher, and the next day the USS *Saratoga* was found by *kamikazes*. The escort carrier USS *Bismarck Sea* was also attacked and sunk. On February 16, by which time the marines had gained the upper hand on the island, Mitscher was able to withdraw, returning to his base at Ulithi Atoll.

The first B-29 emergency landing on Iwo Jima occurred on March 4, at which time roughly a quarter of the island remained under Japanese control. The first P-51 Mustangs of the Seventh US Air Force were using the airfield in April, and first escorted B-29s on March 7. Already, however, American thoughts had turned to the next island.

Okinawa was only 350 nautical miles (630km) from the Japanese home island of Kyushu and, as equally as significant, contained two fleet anchorages – the only ones available between Kyushu and Formosa. These would obviously be needed in the final invasion of Japan (Operation *Cornet*) which the American Joint War Plans Committee had set for December 31, 1945.

The American assault on the island had originally been planned for March 1, 1945, but because the campaign on Iwo Jima took longer than expected the timetable was pushed back. The ground forces commander was Gen. Simon Bolivar Buckner, commander of the Tenth Army. Under him were the III Amphibious Corps led by Maj. Gen. Roy Geiger, and XXIV Corps under Maj. Gen. Courtney Hodges. By this stage in the war, the men under their command were experienced fighters; the various marine and infantry divisions had seen service on Guadalcanal, Guam, the Gilberts, Marianas and the Philippines. The naval force included many of the individuals who had successfully worked together in the assault on Iwo Jima, with Spruance in overall command and Vice Adm. Marc Mitscher commanding the Fast Carrier Force, and Vice Adm. Kelly Turner the Joint Expeditionary Force. After much discussion, the British Pacific Fleet was allowed to participate under Vice Adm. Sir Bernard Rawlings. The scale of the operation was huge, with the Americans leaving little to chance – the Joint Expeditionary Force numbered over 1,450 ships – an American historian of the campaign has commented that by this stage of the war there was no shortage of equipment and accordingly, "It is probably true to say that no military force in history went into action better equipped and better supported than Gen. Buckner's Tenth Army." British observers were also to comment that, "This operation was the most audacious and complex enterprise which has yet been undertaken by the

Above: The US Navy Distinguished Service Medal.
Andrew L. Chernak Collection

Below: In the week before the landings, the US Navy poured an enormous weight of fire onto Okinawa: complemented by 3,095 bombing sorties, this gunfire amounted to more than 13,000 rounds of 6inch caliber or greater.

Above: An F4U Corsair fighter-bomber unleashes a salvo of eight 5-in underwing rockets, equivalent to the broadside of a US Navy destroyer, against Japanese defensive positions on the island of Okinawa.

Below: A Japanese soldier's personal patriotic flag. The hand-written slogans congragulate him on his enlistment and encourage him to keep to the suicide spirit.
Eugene C. Gibson Collection

American Amphibious Forces." Even so, it is worth pointing out that American intelligence was poor as late as January 1945. Japanese strength on Okinawa was estimated at 66,000, this figure rising to 87,000. However, Benis Frank claims that "in all truth, the Tenth Army was never able to arrive at a firm enemy troop estimate". To add to the American problems, this would be the first Pacific operation in which large numbers of enemy civilians would be encountered. In that sense, the invasion of Okinawa would be an important testing ground for procedures when Japan itself was occupied.

Finally, if Okinawa was remote from American bases, it was very close to Japanese bases. Kyushu, with at least 55 airfields, was a mere 350 miles (560km) northeast, while Formosa with some 65 airfields lay 360 miles (576km) southeast. The air threat was the main concern of Nimitz; the Allied carrier forces would have to remain in the combat zone for a considerable period of time. As events would prove, this concern was wholly justified.

The Japanese objective was to involve the Americans in an attritional assault, inflicting heavy casualties and forcing the United States to think again about invading the homeland. But the Japanese were unsure as to where the next American offensive would be: Formosa or Okinawa? This, in fairness, is hardly surprising as the Americans themselves were divided over strategy. But, as is so often the case, this confusion over strategy led to chronic indecision, seen by the movement of the crack Japanese 9th Division from Okinawa to aid the defense of the Philippines.

In August 1944, Lt. Gen. Mutsuru Ushijima arrived on Okinawa to prepare the island's defenses for any American assault. With Japan coming under intense pressure in the southern Pacific, Burma and in

Manchuria, it was unlikely that Ushijima was ever going to have sufficient men and, to a degree, the substantial supplies of artillery given to him were to fill the man-power shortage. Besides losing the 9th Division in December, the 44th Independent Mixed Brigade was torpedoed on its way to Okinawa with the loss of 5,000 men. Ushijima did obtain the 15th Independent Mixed Regiment, the 24th Infantry Division and part of the 62nd Infantry Division. Armor was provided by the 22nd Tank Regiment, though its heaviest gun was only 57mm. Artillery was available in quantity, including the ex-cellent 320mm spigot mortar. In addition, there was a naval base force of about 9,000 men and a volunteer Okinawan force numbering 24,000.

The first sorties against Okinawa were on October 10, 1944, the island again being a target on January 3–4, 1945. A Japanese soldier wrote: "The ferocity of the bombing is terrific. It really makes me furious. It is past 15:00 and the raid is still on. At 18:00 the last two planes brought the raid to a close. What the hell kind of bastards are they? Bombing from 06:00 to 18:00!"

On March 26, the Americans attacked the Kerama Re-tto group of islands to the west of Okinawa. By the end of the month, the 77th Infantry Division were able to re-port that all the islands were under American control, providing the Americans with an advanced logistics base and fleet anchorage. In addition, army troops discovered 350 enemy suicide boats which would obviously have been used against the assault force.

Slowly but surely, Okinawa was isolated by the Americans. First the minesweepers were sent in, then the radar picket vessels, both of whom were to be easy targets for the Japanese suicide planes. On April 1, the American invasion began, preceded by an awesome naval bombardment. Ten battleships, nine cruisers, 23 destroyers, and land-based 155mm Long Toms on the island of Keise Shima heralded the approach of the in-vaders. In line with recent Japanese tactics, the oppo-sition was slight as the first American troops stormed Hagushi beach on the western coast of Okinawa; Ushi-jima had chosen not to attack the Americans as they landed; he decided to withdraw, and concentrate his defenses in the south of the island. Accordingly, within an hour, 16,000 American combat troops were ashore

Below: Japanese Arisaka 6.5mm rifle variants. These include (top) a Type 97 (1937) with scope, and (bottom) a Type 44 (1911) cavalry carbine with folding bayonet extended. Also shown are a type 30 (1897) bayonet and scabbard and a hand held periscope.
Eugene C. Gibson Collection

and by the first evening, the airfields at Yontan and Kadena had been secured. At the end of the first day 60,000 troops were on Okinawa with minimal casualties: 28 killed, 104 wounded with a further 24 missing.

By April 6, the east coast had been reached and a potential logistical problem eased as supplies were able to be brought ashore via Chimu Bay (the Americans were in the embarrassing situation of facing logistical problems due to the speed of their success!). On the same day, 6th Marine Division of the III Amphibious Corps commanded by Maj. Gen. Lemuel Shephard had reached Nago, at the base of the Motobu Peninsula in the northwest of the island. Despite the original plan specifying that the southern part of the island be taken first, 6th Marine Division were ordered to clear the northern part of the island. Two days later, the marines attacked the Japanese who were dug in amongst the Yae Tae Hills. After desperate fighting, the Japanese were surrounded, but resistance continued until April 20.

In the south of the island, XXIV Corps reached the Japanese network of defenses on April 9, and with no immediate prospect of success, Gen. Hodges halted the advance to plan a knockout punch to be delivered on the 19th. In the intervening period, the Japanese were subjected to an intense bombardment. However, the Japanese held their ground, and it was only on the 24th that any ground was gained as Ushijima pulled his troops back.

While the battle for the southern half of Okinawa raged, it was necessary for the Tenth Army to ensure the security of its flanks by neutralizing the off-shore islands, for example the Eastern Islands guarding Chimn Wan, and Ie Shima on the west coast. Despite the overwhelming superiority, American forces could bring to these operations, it says much for the difficult terrain and the indomitable Japanese fighting spirit that casualties were high; in the capture of Tsugen Shima (one of the Eastern Islands), men of the 27th Infantry Division suffered nearly 100 casualties, while 234 Japanese were killed with no prisoners taken. In securing Ie Shima, the 77th Infantry Division fought for six days taking 1,118 casualties. The defenders suffered even more, Japanese losses on the island were 4,706 killed and a further 149 captured.

On Okinawa, the Japanese tactics were proving successful, as although they were having to fall back, American gains were measured in yards won, lost and then won again. On two occasions, the Japanese actually took the offensive, despite grave misgivings amongst some of the Japanese commanders, including Ushijima himself. It would seem that certain IGHQ officers believed a more positive policy should be adopted in defending Okinawa, and accordingly a three-pronged

Below: This is the scene looking aft along the flightdeck of the "Essex" class fleet carrier *Bunker Hill*, which was hit and severely damaged but not sunk by two *kamikaze* aircraft on May 11, 1945 off Okinawa.

attack was planned involving a massed aircraft attack against the American fleet, an attack by the Special Attack Squadron (Yamato Task Force) and an assault on the Yonton and Kadena airfields by Ushijima's ground forces. In fact, the plan suffered from a lack of coordination and all three operations were dismal failures. However, Ushijima was persuaded, largely by his chief of staff Lt. Gen. Isamu Cho, that while the Thirty-second Army still possessed the ability to attack it should go on the counteroffensive. Accordingly it was planned to use the 24th Division against the American XXIV Corps, while amphibious units would creep around the coast to the east and west. The attack was preceded by a substantial artillery barrage, which inevitably exposed the Japanese artillery positions, but the only significant success was the reoccupation of Tanabaru and Tanabaru Ridge which did cause concern amongst the Americans for a brief period. The offensive was a failure, with the Japanese suffering 5,000 casualties and considerable losses in equipment. Ultimately, the offensive reduced the length of time the Thirty-second Army could delay the Americans.

The sinking of the Yamato Task Force on April 6–7, effectively ended the offensive capability of the once mighty Imperial Japanese Navy. The only recourse was to launch a series of large coordinated *kamikaze* attacks – as one historian of the Pacific War has commented, the suicide attacks represented the use of the sole remaining

Above: The kill/loss ratio of the *kamikaze* concept was potentially very high, but made very great demands even on men brought up in the code of unswerving self-sacrifice in the name of the emperor.

Below: A Japanese identification pennant. The figure of the tiger appears to be purely decorative. *Andrew L. Chernak Collection*

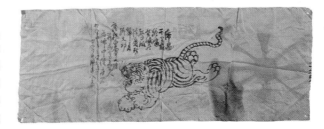

Above: Prisoners of war have always been an emotive issue. This American poster of 1943, by artist A. Brook, simply but effectively urges people to buy war bonds to ensure those early POWs would return.
War Memorial Museum of Virginia

superiority that the Japanese held over their enemies. There were ten such mass raids between April 6 and June 22, and Allied losses totalled 26 ships sunk and another 164 damaged – a considerable tally. In fact, there seems little doubt that by this stage of the war the quality of the Japanese pilots had declined, and pilots dived on the first Allied ships sighted, those in the outer radar perimeter, with the result that there were heavy losses in destroyers but little damage done to transports and carriers. Also, of course, Japanese losses – in aircraft and men – were heavy, and the long-term ability of the Japanese to defend their Home Islands was further diminished.

All through May the battle continued, with American offensives increasingly handicapped by the deteriorating weather situation. In the meantime, extra American units were deployed, for example 8th Marine Division, 2nd Marine Division and the 77th Infantry Division. Hodges' prediction of April that, "it is going to be really tough" and that "I see no way to get the Japanese out, except to blast them out yard by yard" was proving all too true. Gradually, the various Japanese defensive positions were taken – Iwana Ridge, Sugar Loaf Hill, Hill 55, 110 Meter Mill – and on May 29, 5th Marine Division took Shuri Castle. By June, Japanese soldiers were surrendering *en masse*; on June 18 Ushijima ordered his men to disperse and form guerrilla units. On the 21st, he prepared for ritual suicide. Ironically, US ground forces commander Gen. Buckner was already dead, having received a fatal shrapnel wound watching the 8th Marines in action on May 18. Maj. Gen. Geiger, who immediately took over, declared Okinawa secure on May 21, but the

Right: Okinawa was the first island of Japan proper to fall to the Americans, resistance ending on June 21, 1945, but the population's fear of the invaders survived as shown by this photograph of July 9.

mopping up operation continued until the end of the month.

The final casualty figures for the 82-day campaign were high. American estimates for enemy dead were approximately 120,000. American casualties vary from 60,000 up to 85,000 – the larger figure taking into account losses at sea. After the island was secured, considerable controversy arose due to these high American losses. Buckner was criticized for being ultra-conservative in his tactics of frontal attack and for ruling out any amphibious operations. One can, however, argue that considering the length of the campaign, the size of the enemy garrison and the extent to which terrain aided the defender, the losses were not excessive for an island of such strategic importance. One can make the further point that despite American technological superiority, which saw such new technology as armored flame throwers and sound locating devices, this advantage was nullified by the natural terrain and the skillful defence tactics of the Japanese.

The concept of strategic bombing, as put forward by the Italian Guilio Douhet and the American Billy Mitchell, had never received wholehearted support in the United States during the inter-war years. However, by the end of the war in 1945, the raids against Japan probably came closer to vindicating the theories of the air strategists than any others before or since.

Initially, the Americans were confronted with a problem of geography. Up to the end of 1942, the expansion of Japan meant that it was impossible for the Americans to take the war to the Japanese homeland. At this stage in the war, America had few carriers and certainly none to be risked in such a dangerous venture for potentially minimal gain. The option of using China as a base was fraught with logistical difficulties.

By 1943, circumstances had changed, and the idea of basing the bombers in eastern India and merely refuelling in China was gaining ground. The potential arrival of the new Boeing B-29 Superfortress would solve problems of range as well. However, the B-29 was beset with production problems, partly caused by the need for modifications and newly identified requirements arising from flight and combat experience in 1942 and 1943. The program was set back, and it was not until April 1944 that a sufficient number of B-29s were available to be sent to India, originally being stationed at Kharaqpur, Chakulia, Pairdoba and Dudh Kundi in eastern India. As early as April 24, a number flew to forward bases around Chengtu in central China. Finally, the first raid was launched against Japan on June 14, 1944; 75 bombers were sent to attack the iron and steel works on the island of Kyushu. The raid was a dismal failure.

Despite encouragement from President Roosevelt,

Above: A poster of 1944 urging support for the sixth war loan. Its focus is the ultimate objective of the fighting in the Pacific – the Japanese Home Islands. *War Memorial Museum of Virginia*

Above: The shoulder patch insignia of the 20th Air Force; the USAAF force which brought the B-29 and strategic bombing to the Japanese Home Islands.

Right: The final surrender of Japan was made inevitable by the efforts of the B-29 Superfortress bombers, which burned and blasted the heart out of the nation's cities, industries and communications.

logistical problems continued to hamper the campaign, in particular the shortage of fuel. Brig. Gen. Kenneth Wolfe who had done so much to get the campaign off the ground was replaced by Maj. Gen. Curtis Le May in July. Le May had experience of the bombing campaign in Europe and favored the tactics of high-altitude, precision attacks in daylight, and organized the B-29 squadrons into self defending "box" formations. The bombing did improve, but even Le May could not solve the problems of fuel and bombs having to be transported from India to the Chinese bases. The result was that the raids continued to be few in number. It was, of course, the realization that strategic bombing was unlikely to be effectively carried out from bases in China, that was a

factor in the American Central Pacific Campaign; as early as 1943 the capture of the Mariana Islands was recommended: "at the earliest possible date, with the establishment of heavy bomber bases as a primary mission." Indeed, once the Marianas were taken in June/July 1944, work immediately began on the airfields on Saipan, Guam and Tinian. The first B-29s arrived in October, and in November Iwo Jima was bombed. However, the first raids on Japan proved as unsuccessful as those based in China; this is well illustrated by the November 24 raid when 111 B-29s were sent to attack the Nakajima aircraft plant at Musashi, Tokyo. Seventeen aircraft returned early with mechanical trouble, only 24 were able to pinpoint the target, six aborted the mission over Japan, one

Top: The US Distinguished Flying Cross. Above: The US Air Medal. *Andrew L. Chernak Collection*

ditched in the Pacific on the return flight and one was shot down. The vast majority of the B-29s unloaded their bombs indiscriminately over Tokyo, and the specific target was barely touched. It was obvious that the strategic bombing campaign needed rethinking.

Le May, who had been transferred from his command in China, took advice from the local air commander, Maj. Gen. Claire Chennault, and a new strategy of sending the B-29s in low, with incendiaries, was decided upon. The strategy was vindicated immediately with the raid on the Chinese city of Hankow on the Yangtze river. The Far Eastern cities built of wood proved especially vulnerable to area bombing; precision bombing with high explosives was obviously unnecessary. The Japanese port city of Kobe was selected as the target for the first "fire raid". On February 4, 100 B-29s attacked the city and the results were impressive. On February 25, Tokyo was hit and one square mile ($2.5km^2$) of buildings destroyed. A return to the old ways of precision bombing, against the Nakajima plant at Musashi, again proved unsuccessful and Le May had sufficient evidence to adopt area bombing wholesale, to the extent that all guns were removed from the B-29s to make room for more incendiary bombs. The bombers were sent in as low as 5,000 feet (1,500m), at night with special pathfinders to guide them in. The effects were spectacular; the March 9/10 raid on Tokyo levelled 16 square miles ($40km^2$) of buildings, killing an estimated 84,000 people, injuring 41,000 and making a million homeless. American losses amounted to just 14 B-29s. In further raids on May 23 and 25, an additional 18 square miles ($45km^2$) of Tokyo was destroyed. The other industrial centres of Japan

Below: Watched by two US and British generals who had suffered long incarceration after the fall of the Philippines and Singapore, Gen. Douglas MacArthur signs the Japanese surrender on behalf of the Allies.

were also targeted; Nagoya on March 11/12, Osaka on the 14/15th and Kobe again on the 16/17th.

In June, Le May initiated a second campaign against smaller Japanese cities. By now, the B-29s were all but unopposed as the Japanese attempted to hold back a part of their conventional airpower in readiness for the defense of the Home Islands against invasion. It is ironic that due to the lack of Japanese air defense, the fighter escorts from Iwo Jima were discontinued before the end of the war.

Despite America now being able to bomb Japan at will, they still faced the daunting prospect of invading Japan, and fighting a people whose loyalty to their emperor seemed undiminished. It was against this background that President Truman granted permission for the atomic bomb to be used, firstly on Hiroshima on the morning of August 6. On the 9th, the only other atomic bomb in existence was dropped on Nagasaki.

There is still debate as to what extent this new weapon brought the war to a close. Japan surrendered on August 15. Another factor was the Soviet declaration of war on August 9. In a campaign that has received little attention in the West, a Soviet Army of 1.5 million troops invaded Manchuria and decisively defeated the Japanese Kwantung Army. Soviet success has been explained by numerical superiority against an enemy equipped with inferior tanks, aircraft with little or no fuel and artillery short of ammunition. This is somewhat disingenuous as it ignores the ability of the Soviets to complete a "Blitzkrieg" campaign in a country larger than western Europe, for negligible losses.

The Soviets attacked along a frontage of 2,728 miles (4,400km), advancing to objectives between 250 and 560 miles (400–900km) deep in a matter of days. The Soviet armies managed to accomplish strategic surprise by assembling this enormous force in virtual secrecy, during a time of the year when heavy rains made an attack unlikely. In addition, the Soviets' major axis of advance was directed across terrain which the Japanese thought impassable; the Great Hingam Mountains. Tactically the varied terrain, from swamps and rivers to desert, dictated the use of different force packages and almost no two operations at brigade level, or below, worked the same. Even in those areas where the Soviets failed to achieve surprise, the speed of their advance unhinged the Japanese forces, who soon found themselves isolated behind the Soviet advance units.

The Soviet advance continued up to August 23, beyond the date of the Japanese surrender. The Soviet Union claimed 83,737 Japanese killed and 594,000 captured but gave no figures for wounded. The Soviet estimate of their own losses for the campaign was 8,219 killed and 22,264 wounded.

Above: The Japanese surrender was signed on the battleship *Missouri* anchored in Tokyo Bay, and this copy of the document's signature page was displayed on board the great ship even after she was mothballed.

V Fourteen

The Final Horrors

Sean McKnight

The end of World War II may have seen the Allies victorious, but it also revealed in full the depths to which humanity could sink.

Germany formally surrendered to the Allies in Berlin on May 8, 1945, Japan followed on September 2 – the most devastating conflict mankind has ever fought had finally ended. War had cut swathes of destruction across whole continents, and over 50 million people had died. In Germany, heartland of the European continent, ancient cities lay in ruins, and over 13 million refugees scratched a living in the rubble. The pre-war world lay shattered, and a new world was hard to discern from all the destruction.

On August 6 'Enola Gay' was blessed by a Roman Catholic priest. Spiritually fortified for its mission, the B-29 Superfortress took off from the island of Tinian near Guam, and dropped the fruit of the world's finest scientific minds – the atomic device nicknamed "Little Boy" – on the Japanese city of Hiroshima. Three days later another atomic bomb was dropped on Nagasaki. The immediate death toll was not dissimilar from that which conventional bombing could inflict – on March 9–10 incendiary bombs had created a firestorm in Tokyo which killed nearly 100,000 people – but atomic attack seemed more shocking. Over 80,000 people were killed by a single bomb, and the effects of radioactive fallout killed thousands more over the coming decades.

The military possibilities of nuclear fission were known in the 1930s, but it was in the United States that the resources were found to convert theory into weaponry. Not only did the United States possess a plenitude of homegrown talent, it also enjoyed the services of eminent emigré scientists such as Albert Einstein and Enrico Fermi, and in 1942 the British contributed their

Left: Survivors of the Nazis' "Final Solution" at Auschwitz-Birkenau death camp in Poland. The camp was liberated by Soviet troops in January 1945.

expertise to the American project. In August 1942 America set up the "Manhattan Project," which by 1945 employed 150,000 people. Scientists predicted that the atomic bomb would have an explosion equivalent to 1,500 tons (1,524 tonnes) of TNT, but in July 1945 the bomb was tested in New Mexico, and it became clear a yield equivalent to at least 15,000 tons (15,240 tonnes) of TNT could be expected. A military observer of the test, Gen. Farrell, felt "that we puny things were blasphemous to dare tamper with the forces heretofore reserved to the Almighty," and Secretary of War Stimson exulted, "What was electricity? Meaningless. This Atomic Bomb is the Second Coming in Wrath."

Many of the project's scientists had only helped develop the atomic bomb to ensure Germany did not develop the weapon first, and others, such as Einstein, had believed America would have too many scruples to use it, except as a last resort. They were not alone in their doubts; in mid-1945 Gen. Eisenhower told Stimson, "I hate to see our country be the first to use such a weapon."

In retrospect the decision to use the atomic bomb can be criticized, but the arguments take little account of the realities of 1945. Some have argued that the target selected should have been military, or even that a demonstration — perhaps over water — would had sufficed to persuade the Japanese to surrender. However, this ignores the possibility that neither of these events would have broken Japanese resistance, and the fact that the United States had only two weapons available. Japan was on the verge of surrender, but communicating this clearly was the responsibility of the Japanese Government. Continued conventional aerial bombing, and a tightening naval blockade, would have forced Japan to surrender, but it is by no means clear that this would have been morally preferable to atomic attack. Alternatively, America could have invaded Japan's Home Islands but, in the light of the 40,000 casualties suffered invading Okinawa, American planners anticipated 250,000 Allied casualties.

At the end of a bloody war, it is excessively cynical to assume the United States was taking the first shot in a new Cold War, and the military imperatives of the war they were still fighting best explains the decision to use atomic weapons. This does not ease all the moral qualms about the deliberate targeting of the civilian population. The arguments over the morality of using atomic weapons are a smoke screen to the real issue — that of deliberately targeting people who should have been protected by their non-combatant status. The entire Allied campaign of "strategic" bombing was hard to justify in terms of the rules of warfare; it is worth remembering that seven days *after* the Hiroshima bombing,

Below: The world's first atomic device was "Trinity" used to validate the design in which a critical mass of plutonium was created as high explosive "lenses" (nose triggering wires) drove together several small components.

Left: Located at the top of a tower in the desert at Los Alamos, New Mexico, "Trinity" was successfully detonated near dawn on July 19, 1945 with an explosion equivalent to 10,000 tons of TNT: the atom bomb would work.

1,500 Allied planes bombed Tokyo, producing casualty figures similar to those inflicted by the nuclear attack on Nagasaki.

It would be wrong to ignore the horrors which the Allies inflicted on the Axis powers, but not all the participants in World War II were equally guilty. Two of the Axis powers, namely Germany and Japan, committed crimes so hideous as to make subsequent generations reluctant to believe such atrocities could have been perpetrated on such a large scale.

Japanese attitudes to prisoners of war (POWs) had their origins in a culture which regarded surrender as highly dishonorable. This background proved stronger than the legal obligations which Japan had accepted by ratifying the 1907 Hague Convention, and agreeing to reciprocal treatment under the more stringent 1929 Geneva Conventions. Japan systematically ignored these legal obligations; the best a prisoner of the Japanese could expect was brutality and deliberate neglect.

The Japanese illegally put POWs to work on military projects. Schemes such as the Burma–Siam railway were managed so brutally that 16,000 of the 46,000 POWs used on the project died (64 dead for each kilometre of track). In the Philippines the Bataan death march

Above: Located in bowl surrounded by hills that helped to contain the blast, Hiroshima was destroyed when the "Little Boy" atomic bomb detonated at a height of just under 2,000ft (600m) with a yield of some 17 kilotons.

claimed the lives of over 8,000 American and Filipino POWs. At the (mainly British) POW 8 Mile Camp at Sandakan in Borneo, prisoners were punished by being shut in a cage 4ft 6in (1.35m) wide, 6ft (1.8m) long and 3ft (0.9m) high – at one time seven people were simultaneously caged. Eventually, the bulk of these prisoners were marched inland to Ranau; of 2,736 a total of 340 were transferred, six survived and 2,390 died.

The Japanese did not stop at killing through neglect, hard labor and brutality, but in many instances murdered POWs. On the Filipino island of Palawan the Japanese forced 150 American prisoners into cramped shelters, then killed all but five of them. The Nazis, hardly tender jailers, had a mortality rate of 4 percent of British and American POWs in their custody, but the Japanese figure was a horrendous 27 percent.

Chinese soldiers were treated with even less humanity, classified as "bandits," and treated in a bestial manner. It was common practice for these "bandits" to be killed out of hand, or even to be used as bayonet or target practice.

Even worse that this there were incidents of cannibalism, and Japanese orders forbidding troops from eating their comrades failed to extend such protection to POWs. Completing a disgraceful record of criminal treatment of POWs, in Manchuria, Unit 731 conducted experiments with biological weapons, and live POWs were their experimental guinea pigs.

The Japanese also systematically mistreated civilians in their "care." Enemy civilians were interned – a legitimate enough precaution – but the dreadful conditions in which they were kept were criminal. At one camp, Tjideng, at Batavia, on the island of Java the Allies discovered 10,000 civilians confined to 1,000 square yards (800m^2). Virtually all the camps kept their inmates on starvation rations, treated them brutally, and killed by what seems to be deliberate neglect. As badly treated were the citizens of countries "liberated" by the Japanese from the "yoke of imperialism." Thousands of these civilians were carted away in dreadful conditions to be used as slave labor; of 150,000 laborers forced to undertake construction of the Burma–Siam railway at least 60,000 died.

In places where the Japanese believed the local population were less than supportive they resorted to wholesale slaughter. In the Philippines, with liberation imminent in December 1944, orders from Japanese SW Area Fleet Operations stated "when killing Filipinos, assemble them together in one place as far as possible thereby saving ammunition and labor". One of the more unpleasant incidents of the last weeks of the Japanese occupation of Manila was an attack on the Red Cross HQ, in which at least 50 doctors, nurses and patients were killed. The small Suluk tribe who lived in northern Borneo were nearly destroyed when the Japanese punished them; only 179 out of 550 survived the Japanese descent upon their islands in February 1944.

However, it was once again the Chinese who had to endure the worst treatment at the hands of the Japanese. Japan's plans for China were clearly expressed by Prime Minister Hiranuma: "I hope the intention of Japan will be

Above: Personal clothing and personal effects of prisoners of war held in the Philippines. The items include a home made knife and a variety of mess tins. The bugle was used by the Japanese guards.
Milwaukee Public Museum
Bugle: Quartermaster Museum

コレヒドールの地下要塞から出て來た敵、みんな手をあげて

Left: US feelings about the Japanese were conditioned by the Pearl Harbor "sneak attack" and reinforced by the treatment meted out to prisoners such as those seen here at the fall of Corregidor on May 6, 1942.

understood by the Chinese so that they may cooperate with us. As for those who fail to understand, we have no alternative but to exterminate them." Earlier in their war in China, the Japanese had made this clear by slaughtering over 200,000 citizens of Nanjing – stormed in December 1937. This type of brutality continued throughout the war, and with a pacification policy of "Kill All, Take All, Burn All," Japan abandoned any pretence to be conforming to international law. When Singapore fell on February 15, 1942 the Japanese started killing those Chinese regarded as unfriendly to Japan, by the end of the war over 100,000 Singaporean citizens had died. The Japanese had claimed to be the liberators of the Far East, but the reality was a brutal new imperialism.

More shocking to the advancing forces of the Allies was the mounting evidence that Nazi Germany was, if anything, a more diseased state than Imperial Japan. There was a feeling that Nazi rhetoric should not be taken seriously, particularly in the United States where there was widespread scepticism about atrocity stories.

In fighting the war in western Europe, Germany in the main abided by the rules of the Geneva Convention. Most Allied POWs were treated correctly, but there were some exceptions. In 1942, Hitler issued an order that "all quarter is to be denied on principle" to Allied commandos unless they were engaged in "normal hostilities." There were several small scale massacres of POWs, notably in 1940, the machinegunning of 100 soldiers of the British Army's Norfolk Regiment, and the December 1944 Malmedy massacre – both performed by members of the Waffen-SS. Escaping Allied POWs

Right: One of the greatest problems of the immediate post-war period was the vast number of refugees and other displaced persons. These are Poles (probably slave laborers) awaiting transport home in 1945.

were also murdered – 50 escapees of Stalag Luft III following recapture were ordered to be shot.

These criminal acts are dwarfed when compared to the way in which the Germans treated POWs taken on the Eastern Front. As early as June 1941, a directive from the German High Command (OKW) ordered the execution of captured Soviet Political Commissars. Ordinary Red Army POWs fared little better, and their chances of returning alive from the brutal labor camps to which they were sent were less than 30 percent. Germans giving POWs food were officially berated for "misconceived humanitarianism," and senior officers, such as Field Marshal Keitel decried attempts to follow the rules of war in the ideological struggle against the Soviets; Keitel directed that, "The troops have, therefore, the right and the duty to use in this struggle any and unlimited means, even against women and children."

By late 1942, German forces occupied Europe from the Atlantic coast of France to the west bank of the Volga River. For the civilians under the control of Hitler's state, occupation was to be at best a miserable experience. Göring told a conference of German occupation authorities that "this everlasting concern about foreign people must cease now, once and for all. It makes no difference to me if your people starve." In the west the German occupation was "moderate" – "only" 29,000 French hostages were killed as reprisal measures against the Resistance.

In December 1941, Hitler issued the *Nacht und Nebel* (Night and Fog) decree, enabling German occupation authorities to remove suspects by night to Germany, a journey from which few returned. Active resistance was curbed by a systematic policy of reprisals, and in Italy the Germans announced their intention to kill 100 Italians for every German killed. All over the occupied territories, resistance fighters could expect summary execution if caught – understandable perhaps, but nonetheless a breach of the rules of warfare. German forces, however, also killed civilians without even this poor justification. On June 10, 1944, on their way to the Normandy front, troops of the 2nd SS Panzer Division "Das Reich" slaughtered over 600 men, women and children in the village of Oradour-Sur-Glane; to quote a deserter from the division: "everything in our path was killed; and the women undressed, raped and hanged from trees."

One of the largest scale criminal acts in the occupied territories was the forcible export of slave labor to Germany. The treatment these slaves could expect was announced by the Reich Plenipotentiary for Labor, Fritz Sauckel: "All the men must be fed, sheltered and treated in such a way as to exploit them to the highest possible extent at the lowest conceivable degree of expenditure." In total more than five million foreign laborers

Above: Another ghastly aspect of the war that only became fully apparent in 1945 was the German concentration camps. These women in Belsen are sitting among the burning clothing of other prisoners who have died.

were imported into the Reich; the bulk were never to return home. The future for the eastern Europeans was particularly bleak, as the Nazi ideologist Alfred Rosenberg made clear: "We are a master race which must remember that the lowest German worker is racially and biologically a thousand times more valuable than the population here."

There was a more sinister purpose to the German program of slave labor, as "extermination through work" was seen as a way of "solving" the "racial problems" of the greater Reich. Nazi ideology called for the extermination of "inferior" races, in particular the Slavs who were seen as fit only for exploitation and death. Although other groups were also deliberately targeted for death (for example, homosexuals, gypsies, political opponents, the handicapped) the group which was marked down for the most systematic slaughter was, of course, the Jews.

Hitler's racial goal in 1939 was "extermination of the Jewish race in Europe" and the SS was the organization that implemented the policy. Behind the (front line) troops invading the USSR in 1941 came the Einsatzgruppen (Action Squads). These SS-led formations killed those their Nazi masters regarded as racially polluting. However, there were practical limits to the numbers of defenseless people who could be shot or beaten to death, and Einsatzgruppe D demonstrated that gas vans could make the killing more efficient – an innovation that enabled them to claim 229,052 victims by 1942.

Despite the scale of death inflicted by the Einsatzgruppen, they simply could not kill at the pace which

Below: The gate at Auschwitz, surmounted by the motto "Work Makes You Free," gives little indication that this was the entry to an extermination camp that received and killed thousands of innocent victims.

Reichsführer Heinrich Himmler demanded. At the Wannsee Conference in Berlin, on January 20, 1942, it was therefore decided to expand the concentration camp system, and include the Jews of all Germany's satellites, in the "Final Solution." As an interim measure hundreds of thousands of western European Jews were transported east (many died as a result of dreadful conditions on the journey) and were kept in the ghettos of eastern Europe. This was not the end of their journey, and when preparations had been made the survivors were moved to camps. All these camps were intended to kill their inmates, some quickly using methods of mass extermination, other slowly, through brutality, neglect and hard labor. Theresienstadt in Czechoslovakia is described as a privileged concentration camp, but only 16 percent of its "privileged" inmates survived the war.

Although unusual in that it was for women only, Ravensbruck was typical of the camps which killed by neglect. A Norwegian, Sylvia Salvesen, was sent to this camp because she was a friend of the Norwegian King, and describes her first sight of the camp: "a picture of hell – not because I saw anything terrible happen but because I then saw, for the first time in my life, human beings whom I could not distinguish whether they were men or women." She survived the war, but 50,000 inmates of Ravensbruck did not.

The first "purpose built" death camp was at Treblinka in eastern Poland, where the first three gas chambers were completed in July 1942. Using carbon monoxide gas, Treblinka managed on exceptional days to kill 12,000 people, and by the time it had ceased operating in 1944 it had killed nearly 800,000. The inmates of the

Above: Even when they were not immediately murdered in the gas ovens, the inmates of Auschwitz had to face other enemies in the form of starvation, cold, disease and the brutality of the camp guards.

camp knew their fate, and often the SS guards had to drive their victims into the gas chambers with whips.

Perhaps even more horrible than the policy of extermination was the German belief that the inmates of their camps could be subjected to any torment that they chose to inflict upon them. In numerous camps German doctors used their inmates for experiments. At Dachau inmates were subjected to excruciatingly painful levels of air pressure, emersed in ice cold water and injected with pus, and in one experiment 1,200 prisoners were deliberately infected with malaria. At Neuengamme in Germany, Jewish children were injected with TB bacilli, and subsequently hung to destroy any evidence. At Buchenwald, also in Germany, prisoners were drowned in manure, castrated and even skinned in order to provide Ilsa Koch, the commandant's wife with interesting lampshades.

By 1945 the western Allies had liberated some of the "better" camps located in Western Germany. Brig. Glynn Hughes, director of medical services for the British Army of the Rhine said of Belsen: "No description nor photographs could really bring home the horrors that were there outside the huts, and the frightful scenes inside were much worse." (He estimated that a further 10,000 would die even after liberation.) The British and the Americans filmed the camps they had liberated, and without these records it would be all too easy to

Above: The commandant of Belsen was Josef Kramer, the "Beast of Belsen." He was tried by the British for crimes against humanity, found guilty, sentenced to death, and hanged.

Below: Appalled by what they found when they reached Belsen, the British set the captured SS guards to interring the large number of unburied dead.

Left: Many Germans refused to believe that the concentration and extermination camps had existed. Here British troops herd citizens of Burgsteinfurt into a cinema to see film proof of the atrocities in Belsen and Buchenwald.

convince oneself that something so dreadful could not have happened; prior to viewing these films, during the subsequent war crimes' trials, the American, Judge Parker, commented to an aide, "You know Jim, they're going too far in this trial. They [the prosecution] claimed today that the guards threw babies up and shot them in the camps. You know nobody would do that."

It was in the remote marshlands around the Polish town of Oswiecien that the most terrible death camp of all was established. Auschwitz was ideal for the purpose – remote, well east of Germany, but near the junction of four railway lines. The man selected as camp commandant, Hauptsturmführer Hoss, was a meticulous administrator who had already worked in camps at Dachau and Sachsenhausen. He took his new appointment very seriously, and in the spring of 1942 visited Treblinka to see how its operations ran. Hoss was critical of Treblinka as he felt their "output" was low, terror in the victims slowed the process of execution, and carbon monoxide was not the ideal gas. At Auschwitz, the gas chambers were elaborately concealed, and Hoss claims that most prisoners went docilely to their deaths where a new gas – Zyclon B – was used, and the ovens were able to incinerate 10,000 corpses a day. Nearby, at the Birkenau labor camp, POWs, Jews and other victims, still capable of working "enjoyed" a brief stay of execution. Hoss, the perfect bureaucrat of death, kept records, and later told his Allied captors that Auschwitz had exterminated at least three million people. The figure seems unbelievable, but six of the 35 storage buildings at Auschwitz survived the Germans' attempt to destroy them; the Red Army discovered 348,820 suits, 836,255 complete women's outfits and 5,525 pairs of women's shoes.

During the war nearly 12 million people died under German occupation, of these eight million died in concentration camps. Precise figures are impossible to ascertain, but it seems that the "Final Solution" claimed the lives of at least five million Jews – not less than two-thirds of Europe's Jewish population in 1939.

Given the ferocity of World War II, it was inevitable that the victors would punish the vanquished. At the 1943 Tehran Conference, Stalin offered the opinion that the summary execution of 50,000 to 100,000 Germans would suffice, and for a while the American President, Franklin Delano Roosevelt, supported the Morgenthau Plan, which aimed to punish all Germans through the destruction of their entire industrial base. In 1945, it was tempting to administer summary justice in liberated countries, and in France official estimates suggest that at least 4,500 "collaborators" were executed without trial. Given the events of the war years, the German people could not have expected their occupiers to treat them with generosity.

The idea of trying individuals for breaches of the "rules of war" was not new, but hitherto only minor figures had been punished. National leaders had not been arraigned for such crimes, and misguided attempts to try German leaders after 1918 had rather discredited the concept. However, the horrors revealed by the Allied advance made it impossible to punish only those who had killed with their own hands. The Allies established a United Nations War Crimes Commission in 1942, but until 1944 it was denied the resources to do the job. The real drive for a proper legal process came from the United States, where opponents of the Morgenthau Plan saw a war crimes' trial as a much more discriminating procedure. Once Roosevelt had been won over, American legal experts saw a trial as a chance to strengthen the concept of international law, and in so doing, deter future wars. The British, who felt a trial would be seen as "victor's justice," were forced in 1945 to accept American views, and in August 1945 the Allied conference at Potsdam approved the Charter establishing an International Military Tribunal.

There were objections to the Allies' trial procedure. Legal experts at the time, and since, have argued the Allies charged individuals with crimes against international laws which did not exist prior to 1945. Robert H. Jackson (US Supreme Court Judge and chief American war crimes' prosecutor), argued that the charges were

Below: Overcome by grief, a Polish woman weeps over a pile of charred bone fragments, all that remained of many thousands of prisoners killed in Maidanek, one of the five main camps in German-occupied Poland.

based on existing laws which had hitherto not been enforced. Germany had signed the 1907 Hague and 1929 Geneva Conventions, which had both been broken, and in 1928 Germany had signed the Kellog–Briand Pact outlawing war. The major defendants were charged with conspiracy, a concept recognized in Anglo–American law though not in continental law, creating another source of complaint. The Allied legal experts worried about many of these problems, and the Americans in particular argued that a not guilty verdict should be feasible.

A more fundamental objection raised against the notion of trying Axis war criminals might be that the Allies were hardly innocent. Göring said during the trial: "What about the grabbing of California and Texas? That was plain aggressive warfare for territorial expansion too." Soviet participation in the trial adds force to these criticisms, a point underlined by Stalin's insistence that Germany be charged with the Katyn massacres in Poland (which were actually conducted by the Soviets). The Allies' hands were far from clean: carpet bombing, Stalin's own death camps and the atomic bomb all make

Above: In January 1945 the Soviet forces reached Auschwitz, where as many as 6,000 people had been gassed every day. Among the living were numbers of children wearing the same striped uniform as the other prisoners.

one wonder if they were fit to judge others, but this hardly constitutes an argument that the defendants at Nuremberg were innocent.

Several Nazi leaders committed suicide: Hitler and Goebbels as Berlin fell, and Himmler a few weeks later. In the chaos of Germany in 1945, some important Nazis disappeared. Nonetheless, the Allies indicted 21 German leaders including senior Nazi political leaders such as Göring, "respectable" political conservatives – who had sustained the Nazi regime – such as von Papen, senior representatives of the armed forces like Keitel, and Kaltenbrunner the most prominent SS man held by the Allies.

The Allies established their International Military Tribunal at Nuremberg, where the Nazis had staged spectacular pre-war rallies. This decision was not just symbolic; Nuremberg had the practical advantage of being in the American zone of occupation, which not only meant that United States paid the bulk of the costs, but also enabled the legal teams to enjoy the relative luxury of American rations!

Preparing the prosecution case was a daunting task. The Nazis had made arrangements to destroy much of the physical evidence, and only the speed of the Allied advance had partly frustrated these intentions. Many of those involved in the more dreadful excesses of the regime evaded capture, and others less directly implicated claimed to have no knowledge of the shocking events. Fortunately millions of documents had fallen into the Allies' hands (German Foreign Office documents alone weighed 485 tons (495 tonnes). Ironically, it was the meticulous records maintained by German bureaucrats which provided the prosecution with the central evidence for their case.

Below: For the trial of the major German war criminals at Nuremberg between November 20, 1945 and October 1, 1946 the tribunal of eight judges provided by the Allies comprised, from left to right, Lt. Col. A.L. Volchkov (USSR), Maj. Gen. I.T. Nikitchenko (USSR), Lord Justice Norman Birkett (UK), Lord Justice Geoffrey Lawrence (UK, president), Hon. Francis A. Biddle (US), Hon. John Parker (US), Henri Donnedieu de Vabres (France) and Robert Falco (France).

While the prosecution prepared their arguments the Allies treated the defendants humanely. Göring even found that prison restored his health (he was helped to give up his addiction to paracodeine tablets, and lost over 2 of his 19 stone (11 of 106kg) in weight). Several imprisoned Nazis displayed remorse at their crimes; von Schirach (leader of the Hitler Youth and Gauleiter of Vienna) proclaimed: "I just want to speak before a court of law and take the blame on myself, then let them hang me." Others claimed they were unaware of the atrocities perpetrated by the regime, while some of the traditional conservatives could not understand why they had even been arrested. Similarly, the military men indicated did not understand why they had been charged, and believed they should not be tried for executing orders from their superiors.

On November 20, the International Military Tribunal opened with the prosecution's indictment. The prosecution case took 73 days to present, and, despite the horrifying nature of most of the evidence, the process

Above: At Nuremberg were – with their sentences: Hermann Göring (death), Rudolf Hess (life imprisonment), Joachim von Ribbentrop (death), Wilhelm Keitel (death), Alfred Rosenberg (death), Ernst Kaltenbrunner (death), Hans Frank (death), Wilhelm Frick (death), Julius Streicher (death), Walter Funk (life imprisonment), Hjalmar Schacht (acquitted), Karl Dönitz (10 years), Erich Raeder (life imprisonment), Baldur von Schirach (20 years), Ernst Sauckel (death), Alfred Jodl (death), Franz von Papen (acquitted), Arthur Seyss-Inquardt (death), Albert Speer (20 years), Constantin von Neurath (15 years) and Hans Fritsche (acquitted). In the front row from left to right, Göring, Hess, von Ribbentrop, Keitel, Kaltenbrunner and Rosenberg, and in the rear row from left to right Dönitz, Raeder, von Shirach, Sauckel and Jodl.

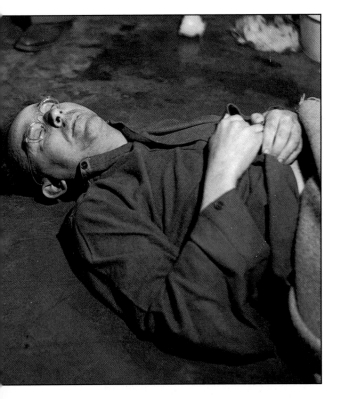

Above: A major war criminal who escaped the trial was Heinrich Himmler, head of the SS. Himmler was captured on May 21, 1945 but two days later killed himself by biting a vial of cyanide he had concealed in his mouth.

rapidly became tedious. With legal representatives from the United States, Britain, France and the Soviet Union all present, the multi-national nature of the prosecution led to frequent repetition, while the documentary evidence was unselectively presented. The judges were irritated by these problems, and the stream of horrible events exhausted their capacity to feel moral outrage. Nonetheless the films made by the Allies of the "better" concentration camps in western Germany shocked the court, and many of the defendants.

The defense were allowed 110 days to attempt to refute the charges. Despite the chaos of post-war Germany they were able to summon nearly 60 witnesses, and took statements from others who were unable to attend. Probably the most dramatic event of the whole trial was Göring's testimony, and the Reichsmarshal threatened to undermine the trial with his combative statement. Worse followed, as Göring dealt easily with Robert Jackson's attempt at cross-examination, and the British alternate judge, Norman Birkett, commented: "the prosecution has not really advanced its case at all." Fortunately for the prosecution, Sir David Maxwell-Fyfe, the *defacto* leader of the British prosecution team, was up to the challenge, and, picking up the cross-examination from Jackson, succeeded in discrediting Göring. Although the spirit behind the trial had been American, in the conduct of the prosecution case the courtroom expertise of the small British team was essential.

The Military Tribunal announced the verdicts on October 1; there were three acquittals, seven prison sentences, and eleven defendants were condemned to death (as was Martin Bormann in his absence). These verdicts demonstrated that the Military Tribunal had undertaken a genuine legal process, in which guilt had not automatically been assumed. However, there were some dubious judgements; Grand Adm. Dönitz's conduct of the U Boat campaign was similar to that of his Allied counterparts in the Pacific, but he was found guilty of war crimes; nowadays hanging Field Marshal Jodl, an ambivalent if ultimately faithful servant of the Nazi regime, seems harsh. Most of the verdicts have stood the test of time, and the ten men hung (Göring escaped being the eleventh by committing suicide) were all deeply implicated in the more horrible acts of the regime.

It was not just at Nuremberg that trials took place. In the US zone of occupation, 26 sentences of death were handed out (though another 35 acquittals suggested that the legal process was fair). Smaller numbers were tried in the British and French zones, but a wider ranging summary "justice" operated in the Soviet zone. Germany was also collectively punished, and especially in the Soviet zone, German industrial plant was taken in

reparations. It seems probable that only the onset of the Cold War saved the Germans from a lengthier period of hardship.

The vast majority of the Japanese leaders fell into Allied hands in 1945, and 28 were indicted to appear before a military tribunal in Tokyo (one was subsequently judged to be incapable of defending himself). These included three ex-prime ministers of Japan headed by Gen. Hideki Tojo, who was seen by the Allies as the foremost defendant, military figures such as Gen. Matsui whose troops were responsible for the massacres in Nanjing, and civilian politicians such as Koichi Kido, the Lord Keeper of the Privy Seal.

The procedure for the Tokyo trials was similar to that established by the Allies at Nuremberg. However, in Tokyo there was not the wealth of documentary evidence available at Nuremberg, and the private diary of Kido had to fill in the gaps caused by Allied bombing and deliberate destruction. As in Nuremberg, the Tribunal allowed the defense latitude in presenting their case, which took 11 months, and the entire trial took a marathon 29 months. The trial lasted so long that two of the defendants died before the verdicts were

Above: "The Last Figure" was a highly apposite and telling cartoon by the Kukryniksy group from the USSR. Eleven of the 20 defendants in the dock at Nuremberg were sentenced to death by hanging.

announced. In contrast to the Nuremberg trials, all the surviving 25 accused were judged guilty. At least one of these verdicts reflected poorly on the Tribunal: Mamoru Shigemitsu while ambassador in London opposed the war party in Japan, and accepted the post of foreign minister primarily to negotiate an end to the war; it seems hard to judge him a criminal for his failure to prevent the ill-treatment of POWs. The seven sentences of death were not as controversial; all of these men, headed by ex-Prime Minister Tojo, were deeply implicated in the decision to go to war and the methods used by Japanese forces.

In other parts of what had been the Japanese Empire, thousands of Japanese were tried for specific war crimes. Many of these trials took place in Singapore, including the seven most senior Japanese officers in command of the occupied island, two of whom were executed. About 5,000 Japanese were found guilty of war crimes and 900 were executed – a figure much higher than its German

equivalent. Despite the intensity of feeling against the Japanese, especially from those who experienced their brutality during the war, these trials were a genuine judicial process, the Australians, for instance, tried over 800 Japanese and acquitted nearly a third.

Japan, like Germany, was occupied, and subjected to a sustained attempt to remodel its society. The United States successfully supervised Japan's transformation into a constitutional monarchy; it even forced Japan, in Article 9 of the new constitution, to declare: "The right of belligerency of the state will not be recognized." Nearly 200,000 Japanese associated with the old regime were purged, but as with Germany the onset of the Cold War in the late 1940s rapidly changed Japan from occupied enemy to valued ally, and most of those removed eventually returned to public life. However, these post-war changes, and the actual experience of war, seem to have made many Japanese into determined pacifists – even in the 1990s public opinion has resisted attempts to

Left: Thousands of deliriously happy Americans gathered in Times Square, New York City, to celebrate VE Day on May 5, 1945. An incongruous note is struck by the advertisement behind this part of the crowd.

Right: Little more than three months after VE Day, New York's Times Square was totally packed once more with exuberant Americans, this time celebrating VJ Day and the end of World War II on August 15, 1945.

restore Japan's armed forces to great power status.

World War II had been a horrible war, and it might have ended in a descent of all the belligerents into barbarism. That the Allies in the main treated the defeated with humanity, and subjected their leaders to a judicial process – if an imperfect one – was at least symbolic of their desire not to have all their civilized values consumed in the fire of total war. It had been all too easy for the belligerents to submerge their humanity in the need

to win; the Allies had deliberately bombed civilians; Roosevelt had taken seriously "scientific" evidence that the Japanese were not quite human, and actually discussed sterilizing the entire Japanese nation. The capacity to commit acts of such evil is not a uniquely German or Japanese quality; history since 1945 – despite the hopes of the most decent of those who made the peace – tells us that people in the wrong circumstances can do the most terrible things.